CHARMING
SMALL HOTEL
GUIDES
ITALY

INCLUDING
SICILY & SARDINIA

CHARMING
SMALL HOTEL
GUIDES
ITALY

INCLUDING
SICILY & SARDINIA

Edited by Chris Gill

HUNTER
PUBLISHING INC

300 Raritan Center Parkway,
CN 94, Edison, N.J. 08818

Published by Hunter Publishing Inc, 300 Raritan
Center Parkway, CN 94, Edison, N.J. 08818. Tel 201 225
1900.

First published 1988 by
Papermac, a division of Macmillan Publishers Limited
and subsequently
by Duncan Petersen Publishing Ltd,
5 Botts Mews, London W2 5AG

Conceived, designed and produced by
Duncan Petersen
Edited by Fox and Partners, The Old Forge,
Norton St Philip, Bath, U.K.

Typeset by Fox and Partners, Bath, and PCS Typesetting,
Frome
Originated by Reprocolor International S.R.I., Milan
Printed by G. Canale & C. SpA, Turin

ISBN 1-55650-467-5

Contents

Introduction

This guide to hotels in Italy – completely revised for 1991, with almost 30 new entries – is part of a series also covering Britain and Ireland, France, and Spain. The *Charming Small Hotel Guides* – are different from other accommodation guides on the market. They are designed to satisfy what we believe to be the real needs of today's traveller; needs which have been served at best haphazardly by other guides.

The most fundamental difference is suggested by the title: we aim to include only those hotels and guest-houses which offer notable character and warmth of welcome, and which are small enough to offer truly personal service, usually from the owner. In Italy, most of our recommendations have fewer than 30 rooms, and only a few have more than 40.

The guides are different in other ways, too. Their descriptive style is different, and they are compiled differently. Our entries employ, above all, words: they contain not one symbol. They are written by people with something to say, not a bureaucracy which has long since lost the ability to distinguish the praiseworthy from the mediocre. The editorial team is small and highly experienced at assessing and writing about hotels, at noticing all-important details. Although we place great emphasis on consistency, we have made use of reports from members of the public, and would welcome more of them (see page 203). Every entry aims to give a coherent and definite feel of what it is actually like to stay in that place.

These are features which will reveal their worth only as you use your *Charming Small Hotel Guide.* Its other advantages are more obvious: it contains colour photographs of a hundred or so of the most appealing entries; the entries are presented in clear geographical groups; and each entry is categorized by the type of accommodation (for example, country inn).

Small Italian hotels

Small hotels have always had the special appeal that they can offer the traveller a personal welcome and personal attention, whereas larger places are necessarily more institutional. But the distinction has become particularly clear in Italy during recent years with the energetic restoration of historic buildings to create singular hotels. Of course, Italy's cities and towns have always had their share of pensioni which, at their best, are the stuff of a guide such as this; but you do need a guide like this to distinguish the seedy from the delightful.

The establishments described in this guide are simply the 275 small hotels, pensioni and bed-and-breakfast

Introduction

places that we believe most discriminating travellers would prefer to stay in, given the choice. Some undeniably pricey places are included – Italy is no longer a particularly cheap destination – but the majority of places in the guide offer double rooms for under L100,000.

Italy is peculiar in having some significant areas notably lacking in hotels of our type. These areas – and some other areas where we know of potential entries that cannot be accommodated in this edition – are discussed in special Area introductions.

Our ideal hotel has a peaceful, pretty setting; the building itself is either handsome or historic, or at least has a distinct character. The rooms are spacious, but on a human scale – not grand or intimidating. The decorations and furnishings are harmonious, comfortable and impeccably maintained, and include antique pieces that are meant to be used, not revered. The proprietors and staff are dedicated, thoughtful and sensitive in their pursuit of their guests' happiness – friendly and welcoming without being intrusive. Last but not least, the food, whether simple or ambitious, is fresh, interesting and carefully prepared. Elaborate facilities such as saunas or trouser-presses count for little in these guides, though we do generally list them.

Of course, not every hotel included here scores top marks on each of these counts. But it is surprising how many do respectably well on most fronts.

Going to Italy

We are pleased to acknowledge the assistance of a UK tour operator in preparing this third edition. Our inspectors travelled to Italy with the help of Magic of Italy, who operate a large and varied programme featuring many of the hotels in the guide. Telephone (081)-748 7575.

How to find an entry

In this guide, the entries are arranged in convenient geographical groups, and these groups are arranged in a sequence starting in the extreme north-west and working west to east and south to north. Sicily and Sardinia come last.

To find a hotel in a particular area, simply browse through headings at the top of the pages until you find that area – or use the maps following this introduction to locate the appropriate pages. To locate a specific hotel or a hotel in a specific place, use the indexes at the back, which lists the entries alphabetically, first by name and then by placename.

Introduction

How to read an entry

At the top of each entry is a coloured bar highlighting
the name of the town or village where the establishment
is located, along with a categorization which gives some
clue to its character. These categories are as far as
possible self-explanatory. The term 'villa' needs, perhaps,
some qualification: it is reserved for places with gardens
which have something of the air of a country house,
whether in a town or at the seaside.

Fact boxes

The fact box given for each hotel follows a standard
pattern which requires little explanation; but:

Under **Tel** we give the telephone number starting with
the area code used within the country; when dialling
from another country, omit the initial nought of this
code.

Under **Location** we give information on the setting of the
hotel and on its parking arrangements, as well as pointers
to help you find it.

Under **Food & drink** we list the meals available.

The **Prices** in this volume – unlike our volume on Britain
and Ireland – are per room, including tax and service.
Wherever possible we have given prices for 1991, but for
many hotels these were not available; actual prices may
therefore be higher than those quoted, simply because of
inflation. But bear in mind also that the proprietors of
hotels and guest-houses may change their prices from
one year to another by much more than the rate of
inflation. Always check before making a booking.
  Normally, a range of prices is given, representing the
smallest and largest amounts you might pay in different
circumstances – typically, the minimum is the cost of the
cheapest single room in low season, while the maximum
is the cost of the dearest double in high season.
  After the room price, we give either the price for
dinner, bed and breakfast (DB&B), or for full board (FB
– that is, all meals included) or, instead, an indication of
the cost of individual meals. After all this basic
information comes, where space allows, a summary of
reductions available for long stays or for children.

Under **Rooms** we summarize the number and style of
bedrooms available. Our lists of facilities in bedrooms
cover only mechanical gadgets and not ornaments such
as flowers or consumables such as toiletries or free drinks.

Introduction

Under **Facilities** we list public rooms and then outdoor and sporting facilities which are either part of the hotel or immediately on hand; facilities in tbe vicinity are not listed, though they sometimes feature at the end of the main description in the **Nearby** section, which presents a selection of interesting things to see or do in the locality.

We use the following abbreviations for **Credit cards**:

AE American Express
DC Diners Club
MC MasterCard (Access/Eurocard)
V Visa (Barclaycard/Bank Americard/Carte Bleue etc)

The final entry in a fact box is normally the name of the proprietor(s); but where the hotel is run by a manager we give his or her name instead.

Unfamiliar terms
Some visitors, particularly from North America, may be mystified by some terms. 'Self-catering' means that cooking facilities such as a kitchenette or small kitchen are provided for making your own meals, as in a rental apartment. 'Bargain breaks' or 'breaks' of any kind mean off-season price reductions are available, usually for a stay of a specific period.

Hotel location maps

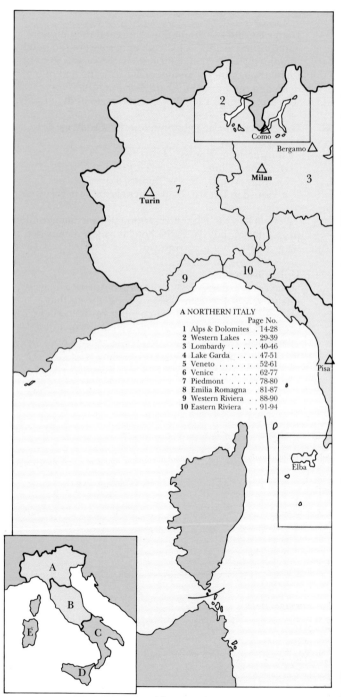

(Continued on following two pages)

B CENTRAL ITALY

11

Hotel location maps

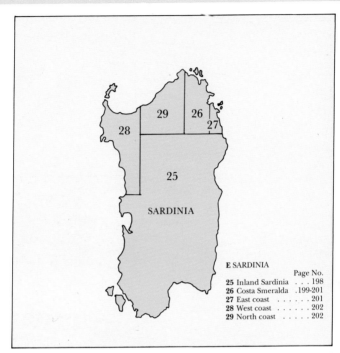

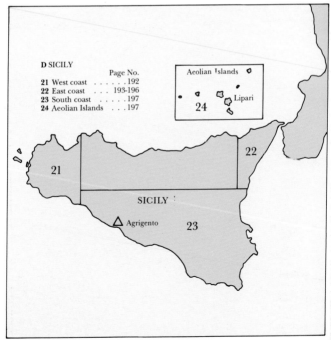

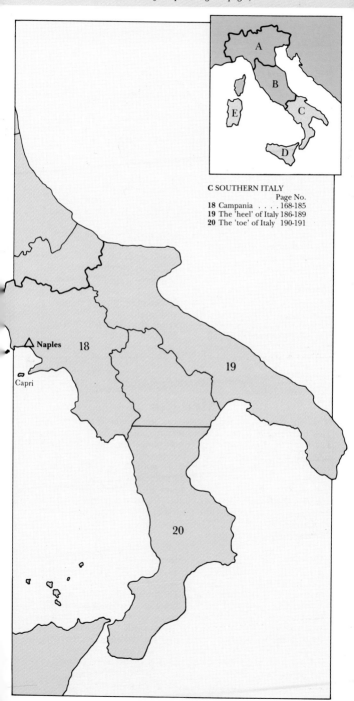

C SOUTHERN ITALY

Naples

Capri

18

19

20

Alps & Dolomites

Cappella

This is a good (and unusually small) example of the classical Sud Tirol hotel – modern (less than 20 years old), but built in Alpine chalet style; thoroughly comfortable and welcoming, with richly traditional furnishings and decoration; well equipped with sports facilities; and set in spectacular mountain scenery (it's close to the Sella massif), with skiing or walking from the door, depending on the season, and beautiful views from the bedroom balconies and the grassy garden.

Nearby Sella group and other Dolomites.

Colfosco, Val Badia 39030 Bolzano
Tel (0471) 836183
Location 2 km NW of Corvara; car parking
Food & drink breakfast, lunch, dinner
Prices rooms L39,000-L140,000; reduction for children
Rooms 30 double, 13 with bath, 18 with shower; 6 single, 2 with bath, 4 with shower; 4 family rooms with bath; all rooms have central heating, phone, radio, TV
Facilities dining-room, bar, TV, playroom; beauty parlour, sauna; covered swimming-pool, table tennis, tennis, bowls
Credit cards DC, V
Children welcome over 3
Disabled no special facilities
Pets small ones only accepted
Closed mid-Apr to mid-June, end Sep to mid-Dec
Proprietors Josef and Renata Pizzinini

Menardi

This old farmhouse has long served the needs of travellers on the road north from Cortina, which over the years has been extended up the valley until it now almost embraces the hotel. The Menardi family has seen the place evolve over the years, from country inn to restaurant to *pensione* to hotel, without losing its rustic warmth and essentially Tyrolean style – despite the introduction of elegant antiques and modern comforts. In size it is slightly over our usual limit, but there is no question that the Menardi also retains the atmosphere of a small family-run establishment.

Nearby Dolomite mountains.

Via Majon 110, Cortina d'Ampezzo 32043 Belluno
Tel (0436) 2400
Location 1.5 km from middle of resort, on road to Dobbiaco; ample car parking and covered garage
Food & drink breakfast, lunch, dinner
Prices rooms L60,000-L175,000; FB L89,000-L140,000
Rooms 40 double, 8 single; all with bath; all rooms have central heating, phone
Facilities dining-room, bar, reading-room, cards room, TV room, taverna
Credit cards V **Children** accepted **Disabled** access difficult **Pets** not accepted
Closed Oct to mid-Dec and mid-Apr to mid-June
Proprietors Menardi family

14

Alps & Dolomites

Elefante

Bressanone is a pretty little town at the foot of the Brenner Pass, more Austrian than Italian in character. The same is true of the charming old Elefante, which owes its name to a beast which was led over the Alps for the amusement of Emperor Ferdinand of Austria. The only stable which could house the exhausted creature was that next to the inn, and the innkeeper, quick to see the possibilities, painted an elephant on the side of his inn and changed its name.

There is an air of solid, old-fashioned comfort throughout. Green-aproned staff lead you through corridors packed with heavily carved and beautifully inlaid pieces of antique furniture. The colours here are rich and sumptuous: scarlets, greens, copper, gold; turn a corner, and you may encounter an enormous display of purple iris and tulips in a simple iron pot. The bedrooms are generous and handsomely furnished with graceful antiques and solid old pieces.

The breakfast room is panelled entirely in intricately carved wood – very Tyrolean – and the main restaurant is wood-floored, with a moulded ceiling and windows looking out on to a little garden area. Much of the produce served here comes from a large walled garden across the street, and from the adjacent farm belonging to the hotel. The formal sitting-room has been decorated in an elegant 18thC style, with mirrors, chandeliers and plush armchairs.

Nearby cathedral; Novacella monastery (3 km); the Dolomites.

Via Rio Bianco 4, Bressanone
39042 Bolzano
Tel (0472) 32750
Location at N end of town, in gardens with car parking and garages
Food & drink breakfast, lunch, dinner
Prices rooms L95,000 -L190,000 with breakfast
Rooms 28 double, all with bath and shower; 16 single, 15 with bath, one with shower; all have central heating, colour TV, phone
Facilities 2 dining-rooms, sitting-room, bar; outdoor swimming-pool
Credit cards V
Children welcome
Disabled not suitable
Pets accepted by arrangement
Closed Jan to Feb **Proprietor** Wolfgang Heiss

Alps & Dolomites

Locanda al Castello

Cividale is a small town in the hills east of Udine, not far from the Yugoslav border. This crenellated red-brick building in a dominant hilltop position, though properly described as a restaurant with rooms, is a quiet, welcoming and restful place to stay, with a large terrace accommodating easy chairs and sunshades. Much of the food is grilled over open fires. Both dining-rooms are rather large and lacking in character, but the bedrooms more than compensate. They are simply decorated but spacious, with honest rustic wooden furniture which gives a somewhat Alpine feel, and fabrics chosen to add to the rusticity. The tiled bathrooms are spotlessly clean.

Nearby cathedral, archaeological museum and Tempietto of Cividale del Friuli; Venice (17 km).

Via del Castello 18, Cividale del Friuli 33043 Udine
Tel (9432) 733242
Location 1.5 km NW of middle of Cividale del Friuli; with private car parking
Food & drink breakfast, lunch, dinner
Prices rooms L44,000- L72,000
Rooms 10 rooms, all with bath or shower; all rooms have phone
Facilities 2 dining-rooms, large terrace
Credit cards V
Children accepted
Disabled no special facilities
Pets dogs not accepted
Closed few days in Nov
Proprietor Roberto Cidarmas

Castel Pergine

A tiny winding mountain road leads you to the hilltop on which is perched Castel Pergine – a medieval castle, surrounded by woods, with marvellous views in all directions. Inside, two enormous, vaulted rooms with rustic chairs and tables and mullioned windows serve as a restaurant. The bedrooms are simple, some with whitewashed stone walls, some panelled in a soft tan wood. Window boxes with bright geraniums add a splash of colour, and the old carved wooden beds are lightened by gay duvets. There is a tranquil walled garden for the use of guests only – the main tower of the hotel and its capacious restaurant and bar are open to the public.

Nearby Lago di Caldonazzo (2.5 km), Trento (10 km).

Pergine 38057 Trento
Tel (0461) 531158
Location 1.5 km S of Pergine on road to Levico Terme, with private walled garden and car parking at gates
Food & drink breakfast, lunch, dinner
Prices FB L50,000- L58,000; 40% reduction for children under 6
Rooms 18 double, 8 with shower; 5 single, 4 with shower; all rooms have phone
Facilities dining-room, bar, sitting-room
Credit cards not accepted
Children welcome **Disabled** not suitable **Pets** accepted
Closed mid-Oct to Apr; restaurant only, Mon
Proprietor Luigi Fontanara

Alps & Dolomites

Converted castle, San Paolo

Schloss Korb

Rising up above the fertile vineyards and orchards that surround the outskirts of Bolzano is the 11thC medieval tower which forms the centrepiece of Schloss Korb.

The entrance to the hotel is a riot of colour – flowering shrubs and plants set against walls of golden stone and whitewash. Inside, furnishings and decorations are in traditional style, and antiques and fresh flowers abound. Reception is a cool, dark, tiled hall, set about with brass ornaments and armoury – the oldest part of the hotel. Surrounding the main restaurant areas is a terrace, hanging out over the valley and awash with plants, where breakfast and drinks can be enjoyed.

The bedrooms in the castle are generous in size, with separate sitting-areas and lovely views out over the vineyards. Duvet covers give a warm, friendly feel. The detached annexe behind the main building has its own dining-room, heated indoor pool and lift/elevator – the last being the attraction for some of the guests.

The daughter of the family (shadowed everywhere by her enormous Great Dane) speaks fluent English.

Nearby sights of Bolzano; Merano within reach; the Dolomites.

Missiano, San Paolo 39050 Bolzano
Tel (0471)633222
Location 8 km W of Bolzano, in gardens on estate with vineyards and large car park
Food & drink breakfast, lunch, dinner
Prices rooms L80,000-L165,000 with breakfast; reductions for children in family room
Rooms 54 double, 2 single, all with bath or shower; all rooms have central heating, phone

Facilities dining-room, conference rooms, bar, sitting-rooms (one with TV); sauna, beauty salon, outdoor and heated indoor swimming-pools, tennis
Credit cards not accepted
Children welcome
Disabled lift to annexe bedrooms, but access awkward for wheelchairs
Pets accepted
Closed Nov to Mar
Proprietors Dellago family

Alps & Dolomites

> **Converted castle, Merano**

Castel Labers

On the hillside to the east of Merano, Castel (or Schloss) Labers is surrounded by its own vineyards, orchards and mountain walks through alpine pastures. The hotel has been in the Neubert family since 1885, but the building itself dates back to the 11th century.

An impressive stone staircase with wrought-iron balustrades leads from the white-walled entrance hall and up to the bedrooms. These all have charming wooden double doors, with sealed wooden floors, simple old furniture, and goose feather duvets in crisp white cotton covers.

The castle gardens are packed with trees and flowering shrubs, which can be admired from the conservatory restaurant, whose windows are draped in country cottons. Leading off this is another restaurant area, with a church-like vaulted wooden ceiling and old panelling round the walls. Fresh local produce is well presented and deliciously cooked.

Nearby promenades along the Passirio river in Merano; Tirolo Castle (5 km); Passirio valley, the Dolomites.

Via Labers 25, Merano 39012 Bolzano
Tel (0473) 34484
Location 2.5 km E of Merano, with private grounds, gardens and vineyard; garage and court yard car parking (locked at night)
Food & drink breakfast, lunch, dinner
Prices rooms L85,000-L130,000; DB&B L80,000-L100,000; reductions for children sharing parents' room
Rooms 22 double, 20 with bath, 2 with shower; 9 single, 2 with bath, 7 with shower; 10 family rooms, all with bath; all rooms have central heating, phone
Facilities dining-room, dining/conservatory, bar, music/reading room, conference room; outdoor heated swimming-pool, tennis
Credit cards AE, DC, MC, V
Children welcome
Disabled not suitable
Pets dogs accepted, but not in the dining-room in evening
Closed Nov to mid-Mar
Proprietors Stapf-Neubert family

Alps & Dolomites

Castel Freiberg

The Freiberg is every inch the grand medieval castle. It commands an exposed hilltop position high above Merano, but its ramparts enclose a beautiful sheltered garden with sweet-scented shrubs, and its walls conceal a hotel which is at once luxurious, welcoming and full of character. The entrance is very grand, with suits of armour and ancient weapons along the whitewashed walls, and vaulted ceilings. Throughout the castle there are small sitting-areas, usually by a window with superb eagle's-eye views down over the valley. The small, intimate bar with an old painted wooden bench adjoins a tiny chapel, but by far the most stunning rooms are the dining-rooms, completely panelled in honey-coloured pine with enormous wood-burning stoves clad in turquoise ceramic tiles.

The house-boys, in black-and-green striped jackets, lead you to the spacious bedrooms – all comfortably fitted out in an opulent, antique style.

Nearby Promenades along Passirio River in Merano; Passirio valley, the Dolomites.

Via Fragsburg, Merano 39012 Bolzano
Tel (0473) 44196
Location 8 km NE of Merano, with walled garden and park; car parking close to hotel, and garaging available
Food & drink breakfast, lunch, dinner
Prices rooms L135,000-L160,000
Rooms 28 double, all with bath and shower; 7 single, all with bath and shower; all rooms have phone, radio, sitting-area; TV on request
Facilities 3 dining-rooms, basement taverna, TV room, 2 sitting-rooms, bar, chapel, veranda; indoor and outdoor heated swimming-pools, fitness room
Credit cards AE, DC, MC, V
Children not suitable
Disabled not suitable
Pets not accepted
Closed Nov to mid-Apr
Proprietors Bortolotti family

Alps & Dolomites

Fragsburg

A lovely drive along a narrow country lane, through mixed woodland and past Alpine pastures where goats and cattle graze, brings you to the wooded outcrop, high up to the east of Merano, where sits the Hotel Fragsburg (or Castel Verruca).

The original building is 300 years old, in traditional chalet style with carved wooden shutters and balconies decked with flowering plants. Recent extensions to provide more bedrooms are sympathetic in style. It enjoys splendid views (notably of the Texel Massif), shared by many of the bedrooms; these are decorated in sparkling white, with abundant wood panelling, some old and some new. Downstairs, the low-ceilinged dining-areas are panelled, with gay table-cloths and rustic benches and chairs. Hearty Italian/Tyrolean meals can also be enjoyed on the balcony which runs the length of the hotel. Below are what appear to be dolls' houses; actually they house the bees which provide honey for the wholesome buffet breakfast. In the extensive wooded garden there are areas for lazing in the sun – including a wooden shelter reserved for all-over tanning.

Nearby Promenades along the Passirio river in Merano; Passirio valley, the Dolomites.

Via Fragsburg 3/a, PO Box 210, Freiberg, Merano 39012 Bolzano
Tel (0473) 244071
Location 6 km NE of Merano, with gardens; ample car parking space, and garages available
Food & drink breakfast, lunch, dinner
Prices rooms L63,000-L130,000 with breakfast; DB&B L70,000-L100,000; FB L85,000- L115,000
Rooms 14 double, 10 with bath, 4 with shower; 3 single,

all with shower; 2 family rooms; all rooms have central heating, phone, balcony, TV, safe
Facilities dining-rooms, sitting-room, terrace; table-tennis, heated outdoor swimming-pool
Credit cards not accepted
Children welcome
Disabled not suitable
Pets dogs accepted by arrangement
Closed Nov to Easter
Proprietors Ortner family

Alps & Dolomites

Medieval manor, Merano

Castel Rundegg

Despite its smart facilities, this ancient white-painted house retains a lot of charm. The pretty sitting-room, with plush seats and antiques, overlooks the garden through delicate wrought iron gates. The restaurant has a cellar-like atmosphere, with its stone-vaulted ceiling and alcove rooms. The bedrooms are luxurious, and many of them have special features – the turret room, reached up spiral steps, commands a 360-degree view.

Nearby promenades along Passirio river; Passirio valley, the Dolomites.

Via Scena 2, Merano 39012 Bolzano
Tel (0473) 34100
Location on E side of town; in gardens, with car parking and garages
Food & drink breakfast, lunch, dinner
Prices rooms L100,000-l240,000 with breakfast; reductions for children under 12
Rooms 22 double, 20 with bath, 2 with shower; 5 single, all with shower; 2 family rooms, both with bath; all rooms have central heating, colour TV, radio, minibar, phone
Facilities 3 dining-rooms, bar, sitting-room; heated indoor swimming-pool, health and beauty farm
Credit cards AE, DC, MC, V
Children welcome
Disabled lift/elevator available
Pets small dogs accepted on request
Closed last 3 weeks Jan
Proprietors Sinn family

Alps & Dolomites

Villa Mozart

Here is a truly extraordinary hotel. Set in a peaceful residential area of Merano, it has been entirely decorated in the Jugend style of art nouveau, with not a single detail overlooked.

The villa was built in 1907 and was renovated to the existing design in the late 1970s. Black and white are dominant throughout the hotel, with splashes of colour sparingly applied. In the airy conservatory, where breakfast is served, gauze curtains throw a soft light on posies of vivid fresh flowers; in the dining-room, a single yellow tulip next to a black candle picks up the soft yellow of the walls. The bedrooms are done out in black, gold and soft yellows, with the honey-coloured parquet floors, giving warmth and contrast to the beautiful black-and-white patterned rugs.

Every last knife, teacup and finger plate in the Villa Mozart is part of a 'homogenous whole', the design principle laid down by Josef Hoffmann in 1901. But this is no museum piece – the seats are for relaxing on, the rugs for walking over and the elegant staff (uniformed in black and white, of course) make a good job of cosseting their guests. And the kitchen too is dedicated to perfection.

Nearby promenades along Passirio river in Merano.

Via San Marco 26, Merano
39012 Bolzano
Tel (0473) 30630
Location in peaceful residential area; with garden and covered car parking
Food & drink breakfast, dinner
Prices rooms L111,000-L222,000; DB&B L189,000
Rooms 8 double, all with bath; 2 single, both with shower; all rooms have colour TV, phone, radio, minibar, health-beds
Facilities bar, restaurant, breakfast conservatory; heated indoor swimming- pool, sauna, solarium
Credit cards AE, MC, V
Children accepted
Disabled lift/elevator
Pets not accepted
Closed Nov to Easter
Proprietors Andreas and Emmy Hellrigl

Photo: Stefaner (facing page)

Alps & Dolomites

Country hotel, Merano

Der Punthof

The original building of the Punthof, which now houses reception, breakfast rooms and a few bedrooms, dates back to the Middle Ages, when it was a farmhouse. To this have been added little detached chalets with kitchen facilities, and a separate restaurant. Despite these alterations, however, much of the charm of the old building has been retained. The breakfast rooms have simple, rustic furniture and traces of the original decorative paintings on the panelled walls. Antiques are dotted around, with plenty of fresh flowers.

Nearby promenades along Passirio River in Merano.

Via Steinach 25, Merano
39022 Bolzano
Tel (0473) 48553
Location about 3 km NW of
Merano, in village; in small
park with parking for 40 cars
Food & drink breakfast,
dinner
Prices rooms L67,800-
L174,000 with breakfast
Rooms 16 double, 3 with bath,
13 with shower; 2 single, both
with shower; all have central

heating, colour TV, radio,
minibar, phone, safe
Facilities breakfast room,
sitting-room, dining-room,
bar; outdoor swimming-pool,
tennis, sauna, solarium
Credit cards DC, V
Children welcome
Disabled no special facilities
Pets accepted in certain rooms
Closed mid-Nov to Feb
Proprietors Wolf family

Mountain chalet, Tires

Stefaner

This relatively modern chalet, standing high up in a beautiful Dolomite valley, is more a home than a hotel: furnishings are simple and cosy, with plenty of plants, comfy armchairs and pretty crockery ornaments. Downstairs on one side is a large sitting-room, and on the other is the restaurant, with gaily striped padded chairs and a ceramic wood-burning stove. The bedrooms are bright and airy, and all have pretty little balconies, decorated with geraniums and carved wood. The views are spectacular. The proprietors have the charm, and the enthusiasm, to make their visitors welcome.

Nearby Bolzano; Dolomite mountains

San Cipriano, Tires 39050
Bolzano
Tel (0471) 642175
Location about 20 km NE of
Bolzano at northern end of
San Cipriano; in garden with
ample car parking
Food & drink breakfast,
dinner
Prices DB&B L42,000- L55,000
Rooms 13 double, 2 with bath,
11 with shower; 2 single, both

with shower
Facilities dining-room,
sitting-room, bar, terrace
Credit cards not accepted
Children welcome
Disabled access possible –
lift/elevator to bedrooms
Pets accepted
Closed mid-Nov to mid-Dec
Proprietor Mathilde Goller-
Villgrattner

Alps & Dolomites

Villa Anna Maria

Champoluc is the main community of a steep-sided valley running up to the Swiss border, between the famous peaks of the Matterhorn and Monte Rosa – a small-time ski resort in winter, a base for mountaineering (and less strenuous walking) in summer. The Anna Maria is a 1920s villa in a quiet wooded hillside setting, close to the village, with flowery terraces outside and wood panelling and country decorations within. Bedrooms are simply furnished but cosy, and most have private bathrooms. Cooking revolves around specialities of the Val d'Aosta.
Nearby Skiing, skating in winter; walking, fishing in summer.

Via Croues 5, Champoluc
11020 Aosta
Tel (0125) 307128
Location on outskirts of village, 27 km N of Verrés on S506; ample car parking
Food & drink breakfast, lunch, dinner
Prices rooms L45,000-L90,000; meals L30,000-L40,000
Rooms 15 double (12 twin), 6 with bath, 4 with shower; 5 single, 2 with shower; all rooms have central heating
Facilities dining-room, sitting-room, TV room, small bar, games room, ski locker; sun terrace
Credit cards V
Children accepted
Disabled no special facilities
Pets not accepted
Closed mid-Sep to Dec, late Apr to late Jun, depending on weather
Proprietor Domenico Origone

Il Capricorno

Sauze d'Oulx is not renowned for attracting discerning travellers – it is a resolutely downmarket ski resort in winter, and not a pretty sight in summer.

But the wooded slopes above the resort are pretty all year round and the Capricorno, isolated among the trees, breaks all the local rules by being small, traditional in style and cosily charming. Outside the chalet looks modern, although built traditionally in wood and stone; inside, it is all rough beams, handmade furniture and blazing log fires.

Mariarosa is the cook, and well able to meet the demands of the gourmets who stray across the nearby border from France.
Nearby walking in summer, skiing in winter

Case Sparse 21, Le Clotès, Sauze d'Oulx 10050 Torino
Tel (0122) 85273
Location in woods above village; car parking in summer
Food & drink breakfast, lunch, dinner
Prices rooms L102,000-L164,000; meals L45,000-L60,000
Rooms 8 double, all with shower; central heating
Facilities dining-room, sitting-room, bar; sun terrace
Credit cards DC, V
Children accepted only by arrangement
Disabled no facilities
Pets not accepted
Closed May to mid-Jun, mid-Sep to Nov **Proprietors** Carlo and Mariarosa Sacchi

Alps & Dolomites

Restaurant with rooms, Masi

Mas del Saügo

Secluded hostelries don't come much more remote than this. A good 2 km up a winding forest track that leads to nowhere but the Lagorai mountains, the Mas del Saügo is surrounded by nothing but open meadow, forest, and fresh air. Donatella Zampoli, a local cook who learned her mother's lessons well, but knows when to depart from their traditions, and Lorenzo Bernardini, a painter and designer with a nose for an excellent wine, embarked on their great adventure in 1985. The derelict barn adjacent to their immaculately restored 17thC farmhouse gives some idea of their achievement. Inside, Lorenzo has combined original features with his own distinctive Tyrolean-Cubist styles. The smaller dining-room is all wood, with the original decorated plaster ceiling and traditional ceramic boiler, while the larger dining-room – once a fodder store – is more formal. There is a Picasso original over the wooden steps that lead to the enchanting bar in the converted cattle stalls below. Everywhere there are gorgeous smells of wood or herbs – or of food.

The bedrooms are individual: some with stone walls and exposed beams, others wood-panelled. All contain Lorenzo originals. The gourmet menus are a six-course sortie into the unknown, each course accompanied by a glass of Lorenzo's recommended wine. Since Lorenzo and Donatella offer a unique and personal hospitality, it is understandable that prior booking is obligatory.

Nearby Mountain walks, winter skiing at Cavalese (4 km).

Masi 38033 Cavalese
Tel (0462) 30788
Location up mountain track, 4 km SW of Cavalese, 40 km SE of Bolzano; in fields, with ample car parking
Food & drink breakfast, lunch, dinner
Prices rooms L120,000-L200,000; lunch and dinner L120,000- L150,000
Rooms 3 double, one single, all with shower; all rooms have central heating, hairdrier
Facilities dining-room, bar
Credit cards V
Children **not accepted under 8 years**
Disabled no special facilities
Pets not accepted
Closed hotel never; restaurant Thurs
Proprietors Donatella Zampoli, Lorenzo Bernardini

Alps & Dolomites

Town hotel, Trento

Accademia

The old centre of Trento is much quieter now that traffic restrictions are in force, and this recently converted medieval house lies on a tiny street right in the heart of it. Quaint wooden shutters and geranium-filled window boxes break up the four storeys of the elegant cream-stucco façade. Inside, all is in the best contemporary taste: white vaulted chambers, parquet floors, classic modern furniture, and strategically placed antique pieces and old maps. There are plenty of comfortable sofas, some on a small wooden gallery above the bar – ideal for a quiet drink. The smart staff have an air of calm efficiency about them. The atmosphere is carried through to the bedrooms which are bright and airy, only the singles being a bit on the small side. You will find all the facilities you could wish for – tastefully presented, of course – right down to the electric shoe polishing machine on the landing.

Breakfast is a particular pleasure when taken on the walled terrace, shaded by a giant horse-chestnut tree. The restaurant – another white vaulted room, with crisp white table-cloths and simple wooden and wicker chairs – is a Trento favourite. The *gnochetti di ricotta* are not to be missed.

Nearby Church of Santa Maria, Piazza del Duomo.

Vicolo Colico 4/6, 38100 Trento
Tel (0461) 233600
Location in historic middle of town, between *duomo* and Piazza Dante
Food & drink breakfast, lunch, dinner
Prices rooms L140,000-L200,000; meals from L50,000
Rooms 28 double, 12 with bath, 16 with shower; 9 single, all with shower; 5 family rooms, all with bath; all rooms have central heating, telephone, TV, minibar, hairdrier
Facilities dining-room, sitting-room, bar, breakfast room, terrace
Credit cards AE, DC, V
Children accepted
Disabled lift/elevator
Pets accepted
Closed hotel never; restaurant Mon
Proprietor Sig. Fambri

Alps & Dolomites

Country hotel, Rasun di Sopra

Ansitz Heufler

This converted 16thC castle is a bit too close to the road up the Anterselva valley to rate as truly idyllic. But it is undoubtedly one of the most beautiful buildings in the area, both inside and out. Fir trees shelter the chairs and tables scattered on the lawn in front and, once inside, traffic is soon forgotten: a large pine table, with drawers set into the white-washed wall behind, serves as the reception where guests are met by the young and cheerful staff.

All the public rooms are pine-panelled, with rugs and skins, rustic wooden tables, benches and amply cushioned sofas and armchairs. The main sitting-room on the first floor is the real gem: here the panelling is intricately inlaid, and there is a vast traditional ceramic stove reminiscent of a castle tower. Breakfast is taken in the snug bar, while other meals are served by smart, lace-aproned waitresses in the equally cosy dining-rooms. The *carte* offers good solid Tyrolean fare, with liberal use of alcohol. Chocolate truffles in Grand Marnier can be just what the doctor ordered when it's snowing outside.

The bedrooms, set around a large open hall and gallery, are all of ample size, though you have to mind your head on low door lintels at times. In the majority, the pine fixtures are original.

Nearby Walking, cycling, and winter skiing at Brunico.

39030 Oberraseli
Tel (0474) 46288
Location in wooded Anterselva valley, 10 km E of Brunico; with garden and car parking
Food & drink breakfast, lunch, dinner
Prices rooms L90,000-L140,000 with breakfast; meals L30,000- L56,000
Rooms 9 double, 3 with bath, 6 with shower; all rooms have central heating, telephone
Facilities dining-room, sitting-room, breakfast room, bar
Credit cards AE,DC, MC, V
Children accepted
Disabled no special facilities
Pets accepted
Closed November; 15 May to 15 Jun
Manager Valentin Pallhuber

Alps & Dolomites

Country guest-house, Caldaro

Leuchtenburg

This solid stone-built 16thC hostel once housed the peasant servants of Leuchtenburg Castle, an arduous hour's trek up the steep wooded mountain behind.

Today, guests in the *pensione* are cosseted, while the castle lies in ruins. The young Sparer family do the cosseting, providing good, solid breakfasts and 3-course dinners of regional cuisine in an unpretentious, home-like atmosphere. The white-painted, low-arched dining-chambers occupy the ground floor; above is the reception, with a large table littered with magazines and surrounded by armchairs.

There is a further sitting-area on the second floor, leading to the bedrooms. These have pretty painted furniture, tiled floors and attractive duvet covers; the rooms on the third floor are plainer. All the rooms are of a reasonable size, and some share the wide views of the terrace, across vineyards to the Lago di Caldaro, better known (at least to wine buffs) as Kalterer See.
Nearby Swimming and fishing in lake.

Campi al Largo 100, Caldaro 39052 Caldaro
Tel (0471) 960093
Location 5 km SE of Caldaro (Kaltern), 15 km SE of Bolzano; in courtyard surrounded by vineyards, with adequate car parking
Food & drink breakfast, dinner
Prices rooms L60,000-L80,000 with breakfast; meals L10,000
Rooms 13 double, 2 with bath, 11 with shower; 3 single with shower; 2 family rooms, one with bath, one with shower; all rooms have central heating
Facilities dining-area, sitting-area, bar; private beach
Credit cards none
Children no special facilities
Disabled no special facilities
Pets not accepted
Closed Nov-Easter
Proprietor Paul and Markus Sparer

Western Lakes

Villa Odescalchi

This rather grand 17thC building is popular with business visitors, but it is also worth considering for holiday purposes. The main salon, furnished with antiques and plush sofas and chairs, leads out to the lush gardens and grand park behind. An open gallery runs all around the top of the room, and many of the bedrooms lead off this narrow rectangle – tall, quite spacious rooms, decorated in autumn colours with modern furnishings. The dining-room is pleasantly situated in a modern conservatory extension, with garden views.

Nearby Como (10 km), Milan (43 km), Bergamo (46 km)

Via Anzani 12, Alzate Brianza 22040 Como
Tel (031) 630822
Location close to middle of town off road for Como, with large private park and car parking opposite entrance
Food & drink breakfast, lunch, dinner
Prices rooms L97,000-L117,000; FB L140,000
Rooms 14 double, 8 single, 3 family rooms, all with bath or shower; all rooms have phone, minibar, colour TV
Facilities sitting-room, dining-room, 2 conference rooms, bar; outdoor swimming-pool, tennis
Credit cards AE, MC
Children welcome
Disabled not suitable
Pets dogs allowed
Closed never
Managers Federico Bruschini, Gianpaolo Frosace

Belvedere

It is odd to walk into this small old villa on the shore of Lake Como and find an English-style bar upholstered in tartan. But when you meet the jolly owner and discover that his wife is a Scot, the friendly British guest-house atmosphere is explained.

In front of the house is a sunny, gravelled terrace where you can enjoy a drink, or eat out if the weather permits. In the sitting-room (with views out over the lake), the old painted ceiling remains, and antiques are scattered around. The bedrooms are simply, even basically furnished, and some are a little cramped; those at the back are possibly rather noisy, but those at the front have splendid views of the lake.

Nearby Valle di Intelvi; boat trips on lake.

Via Milano 8, Argegno 22010 Como
Tel (031) 821116
Location on shores of Lake Como; private car parking
Food & drink breakfast, lunch, dinner
Prices rooms L40,000-L80,000 with breakfast; meals L35,000
Rooms 17 double (7 twin), 11 with bath or shower; one single
Facilities dining-room, bar, sitting-room; boat for hire
Credit cards DC, MC, V
Children welcome
Disabled not suitable
Pets accepted (not in dining-room) **Closed** Nov to Mar
Proprietors Giorgio and Jane Cappelletti

Western Lakes

Lakeside hotel, Cannero Riviera

Cannero

Cannero is one of the quietest resorts on Lake Maggiore and its most desirable hotels lie right on the shore. Only the ferry landing-stage and a quiet dead-end road separate the Cannero from the waters of Maggiore.

The building was once a monastery, though only an old stone column, a couple of vaulted passageways and a quiet courtyard suggest it is anything other than a modern hotel. The emphasis is on comfort and relaxation and the atmosphere is very friendly, thanks largely to the smiling Signora Gallinotto. Downstairs, big windows and terraces make the most of the setting. The restaurant focuses on the lake, with an outdoor terrace running alongside.

The bedrooms are light and well cared for, and have adequate bathrooms. There are gorgeous views of lake and mountains from the front rooms, though many guests are just as happy overlooking the pool at the back – which, if anything, is quieter. By day this provides a delightfully peaceful spot to take a dip or lounge under yellow and white parasols.

Nearby Borromean Islands – daily connections by boat; Ascona (21 km), Locarno (25 km) and other resorts of Lake Maggiore.

Lungo Lago 3-2, Cannero Riviera, Lago Maggiore 28051 Novara
Tel (0323) 788046
Location in resort, overlooking lake, with garden and 2 car parks
Food & drink breakfast, lunch, dinner
Prices rooms L55,000-L90,000; DB&B L70,000; FB L80,000; 10% reduction for children under 10
Rooms 30 double, 15 with bath, 15 with shower; 6 single, 3 with bath, 3 with shower; all rooms have central heating,

phone
Facilities sitting-room, piano bar, dining-room, lakeside terrace; tennis, pool, solarium, boat, windsurfing, 2 bicycles
Credit cards AE, DC, MC, V
Children welcome; separate dining-room for children, baby-sitter on request
Disabled 8 rooms accessible; lift/elevator
Pets accepted if well behaved, but not in main sitting-room
Closed Nov to mid-Mar
Proprietors Sga Gallinotto and sons

Western Lakes

Giardino

There is little point in staying in Arona without views of Lake Maggiore, and the Giardino's great attraction is a large terrace shaded by a magnificent awning of well-trained wisteria, looking across the road to the waterfront. Rooms (with lake views for a modest premium) have been decorated with a modest attempt at individuality – for example tartan carpets, marble tops, brass and china lamp fittings. The dining-room is strictly average in ambience and decoration, but in season there will be the Piedmontese speciality of *porcine* (*cèpe* mushrooms) in several guises. It is a family business with friendly, willing staff.
Nearby Colosso di San Carlone (1.5 km); Stresa (16 km); Borromean Islands (regular boats); Baveno, Pallanza.

Via Republica 1, Arona 28041 Novara
Tel (0322) 45994
Location five minutes from station; car parking nearby on and off road
Food & drink breakfast, lunch, dinner
Prices rooms L78,000-L82,400; meals L35,000-L50,000
Rooms 56 double, all with bath and shower; all rooms have central heating, TV, minibar, phone
Facilities dining-room, sitting-room, TV room, bar, disco in basement; tennis
Credit cards AE, DC, V
Children welcome
Disabled no special facilities
Pets welcome
Closed never
Proprietor Ezio Bertalli

Al Sorriso

The village of Soriso lies some way from the lake of Orta and has no special charm (despite its name which, with the addition of an 'r' – as in the name of the hotel – comes to mean 'smile'). The real reason for coming here is the food. In the whole of Italy there are fewer than a dozen restaurants which are awarded two or more Michelin stars, and this is one of them. Among the specialities are pumpkin flowers with truffle sauce, celery soup with prawns in thyme and slices of lamb with marjoram. The dining-room is the picture of elegance and the service is highly professional. The bedrooms are quite plush, but unremarkable.
Nearby Orta San Giulio (8 km), Milan (78 km).

Soriso 28018 Novara
Tel (0322) 983228
Location in village of Soriso, S of Lake Orta; car parking on road
Food & drink breakfast, lunch, dinner
Prices rooms L90,000-L170,000; meals about L130,000-L300,000; breakfast L10,000
Rooms 5 double, 2 single; all with bath or shower; all rooms have phone, TV, minibar
Facilities bar, dining-room
Credit cards MC, V
Children not suitable
Disabled no special facilities
Pets dogs not accepted
Closed 2 weeks Jan, 3 weeks Aug; restaurant only, Mon and Tue lunch
Proprietors Angelo and Luisa Valazza

Western Lakes

Lakeside hotel, Bellagio

Florence

Bellagio is the pearl of Lake Como. It stands on a promontory at the point where the lake divides into two branches, and the views from its houses, villas and gardens are superb. The Florence is a handsome 18thC building occupying a prime position at one end of the main piazza, overlooking the lake. A terrace under arcades, where drinks and snacks are served, provides a welcoming entry to the hotel and the interior is no less appealing. Whitewashed walls, high vaulted ceilings and beams create a cool, attractive foyer; to one side, elegant and slightly faded seats cluster round an old stone fireplace. The atmosphere of rustic old-world charm is carried through to the vaulted dining-room.

Bedrooms have the same old-fashioned charm as the public rooms, furnished with cherry-wood antiques and attractive fabrics; the most sought after, naturally, are those with balconies and views over the lake (best from the upper floors). Breakfast can be taken on a delightful lakeside terrace under shady trees across the street from the hotel.

In the evening there is jazz in the elegant cocktail bar – one of Lake Como's smarter nightspots. The hotel has been in the same family for 150 years, and is now in the hands of brother and sister Ronald and Roberta, who speak good English. Ronald is fiercely proud of his hotel, but it has not been universally approved by readers in the past. More reports welcome.

Nearby Villa Serbelloni (in Bellagio); tour of the Madonna del Ghisallo (37 km); ferry and motor boat trips around Como.

Piazza Mazzini, Bellagio 22021 Como
Tel (031) 950342
Location on main piazza overlooking lake, with waterside terrace and garage
Food & drink breakfast, lunch, dinner
Prices rooms L95,000-L103,000; DB&B L70,000-L80,000; FB L75,000-L85,000
Rooms 32 double, 23 with bath, 8 with shower; 6 single; all rooms have central heating
Facilities dining-room, bar, reading and TV room, terrace
Credit cards AE, DC, MC, V
Children accepted
Disabled no special facilities
Pets well behaved ones accepted, but not in restaurant
Closed 20 Oct to 15 Apr
Proprietor Ronald Ketzlar

Western Lakes

Lakeside hotel, Bellagio

Du Lac

A congenial family atmosphere, light sunny rooms and, above all, a delightful setting on the central piazza combine to make the Hotel du Lac one of the most popular hotels in Bellagio. One of the most inviting features is the arcaded terrace, where drinks are served to guests and passers-by. Clients seeking more privacy have sole use of a roof garden for sunbathing and admiring the views. The decoration is essentially modern and not altogether inspiring, but the dining-room is particularly spacious and light, overlooking the lake, and several of the bedrooms have their own terrace or balcony.

Nearby Villa Serbelloni (in Bellagio).

Pza Mazzini 32, Bellagio 22021 Como
Tel (031) 950320
Location overlooking lake, in middle of resort
Food & drink breakfast, lunch, dinner
Prices rooms L85,000-120,000; reductions for children
Rooms 33 double, 30 with bath, 3 with shower; 10 single, 6 with bath, 4 with shower; 5 family rooms, all with bath; all rooms have central heating, phone, hairdrier
Facilities dining-room, sitting-room, bar, TV room, terrace, roof garden
Credit cards MC, V
Children welcome
Disabled no special facilities
Pets not accepted in dining room
Closed end-Oct to Easter
Proprietors Leoni family

Lakeside hotel, Bellagio

La Pergola

While most hotels in Bellagio are concentrated around the main piazza and waterfront, La Pergola is tucked away in the tiny, quiet village of Pescallo just to the south. It faces the eastern shores of Como, its lakeside terrace commanding beautiful views. Parts of the house are 500 years old. There are handsome flagstone floors, antiques, vaulted ceilings and an air of rustic simplicity. It is a small, modest family-run place where mother does the cooking (mainly fish from the lake) and the rest of the family look after the hotel. The bedrooms are all simple and old-fashioned but not without charm. And, being some of the cheapest rooms in one of the most popular resorts of the lakes, they are booked up well ahead in season.

Nearby Villa Serbelloni at Bellagio; lake tours.

Pescallo, Bellagio 22021 Como
Tel (031) 950263
Location one km S of Bellagio, overlooking lake; ample car parking
Food & drink breakfast, lunch, dinner
Prices rooms L26,500-L51,000
Rooms 12 double, 2 with bath; 2 single
Facilities dining-room, bar, terrace
Credit cards AE, DC, MC, V
Children accepted
Disabled no special facilities
Pets accepted
Closed Nov to Mar; restaurant only, Tue
Proprietor Sga M Mazzoni

Western Lakes

Lakeside guest-house, Isola dei Pescatori

Verbano

The Isola dei Pescatori, a tiny dot in Lake Maggiore, may not have the *palazzo* or gardens of neighbouring Isola Bella (unlike the other islands, it has never belonged to the wealthy Borromean family), but it is just as charming in its own way. The cafés and the slightly shabby, painted fishermens' houses along the front are, perhaps, reminiscent of a Greek island – though not an undiscovered one.

The Verbano is a large russet-coloured villa occupying one end of the island, its garden and terraces looking across the lake to Isola Bella. It does not pretend to be a hotel of great luxury, but it can offer lots of character and local colour, and the Zacchera family are friendly hosts. There are beautiful views from the bedrooms, and 11 of the 12 have balconies. Each room is named after a flower; most are prettily and appropriately furnished in old-fashioned style, with painted furniture; those which were a little tired-looking have apparently been refurbished.

But the emphasis in this small hotel is really on the restaurant. The cook has been here for about 30 years and home-made pastas are her speciality. If weather prevents eating on the terrace you can still enjoy views of the lake through the big windows of the dining-room.

Nearby Isola Bella (5 minutes by boat); Stresa, Pallanza, Baveno all linked to the island by regular ferry service

Via Ugo Ara 2, Isola dei Pescatori, Stresa 28049 Novara
Tel (0323) 30408
Location on tiny island with waterside terraces; regular boats from Stresa, where there is ample car parking space
Food & drink breakfast, lunch, dinner
Prices rooms L120,000 with breakfast; DB&B L90,000; FB L120,000

Rooms 12 double, 8 with bath, 4 with shower; all rooms have central heating
Facilities dining-room, sitting-room, bar, terrace
Credit cards AE, DC, MC, V
Children accepted
Disabled no special facilities
Pets accepted
Closed never
Proprietors Zacchera family

Western Lakes

Leon d'Oro

In itself, the Leon d'Oro is unremarkable. The bedrooms, although comfortable, are small, their furnishings are modern and anonymous, and as a room the restaurant is nothing more than pleasant. But the hotel enjoys a position which is unbeatable for beautiful lake views. From its shady vine-clad terraces on the water's edge, there are superb and commanding views of the enchanting little island of San Giulio and the wooded shore rising up behind – and the big windows provide views that are almost as wide as from within the restaurant. Another bonus of the location is the adjoining Piazza Motta, an animated square of extraordinary beauty.

Nearby island of San Giulio (quick trip by boat).

Orta San Giulio, Lago d'Orta 28016 Novara
Tel (0322) 90254
Location just off main piazza, with terrace right on lake; some car parking 100 m away
Food & drink breakfast, lunch, dinner
Prices rooms L48,000-L68,000; meals L20,000-L35,000
Rooms 26 double, 4 with bath, 22 with shower; 5 single, all with shower; one family room with shower; all have central heating; phone in 12 rooms
Facilities restaurant, lake terrace, bar, TV, solarium
Credit cards AE, MC, V
Children accepted
Disabled access difficult
Pets accepted
Closed Jan
Proprietors Maddalena and Giuseppina Ronchetti

Orta

Lying on the main square of Orta San Giulio, the Orta enjoys beautiful views across the lake. Its endearingly shabby classical façade flanks the southern side of the piazza, and the tables of its flowery terrace spill out on to the square. On the lakeside, the tables along the restaurant terrace have a bird's-eye view of the cluster of houses forming the lovely little island of San Giulio. Sitting areas are light and surprisingly spacious for a hotel of its size, though furnishings are rather old-fashioned and the atmosphere a trifle staid.

Nearby island of San Giulio (quick trip by motor or rowing-boat from the piazza).

Orta San Giulio 28016 Novara
Tel (0322) 90253
Location on central square of Orta San Giulio, overlooking lake; garage
Food & drink breakfast, lunch, dinner
Prices rooms L55,000-L100,000 with breakfast; meals L30,000
Rooms 24 double, 9 with bath, 15 with shower; 5 single with shower; 6 family rooms, 2 with bath, 4 with shower; all rooms have central heating, phone, view of lake; TV on request
Facilities dining-room with lakeside terrace, bar, TV room, sitting-room
Credit cards AE, DC, MC, V
Children accepted
Disabled some rooms suitable
Pets accepted
Closed Nov to Feb
Proprietors Marina Bianchi and Adriano Oglina

Western Lakes

La Bussola

The modern building and decoration of this hotel are not special, but the setting certainly is – in a splendid position, amid lawns, flowering shrubs and shady trees, on a hill looking down on lake Orta and the little island of San Giulio – and La Bussola has been built to make the most of the views.

Few of the bedrooms match up to the expectations aroused by the reception area, where antique features like beams and stone walls merge successfully with modern furnishings. The restaurant is simple, light and spacious, and there is understandable competition for space on the narrow lakeside terrace.

Nearby old town of Orta; San Giulio island.

Orta San Giulio 28016 Novara
Tel (0322) 90198
Location on hillside, above Orta; plenty of open car parking
Food & drink breakfast, lunch, dinner
Prices rooms L45,000-L49,000 (half board only, Jun-Sep)
Rooms 14 double, 2 single; 11 with bath, 5 with shower; all rooms have phone; 7 rooms have minibar
Facilities dining-room with terrace, bar, TV room; outdoor swimming-pool
Credit cards AE, MC, V
Children welcome; baby listening
Disabled not suitable
Pets dogs not accepted in dining-room
Closed Nov
Proprietor Mario Tassera family

Sole

The Sole at Ranco has been in the Brovelli family for over a century. It started off as a coaching inn and 'casa del vino' in 1872; now it is an elegant restaurant, renowned for the fish specialities created by Carlo Brovelli (now assisted by the sixth generation – Carlo's son Davide). Meals are served in friendly but formal style on the terrace or in the refined setting of the restaurant, smartly combining modern and antique furnishing. Bedrooms are swish suites, all with terrace and lake view.

Nearby castle at Angera (3 km), Arona (19 km).

Piazza Venezia 5, Ranco, Lago Maggiore 21020 Varese
Tel (0331) 976507
Location 10 km NW of Sesto Calende, in village, with garden and ample private car parking
Food & drink breakfast, lunch, dinner
Prices rooms L220,000; meals about L110,000
Rooms 8 twin-bedded suites, all with bath; all rooms have central heating, minibar, lake-view terrace, air-conditioning, safe, TV
Facilities dining-room, reading-room, conference room, bar, lakeside terrace
Credit cards AE, DC, MC, V
Children accepted if well behaved
Disabled no special facilities
Pets accepted, but not in dining-room or some bedrooms
Closed Jan
Proprietor Carlo Brovelli

Western Lakes

Lakeside hotel, Lenno

San Giorgio

This large white 1920s villa on the shores of Lake Como stands out against a backdrop of wooded hills and immaculate gardens running right down to the shore.

The San Giorgio's gardens are a delight. A path lined with potted plants leads down through neatly tended lawns to the lakeside terrace and the low-lying stone wall which is all that divides the gardens from the pebble beach and the lake. There are palm trees, arbours and stone urns where geraniums flourish. For a trip on the lake you need not go far – the ferry landing-stage lies close by.

The interior is no disappointment. The public rooms are large and spacious, leading off handsome halls. There are antiques wherever you go, and attractive touches such as pretty ceramic pots and copper pots brimming with flowers. The restaurant is a lovely light room with breathtaking views and the salon is equally inviting, with its ornate mirrors, fireplace and slightly faded antiques. Even the ping-pong room has a number of interesting antique pieces.

Bedrooms are large and pleasantly old-fashioned. Antiques and beautiful views are the main features, but there is nothing grand or luxurious about them – hence the reasonable prices. Half-board terms are available for stays of several days.

Nearby Tremezzo, Cadenabbia, Villa Carlotta (2-4 km); Bellagio (10 min boat crossing from Cadenabbia).

Via Regina 81, Lenno, Tremezzo 22019 Como
Tel (0344) 40415
Location on lakefront in private park, with parking for 30 cars, garage for 6
Food & drink breakfast, lunch, dinner
Prices rooms L40,000-L95,000; meals L28,000
Rooms 26 double, 20 with bath, 6 with shower; 3 single, one with bath; all rooms have central heating
Facilities dining-room, hall, reading-room, ping-pong room, terrace; tennis
Credit cards MC, V
Children accepted
Disabled access difficult
Pets not accepted
Closed Oct to Apr
Proprietor Margherita Cappelletti

Western Lakes

Villa Flora

This is a modest, home-like *pensione* with no pretensions, occupying a large pinkish-orange villa of indeterminate age. Its great asset is the lakeside situation, well below the road which runs through the little medieval village of Torno. Your bedroom could be spacious, with a parquet floor and 1960s furniture, or cramped with smarter laminated units; but it will be simple. The restaurant, too, is functional but spotlessly clean, and has a terrace overlooking the lake. The sitting-room is rather quaint: with its brocade and ornate ceiling, it seems unchanged since the turn of the century.

Nearby cathedral and town of Como; Bellagio (23 km).

Via Torrazza 10, Lago di Como, Torno 22020 Como
Tel (031) 419222
Location 7 km NE of Como; car parking nearby
Food & drink breakfast, lunch, dinner
Prices rooms L70,000-L90,000; meals L22,000-L45,000; reductions for children
Rooms 20 double, all with shower; 3 family rooms, all with shower; all rooms have phone
Facilities restaurant with terrace, breakfast area, sitting-room, bar; jetty, private beach
Credit cards MC, V
Children accepted
Disabled not suitable
Pets accepted
Closed Nov to Feb; restaurant only, Tue
Proprietor Sg Cavadini

Stella d'Italia

Mario Ortelli represents the third generation of his family to run this popular little hotel on the shores of Lake Lugano. Bedrooms are large, and have apparently been prettily refurbished; the little sitting-room has a pleasantly lived-in atmosphere, with pictures, comfy furniture and books – many in English. But the most appealing feature is the slightly unkempt garden and gravelled terrace, shaded by pergolas, which juts right into the lake.

Nearby Lugano (10 km), Menaggio (Lake Como) (20 km), Como (50 km).

Piazza Roma 1, San Mamete, 22010 Como Valsolda; postal address PO Box 46, 6976 Castagnola, Switzerland
Tel (0344) 68139
Location 8 km E of Lugano, 3 km from Swiss border; garage parking for 14 cars
Food & drink breakfast, lunch, dinner
Prices rooms L53,000- L82,000
Rooms 31 double, 4 single; 23 with bath, 12 with shower; all rooms have central heating, balcony, phone
Facilities 2 sitting-rooms, bar, dining-room, terrace; private beach
Credit cards AE, DC, MC, V
Children accepted
Disabled not very suitable
Pets small dogs only accepted
Closed mid-Oct to Apr; restaurant only, Wed
Proprietors Ortelli family

Western Lakes

Lakeside hotel, Varenna

Du Lac

This hotel, tucked away down a tiny alley off the old piazza of Varenna, is so close to Lake Como it seems perilously close to falling in. The villa itself is 19thC, but inside it is mostly modern and lacking character, though comfortable enough. The bedrooms have all the trimmings, right down to shower cap and tissues. It is when you open the balcony window that they come into their own. Dinner on the terrace, suspended above the hotel's private jetty, is the high point. The food is excellent, and the highly attentive staff serve from side-tables with panache.

Nearby Abbey; Ferry to Menaggio, Bellagio, Cadenabbia, Como.

Via del Prestino 4, Varenna
22050 Como
Tel (0341) 830238
Location on lakeside close to centre of village, 22 km NW of Lecco; with parking for about 20 cars (L10,000)
Food & drink breakfast, lunch, dinner
Prices rooms L95,000-L125,000; meals L40,000
Rooms 5 double, with shower; 5 single, with shower; 8 family

rooms, 3 with bath, 5 with shower; all rooms have central heating, phone, TV
Facilities dining-room, sitting-rooms, bar, 2 terraces
Credit cards AE, DC, MC, V
Children welcome
Disabled lift/elevator, easy access to some rooms
Pets in bedrooms only
Closed hotel mid-Dec to Feb; restaurant mid-Oct to mid-Mar
Proprietor Laura Pellizzari

Country villa, San Fedele d'Intelvi

Villa Simplicitas

This saffron-coloured 19thC country villa perches high above lakes Como and Lugano in flower-filled mountain pastures. The relaxed staff maintain its family-home atmosphere; there is only one TV, in the creaking billiard room along with a piano and a collection of books and games. Rough-cast stone stairs lead to the bedrooms, where the furniture is all antique; many of the beds are brass and iron. Even the old silvered radiators have style. Each room has its own particular interest – a rocking chair here, a grand old mirror there – and some have balconies; all have breathtaking views to the lakes or the mountains. You eat in the only modern area – a large sunny conservatory overlooking the valley below; the four-course menu of local produce offers plenty of choice.

Nearby Walks in woods; Lake Lugano (8 km); Lake Como (9 km).

San Fedele d'Intelvi,
Tremezzo 22101 Como
Tel (031) 831132
Location 2 km from San Fedele, NW of Argegno; with large garden and car park
Food & drink breakfast, lunch, dinner
Prices DB&B L95,000
Rooms 10 double, 4 twin; all

with bath; all rooms have central heating
Facilities dining-room, sitting-room, billiard room
Credit cards not accepted
Children accepted
Disabled no special facilities
Pets small ones only accepted
Closed Oct to Apr
Proprietor Sga Caselli

Lombardy

Antica Locanda Solferino

The last thing you might expect to find close to the centre of glossy Milan: a simple and modestly priced hotel of great character and charm, with a rather countrified atmosphere. Bedrooms are on the small side, but are prettily decorated and furnished with rustic antiques, and are not without modern conveniences; unusually for Italy, the bathrooms have not been given the chrome-and-glass treatment. In the past an additional attraction has been the restaurant which formed part of the inn and was highly popular in its own right – cosily traditional in style, with more than a hint of Parisian bistros. We now understand that the restaurant has changed hands, and may close altogether.

Nearby Brera gallery within walking distance.

Via Castelfidardo 2, Milan 20121
Tel (02) 657 0129
Location on tiny street between Arena and Piazza della Republica; no car parking space
Food & drink breakfast, lunch, dinner
Prices rooms L45,000-L91,000; meals from L30,000

Rooms 10 double, one single, all with bath; all rooms have central heating, phone
Facilities dining-room
Credit cards V **Children** accepted **Disabled** no special facilities **Pets** accepted
Closed 10 days in Aug; restaurant only, Sat lunch and Sun mid-July to mid-Sep
Manager Curzio Castelli

Castello di San Gaudenzio

Voghera is a small town south of Milan, where the plain of the Po starts to give way to hills; the Castello lies half-way between the town and the river, convenient for travellers on both the A7 and the A21. It is a brick-built 14thC castle in lush grounds, immaculately restored and sensitively furnished in mainly modern styles, which caters for big banqueting parties but also takes small numbers of guests. The public areas and bedrooms are superbly spacious, and for what you get the prices are modest.

Nearby Pavia (Carthusian monastery) (25 km).

Cervesina, Voghera 27050 Pavia
Tel (0383) 75025
Location 6 km N of Voghera, in hamlet; in large grounds, with ample car parking
Food & drink breakfast, lunch, dinner
Prices rooms L95,000-L160,000, suites L220,000; meals L40,000-L50,000
Rooms 9 double with bath, one single with shower, 2 suites; all rooms have central heating, TV, mini bar, phone, radio
Facilities dining-room, sitting-room/bar, meeting rooms, banqueting hall
Credit cards AE, DC, MC, V
Children welcome
Disabled access difficult
Pets not accepted
Closed never
Manager Stefano Natali

Lombardy

Restaurant with rooms, Bergamo

Agnello d'Oro

The Agnello d'Oro lies in the heart of the old city of Bergamo – a picturesque, tall and incredibly narrow building facing a tiny square with a fountain. The interior exudes charm and character. An antique desk and walls cluttered with ceramics, copper masks (made by the *padrone*) and various trophies for gastronomic excellence make up the tiny reception area, and the dining-room is a cosy trattoria with red-check table-cloths and a collection of bottles and copper pots covering every inch of wall and ceiling. The menu mainly features local dishes including the Bergamo speciality of small birds with *polenta*. Bedrooms verge on the basic; but they are bright and reasonably priced.

Nearby Colleoni chapel, Piazza Vecchia, church of Santa Maria Maggiore (all in upper town); Carrara gallery (lower town).

Via Gombito 22, Bergamo 24100
Tel (035) 249883
Location in the heart of the old upper town, on a small piazza; no private car parking
Food & drink breakfast, lunch, dinner
Prices rooms L40,200-L69,400; meals about L50,000
Rooms 16 double, 4 with bath, 12 with shower; 4 single, all with shower; all rooms have central heating, phone, colour TV
Facilities dining-room, bar
Credit cards AE, DC, MC, V
Children accepted
Disabled no special facilities
Pets accepted
Closed never
Proprietor Pino Capozzi

Restaurant with rooms, Bergamo

Gourmet

Bergamo's reputation for gastronomy is well deserved, and the food at the Gourmet is about as good as you will find anywhere in the upper city. Tagliatelle with artichokes and prawns, turbot with butter and capers, truffle and caviar soufflé – these are just a few of the dishes you might find on the menu. But the Gourmet is also a comfortable place to stay the night – the 12 bedrooms are spacious, light and civilized, with smart furnishings of high quality in modern Italian style, and luxury bathrooms. In summer, meals are taken on a delightful flowery veranda, overlooking the lower city.

Nearby Piazza Vecchia, Colleoni Chapel, Church of Santa Maria Maggiore in upper town; Carrara Academy in lower town.

Via San Vigilio 1, Bergamo Alta 24100
Tel (035) 256110
Location in upper town; private car parking
Food & drink breakfast, lunch, dinner
Prices rooms L84,000; meals about L70,000
Rooms 10 rooms, all with bath or shower, phone, TV, minibar
Facilities dining-room with terrace, sitting-room, bar
Credit cards AE, DC, MC, V
Children accepted
Disabled not suitable
Pets not accepted
Closed restaurant only, Tue
Managers Aldo Beretta and Franco Tassi

Lombardy

Al Duca

Sabbioneta was built in the 16th century by the great Gonzaga family as an ideal fortified city; now it is a sad backwater, but still retains some of its finest monuments. The Al Duca is a family-run, no-frills hotel close to the central square. The façade is classical Renaissance, and the hallway retains the original columns and pink marble stairway, but the rest is almost entirely renovated. Bedrooms are bright and airy with modern light-wood furniture, some of them large. But the main emphasis is on the restaurant – a relaxed, modest trattoria with pink table-cloths, ladder-back chairs and flowers on every table. The dishes are regional and the set meals moderately priced.

Nearby Palazzo del Giardino (gallery of antiquities); Parma, Mantua, Modena all within reach.

Via della Stamperia 18,
Sabbioneta 46018 Mantova
Tel (0375) 52474
Location very close to main
piazza, on fairly quiet street
with car parking available
Food & drink breakfast,
lunch, dinner
Prices rooms L30,000-
L79,000; lunch and dinner
L20,000- L25,000
Rooms 9 double, one single,
all with bath or shower; all
rooms have central heating,
intercom
Facilities breakfast room,
dining-room, bar
Credit cards AE, MC, V
Children accepted
Disabled no special facilities
Pets accepted
Closed Jan
Proprietor Giovanni Savi

Il Sole

On the corner of the lovely Piazza Vecchia, the Sole catches a lot of Bergamo's tourist trade. Primarily this is a place to eat. The restaurant doesn't have quite the same cosy charm as the Agnello d'Oro (page 41) but there is a cheerful atmosphere and you are unlikely to be disappointed either by food or service – and when weather permits you can eat in an attractive courtyard. In comparison to the restaurant standards, the bedrooms are fairly basic and uninspired. But the cost of a night's accommodation is low, and for the location – right in the heart of the old city – it is hard to beat.

Nearby Colleoni chapel, church of Santa Maria Maggiore (both at far end of square); Carrara Accademy in lower town.

Via Bartolomeo Colleoni 1,
Piazza Vecchia, Citta Alta,
Bergamo 24100
Tel (035) 218238
Location in upper town; car
parking awkward
Food & drink breakfast,
lunch, dinner
Prices rooms L59,000 with
breakfast
Rooms 11 double, all with
shower or bath
Facilities dining-room, bar,
courtyard
Credit cards AE, DC, MC, V
Children accepted
Disabled no special facilities
Pets small ones only accepted
Closed restaurant only, Thu
Proprietor Mauro Dipilato

Lombardy

Restaurant with rooms, Capriate San Gervasio

Vigneto

Capriate San Gervasio is a few minutes' drive from the main autostrada from Milan to Venice, convenient for an overnight stop. The Vigneto is a comfortable villa, perched on a river bank, surrounded by a beautifully kept small garden and terrace. The bedrooms are reasonably sized, with modern furniture, decorated in rather sombre beige and tans; those at the front look out over the tree-lined banks of the river. The dining-room is formal, with many pictures on the walls, and looks out over the covered terrace where you can eat in the summer months. The restaurant is popular with the locals.

Nearby Bergamo (17 km); Milan (35 km).

Capriate San Gervasio 24042
Bergamo
Tel (02) 909 39351
Location 12 km SW of
Bergamo, 2 km N of A4, on
banks of River Adda; with
private car parking
Food & drink breakfast,
lunch, dinner
Prices rooms
L80,000-L120,000; meals
L65,000-L80,000

Rooms 12 rooms, all with
shower, phone, TV
Facilities 2 sitting-rooms,
dining-room, conference
facilities
Credit card AE, V
Children accepted
Disabled no special facilities
Pets not accepted
Closed Aug; restaurant only,
Tue
Proprietor Casina Rosella

Lombardy

Broletto

The huge cobbled Piazza Sordello and the arcaded Piazza delle Erbe boast the finest buildings of Mantua, and the little Broletto lies conveniently between the two. It is a new building in an old shell and apart from the façade and stone-arched entrance the only real evidence of age are the old timber beams in a couple of the bedrooms. Elsewhere it is light, modern and essentially functional. Bedrooms are small, bright and spotlessly clean, and there is a modest little breakfast room on the first floor. As a modestly priced and welcoming base, with friendly staff, the Broletto serves its purpose well.

Nearby Apartments of the Palazzo Ducale (Piazza Sordello); Parma, Modena and Verona all within reach.

Via Accademia 1, Mantua 46100
Tel (0376) 326784
Location in heart of city, close to Teatro Bibiena; car parking available
Food & drink breakfast
Prices rooms L58,000-L88,500; breakfast L9,000
Rooms 8 double, 2 with bath, 6 with shower; 9 single, all with shower; all rooms have central heating, air-conditioning, minibar, phone, radio
Facilities breakfast room
Credit cards AE, DC, MC, V
Children accepted
Disabled no special facilities
Pets small ones only
Closed 24 Dec-3 Jan
Proprietor Augusto Bodoardo

San Lorenzo

The San Lorenzo stands close to the famous Piazza delle Erbe, and from its terrace there are fine views of historic Mantua. Although it is comparatively new, the hotel feels old. A simple façade with arcades conceals a rather grand lobby: ornate gilt mirrors, gleaming antiques and chandeliers. The first-floor salon is comfortable, quiet and civilized, with smart furnishings, huge bowls of carnations and coloured urns. The bedrooms have been a trifle gloomy (though a few have original antiques and all are in good taste), but are now being renovated.

Nearby Piazza Sordello, Palazzo; Parma, Modena, Verona all within reach.

Piazza Concordia 14, Mantua 46100 Mantova
Tel (0376) 220500
Location in historic heart of city, with private paying garage 60 m away
Food & drink breakfast
Prices rooms L127,000-L190,000
Rooms 28 double, 18 with bath, 10 with shower; 10 single, 6 with bath, 4 with shower; 3 suites, all with bath; all rooms have central heating, phone
Facilities sitting-areas, bar, TV room, breakfast room, roof-top terrace
Credit cards AE, DC, MC, V
Children accepted
Disabled no special facilities
Pets small ones only
Closed never
Managers Giuseppe and Ottorino Tosi

Lombardy

Restaurant with rooms, Pomponesco

Il Leone

Pomponesco was once a flourishing town under the Gonzaga family. Now it is a shadow of its former self, surrounded by unsightly modern suburbs. But the old part still has a certain faded charm, and just off the main piazza lies the Leone – an old peeling building which once belonged to a 16thC nobleman.

This is primarily a place to eat (it calls itself a trattoria). There are only eight bedrooms, and by far the most attractive features are the dining-areas. The *pièce de résistance* is the coffered 16thC ceiling and frieze in the main restaurant. Elsewhere the decoration is suitably elegant: 'old master' paintings, gilt wall lamps, a terrazzo floor and tables immaculately laid. Food here is among the best in the region, and local specialities include the traditional dish of braised beef with polenta, which was one of the popular dishes of the Gonzagas.

Beyond the restaurant a flower-filled inner courtyard leads to the bedrooms. These are built around an inviting pool and garden area where a country house atmosphere prevails.

In contrast with the Renaissance elegance of the restaurant, the bedrooms have a stark modernity. But they are peaceful, bright, comfortable and well maintained.

Nearby Mantua, Modena, Parma all within reach.

Piazza IV Martiri 2,
Pomponesco 46030 Mantova
Tel (0375) 86077
Location on small piazza, next to river Po, with garden and car parking
Food & drink breakfast, lunch, dinner
Prices rooms L41,000-L67,000; DB&B L63,000
Rooms 6 double, 3 single; all with shower; all rooms have central heating, phone, minibar
Facilities dining-room, bar, TV room; swimming-pool
Credit cards AE, DC, MC, V
Children accepted
Disabled access difficult
Pets accepted
Closed Jan; restaurant only, Sun pm and Mon
Proprietor Fernando Mori

Lombardy

Restaurant with rooms, Maleo

Sole

Franco Colombani fulfilled a lifelong ambition when he completed restoration of this 15thC coaching-inn, six years ago. Today it is reckoned among the finest restaurants in Italy. Franco's wife, Silvana, has brought her own distinctive personality to the traditional regional Italian cuisine that is Franco's quiet obsession. Dark, tasty stews, roast meats and fish are accompanied by fresh vegetables from the Colombanis' kitchen garden and fine wines from Franco's unfathomable cellars.

The building itself displays the same robust restraint as the cooking. The exterior is marked solely by a gilt wrought iron sun. Inside, the walls are white-washed, the ceilings timbered and the arched chambers carefully scattered with antique furniture, copper pots and ceramics. There are three dining-areas: the old kitchen, with its long traditional table, open fire and old gas hobs where on occasions Silvana finishes dishes in front of the guests; a smaller dining-room, with individual tables behind; and the stone-arched portico which looks out on to the idyllic courtyard garden. The bedrooms all have their individual high points, and good bathrooms. Those above the dining-room are the most traditional, while those overlooking the garden have a less impressive mix of old and new furnishings.

Nearby Piacenza; Cremona (22 km).

Via Trabattoni 22, 20076
Maleo
Tel (0377) 58142
Location behind church, off main piazza of village, 17 km NE of Piacenza; car parking available
Food & drink breakfast, lunch, dinner
Prices rooms L170,000-L290,000 with breakfast; meals L70,000

Rooms 8 double, all with bath; all rooms have central heating, phone, TV, minibar
Facilities 2 dining-rooms, sitting-room; garden
Credit cards AE, MC, V
Children welcome
Disabled no special facilities
Pets welcome
Closed hotel Jan and Aug; restaurant Sun eve, Mon
Proprietor Franco and Silvana

Lake Garda

Montefiori

The Montefiori is up the hill-side from Lake Garda, secluded in exotic gardens and parkland. It actually consists of three villas, all built relatively recently, though you would not notice at first glance – the style is distinctly old-world. Bedrooms are tastefully furnished in Venetian or Florentine style and nearly all have balconies facing the lake; the dining-room is a suave combination of modern and traditional styles. In summer, meals on the sheltered terrace are a delight, although the food itself – simple but generous – is not particularly remarkable.

Nearby Walks in the hills; boat trips to Desenzano, Sirmione, Torri del Benaco, Malcesine.

Gardone Riviera, Lago di Garda 25083 Brescia
Tel (0365) 21118/21976
Location 400 m from Gardone Riviera, with 2 private car parks
Food & drink breakfast, lunch, dinner
Prices rooms L80,000-L140,000 with breakfast; FB L110,000-L125,000
Rooms 35 rooms, 7 with bath, 28 with shower; all rooms have central heating, TV, phone, radio
Facilities 3 sitting-rooms, 3 bars, dining-room; outdoor swimming-pool, table-tennis; tennis nearby
Credit cards AE, DC, V
Children accepted
Disabled no special facilities
Pets accepted **Closed** never
Proprietor Giacomini Franca

Villa del Sogno

The Villa del Sogno ('Dream Villa') deserves its name, thanks to a remarkable position, overlooking Lake Garda and secluded in its own luxuriant park (with a pleasant swimming-pool). Inside, the villa is comfortable and traditional, with some handsome turn-of-the-century features and furnishings but also a smart modern 'American' bar; much of the hotel was renovated a couple of years ago. All the bedrooms have a lake view and there is also a vast terrace.

Nearby Gardone Riviera (2 km); boat trips on Lake Garda.

Via Zanardelli 107, Fasano di Gardone Riviera, Lago di Garda 25083 Brescia
Tel (0365) 20228
Location 2 km NE of Fasano di Gardone Riviera; in grounds with garage and ample car parking
Food & drink breakfast, lunch, dinner
Prices B&B L100,000-L165,000
Rooms 31 double, 3 single, all with bath or shower; all rooms have central heating, phone, TV
Facilities dining-room, American bar, sitting-rooms (one with TV), terrace; heated outdoor swimming-pool, tennis
Credit cards AE, DC, MC, V
Children not encouraged
Disabled no special facilities
Pets small dogs accepted in rooms only
Closed mid-Oct to end-Mar
Proprietors Calderan family

Lake Garda

Lakeside hotel, Gargnano

Baia d'Oro

Gargnano is a picturesque resort on the west shore of Lake Garda. The Baia d'Oro is a distinctive old yellow-and-green building, right on the shore, its little pier jutting out into the dark blue waters of Garda and its terrace commanding superb views of the mountains beyond. This outside terrace provides the focal point of the hotel: in the summer months you breakfast, lunch and dine outside. If you are lucky enough to arrive by boat you can moor at the pier and step straight into the hotel.

It is a small, friendly establishment run by the Terzi family. Gianbattista is however first and foremost an artist – you can see some of his water-colours of the lakes in the rooms of the hotel. It is his wife, a naturally warm hostess, who devotes all her time to maintaining high standards in the hotel. In 25 years she has transformed the building, first from a private home to a *pensione* and now to a delightful hotel which retains its former intimacy.

The main public room is the restaurant – a light and inviting area with baskets brimming with fruit, bowls of freshly cut flowers, pretty arches and glass doors opening on to the terrace. The great majority of the main dishes here are fish – either from the sea or straight from the lake. Bedrooms are bright and lovingly cared for, several with lakeside balconies.

Nearby Gardone Riviera, Desenzano, Sirmione, Garda, Malcesine – all reached by hydrofoil or ferry.

Via Gamberera 13, Gargnano 25084 Brescia
Tel (0365) 71171
Location in resort, with private car parking
Food & drink breakfast, lunch, dinner
Prices rooms L60,000-L90,000; meals L40,000-L50,000
Rooms 11 double, all with bath and shower; 2 single with shower; all have central heating, phone, minibar
Facilities dining-room, bar, TV room, sitting-room
Credit cards MC
Children small children not accepted **Disabled** access difficult **Pets** dogs accepted
Closed end Oct to Easter
Proprietors Terzi family

Lake Garda

Lakeside hotel, Gargnano

Giulia

From a *pensione* with no private bathrooms, the Giulia has gradually been upgraded over the years to a three-star hotel. But happily it retains the atmosphere of a family-run guest-house – albeit a large one. It is a beautiful, big spacious villa, built over a hundred years ago in Victorian style with Gothic touches. Signora Bombardelli, the proud owner, has been here for over 40 years, and thanks to all her hard work (for which she has received various awards) the Giulia is one of the most delightful places to stay on the entire lake.

For a start, it has a wonderful location, with gardens and terraces running practically on the water's edge. Inside, light and airy rooms lead off handsome corridors – a beautiful dining-room with Murano chandeliers, gold walls and elegant seats; a civilized sitting-room with Victorian armchairs; and bedrooms which range from light and modern to large rooms with timbered ceilings, antiques and balconies overlooking the garden and lake.

At garden level a second, simpler dining-room opens out on to a terrace with ample space and gorgeous views. At any time of day, it is a lovely spot to linger among the palm trees and watch the boats plying the blue waters of Garda.

Nearby hydrofoil and ferry services to villages and towns around Lake Garda.

Gargnano, Lago di Garda 25084 Brescia
Tel (0365) 71022/71289
Location 150 m from middle of resort, with garden and terrace down to lake; private car park
Food & drink breakfast, lunch, dinner
Prices DB&B L57,500; FB L95,000-L100,000
Rooms 14 double, 3 single; all with bath or shower; all rooms have central heating, intercom, phone
Facilities dining-room, veranda taverna, sitting- room, TV room, terrace; beach, swimming-pool, sauna
Credit cards AE, V
Children accepted
Disabled access difficult
Pets accepted
Closed mid-Oct to mid-Mar
Proprietor Rina Bombardelli

Lake Garda

Grifone

No tour of Lake Garda is complete without a visit to the lovely lakeside village of Sirmione. The massive Castle of the Scaligers, the gardens, beaches and Roman remains bring hoards of day-trippers, which makes it sensible to stay the night and see the quieter side of Sirmione. There is nothing very special about the bedrooms of the Grifone – in fact they are rather spartan and lack the charm evoked by the old stone façade, but the advantages are low prices, a family atmosphere and an excellent location with a small garden and terrace overlooking the castle and Lake Garda. There is a good restaurant in the same building, but a reader recommends cheaper alternatives nearby.

Nearby Castle of the Scaligers, grottoes of Catullus, both at Sirmione; boat tours of Lake Garda.

Via delle Bisse, Sirmione 25019 Brescia
Tel (030) 916014
Location on waterfront, overlooking lake and castle; with small garden; car parking some distance away
Food & drink no meals served
Prices rooms L38,000- L56,000

Rooms 17 rooms, all with bath or shower
Facilities TV room
Credit cards not accepted
Children accepted
Disabled not suitable
Pets not accepted
Closed Nov to mid-Apr
Proprietor Sga Bertaldi

Gardesana

The Gardesana, a great favourite with readers, has a plum position on the main piazza facing the busy little harbour of Torri del Benaco. The building has a long history, but the entire interior was smartly modernized in the late 1970s. Bedrooms are almost all identical – rustic wood furnishings, soft green fabrics, and plenty of little extras – and most have beautiful views of the lake. The historic Hall of the Ancient Council makes a suitably elegant dining-room, and there are a few tables on the balcony which overlooks the lake. Breakfast is sumptuous.

Nearby Bardolino (11 km), Malcesine (21 km).

Piazza Calderini 20, 37010 Torri del Benaco, Lago di Garda (Verona)
Tel (045) 722 5411
Location in middle of resort, on waterfront; private parking 150 m away
Food & drink breakfast, dinner
Prices rooms L55,000-L150,000; DB&B L65,000-L170,000; reduction for children sharing parents' room

Rooms 30 double, 4 with bath, 26 with shower; 3 single, all with shower; all rooms have central heating, air-conditioning, phone
Facilities dining-room, bar, TV room, lakeside terrace
Credit cards AE, DC, MC, V
Children welcome
Disabled no special facilities
Pets not accepted
Closed Nov and Dec
Proprietor Giuseppe Lorenzini

Lake Garda

Lakeside inn, San Vigilio

Locanda San Vigilio

In general the east side of Lake Garda is more downmarket than the west. A conspicuous exception is the Punta de San Vigilio; this verdant peninsula, dotted with olive trees and grazing ponies, is entirely owned by Count Agostino Guarienti, who lives in the impressive 16thC villa that dominates the headland. Visitors to its popular private beach pay dearly for the privilege. To the left of the big house, down a cobbled lane, nestling between the hillside and a miniature harbour, is this secluded inn of more modest proportions. Inside, blue carpets lend sophistication to the rustic furniture, white walls and wooden doors. Bedrooms are decorated in suitable antique style.

It is in the evening that the Locanda really comes into its own. With the day-trippers departed, guests are free to wander the peninsula, take a drink at one of the tables on the harbour wall, or join the Count for the evening meal in the Locanda (he eats here practically every night). The restaurant is candle-lit, and there is a walled garden dining-terrace with giant canvas parasols; both overlook the lake. The menu is cheerfully recited to guests by the smart, cheerful staff. Lake Garda carp is an inevitable house speciality, but there can be no better setting for it. The impression given is that little has changed since the Locanda received its first guests nearly two hundred years ago – except of course the prices, which are very high.

Nearby Garda (2 km).

San Vigilio 37016 Garda
Tel (0457) 256551
Location 2 km W of Garda, on promontory; parking available 150 metres away
Food & drink breakfast, lunch, dinner
Prices rooms L255,000-L300,000 with breakfast
Rooms 10 double, 4 suites, all with bath and shower; all rooms have central heating, air-conditioning, phone, TV
Facilities restaurant, dining-terrace, sitting-room, bar; walled garden
Credit cards AE, DC, V
Children accepted if well behaved
Disabled no special facilities
Pets accepted if well behaved
Closed Dec to Mar
Proprietor Count Agostino Guarienti

Veneto

Villa Michelangelo

This rather severe-looking 18thC villa – a Capuchin college before it was a hotel – was completely renovated in 1987, but there is a certain monastic purity about its modern decorative style even now (with the possible exception of the rather *risqué* mural in reception). Black slate floors and black leather chairs contrast with white walls inside. Bedrooms are similarly chic, with all possible conveniences. The staff are polite to a fault. This is a favourite haunt of the Vicenza business set.

Nearby Vicenza, Padua (33 km).

Via Sacco 19, Arcugnano
36057 Vicenza
Tel (0444) 550300
Location in countryside E of village, 7 km S of Vicenza, on road for Berici hills; in large grounds, with car parking
Food & drink breakfast, lunch, dinner
Prices rooms L120,000-L200,000 with breakfast; meals about L55,000
Rooms 15 double, 13 with bath, 2 with shower; 17 single, all with shower; 2 family

rooms, both with bath; all have central heating, air-conditioning, phone, TV, radio, minibar
Facilities dining-room, sitting-room, bar, terrace; swimming-pool
Credit cards AE, DC, MC, V
Children no special facilities
Disabled lift/elevator
Pets accepted if small, but not in public rooms
Closed hotel never; restaurant Sun eve, Mon
Proprietor Paolo Gobbetti

Villa Margherita

Yet another country villa well placed for excursions into Venice – this one opened as a hotel only since late 1987. Villa Margherita is less imposing than some from the outside, but charmingly furnished and decorated within, particularly in the public areas. The breakfast room is gloriously light, with French windows on to the garden, while the sitting-room has *trompe l'oeil* frescos and an open fireplace. Bedrooms are plainer, but thoroughly comfortable (and some are notably spacious).

Note that the highly regarded restaurant is a short walk from the main building.

Nearby Venice (10 km), Padua (30 km).

Via Nazionale 416, Mira Porte
30030 Venezia
Tel (041) 426 5800
Location on banks of Brenta river at Mira, 10 km W of Venice; ample car parking
Food & drink breakfast, lunch, dinner
Prices rooms L100,000-L180,000; meals from L38,000
Rooms 18 double, 3 with bath, 15 with shower; 1 single with

shower; all have central heating, phone, air-conditioning, TV, minibar
Facilities breakfast room, sitting-room, bar, restaurant (200 m walk); jogging track
Credit cards AE, DC, MC, V
Children accepted
Disabled some rooms on ground floor **Pets** by arrangement **Closed** never
Manager Stefano Maggiolini

Veneto

Country villa, Asolo

Villa Cipriani

Asolo is a beautiful medieval hilltop village commanding panoramic views of the plains below. The Villa Cipriani is a mellow ochre-washed house on the fringes of the village, the entrance leading directly from the street into a tiled hall with Oriental-style rugs and a grandfather clock, brass wall lights and an efficient but warm welcome from reception. The hotel is part of the Cigahotels group, but there is no chain-hotel atmosphere – the staff are friendly and attentive.

A tall covered terrace furnished in rustic style, and with an unusual pierced minstrel's gallery, leads out through glass doors into the prettiest of gardens, well stocked with flowers and partly laid to grass – a mass of roses, azaleas and mature trees. The restaurant areas dog-leg around the outside of the villa, over-hanging the valley below, with views out through plate-glass windows. For cooler evenings, there is a cosy bar.

The bedrooms all have lovely views, and are decorated in comfortably old-fashioned style, with prints, fresh flowers and antiques adding interest and colour. Pretty tiles have been used for the en suite bathrooms. The views, the comfort and the peaceful garden all combine to make this a most relaxing country hotel. Food is reported to be excellent.

Nearby Treviso (35 km); Padua, Vicenza, Venice within reach.

Via Canova 298, Asolo 31011 Treviso
Tel (0423) 55444
Location on NW side of village; with small garden and private car parking
Food & drink breakfast, lunch, dinner
Prices rooms L210,000-L300,000; meals about L87,500
Rooms 31 double; all rooms have colour TV, phone, air-conditioning
Facilities dining-room, bar, conference room
Credit cards AE, DC, MC, V
Children accepted
Disabled lift/elevator
Pets accepted
Closed never
Manager Giuseppe Kamenar

Veneto

Country villa, Cavasagra

Villa Corner della Regina

Driving through the flat agricultural land west of Treviso, it is something of a surprise to come upon this stately Palladian mansion, set in its vast estate and formal grounds at the end of a gravel drive. Lemon trees in huge terracotta pots and an ancient wisteria decorate your path to the entrance on the ground floor, to the side of a vast, sweeping set of stone steps. Once inside, you are greeted with a magnificent floral display, and it is clear that much of the original grandeur of the villa has been preserved, despite the provision of modern comforts.

The grandiose central reception room runs the full width of the villa; intricately carved French windows survey the drive, with floor-to-ceiling drapes trimmed in pink contrasting with the dark panelling and matching the deeply cushioned chairs and sofas. The bedrooms are huge, light and airy. They are all decorated differently and named rather than numbered: 'the Butterfly Room' or 'the Rose Room', for example. They offer a combination of both character and luxury, with period antiques, decorative painted plaster walls, abundant flowers and prints, and thick pile carpets.

The grounds are beautifully kept and the pool beside the villa has plenty of space for relaxation.

Nearby Palladian villas; Venice (40 km).

Cavasagra, Treviso 31050
Treviso
Tel (0423) 481481
Location 15 km W of Treviso, 3 km S of road to Vicenza; in formal gardens and parkland, with ample car parking
Food & drink breakfast, lunch, dinner
Prices rooms L220,000-L340,000 with breakfast
Rooms 4 double, 7 suites in villa and 12 apartments in annexe, all with bath; all have

TV, telephone, minibar
Facilities dining-rooms, breakfast room (in old orangery), sitting-room; heated outdoor swimming-pool, sauna, tennis
Credit cards AE, DC, MC, V
Children accepted
Disabled not suitable
Pets dogs accepted in annexe
Closed never
Proprietor Conte Nicolo and Contessa Dona Dalle Rose

Veneto

Country villa, Mogliano Veneto

Villa Condulmer

For about the price of a two-star hotel in central Venice you can stay in this lovely 18thC villa only a 20-minute drive away, and enjoy the perfect antidote to the hurly-burly of the city. The villa belonged to the last admiral of the Venetian Republic. The splendour of the era is preserved in the delightful rococo frescoes, the extravagant Murano-glass chandeliers, the period furniture and the formal gardens. Bedrooms in the main villa are quite grand, but those that have been converted from the old stables have the advantage of air-conditioning – you may well need it here in the height of summer.

Nearby Venice (18 km), Treviso (12 km)

Via Zermanese, Zerman
Mogliano 30121 Treviso
Tel (041) 457100
Location 4 km NE of
Mogliano Veneto; in large
park, with ample car parking
Food & drink breakfast,
lunch, dinner
Prices rooms L75,000-
L135,000; suites L200,000;
meals L60,000-L80,000
Rooms 45 rooms; all rooms
have phone, minibar; some
rooms have air-conditioning
Facilities dining-room,
sitting-rooms, bar, conference
facilities; swimming-pool,
tennis, 27- hole golf, riding
Credit cards AE, DC, MC, V
Children accepted
Disabled ground-floor
bedrooms suitable
Pets not accepted
Closed 8 Jan to 15 Feb
Proprietor Paolo Magrino

Country villa, Paderno di Ponzano

El Toulà

An old farmhouse lovingly converted by Alfredo Beltrame some 15 years ago, now a member of the Relais & Chateaux group and living up to the five C's of character, courtesy, calm, comfort and cuisine. People come from far and wide to experience the restaurant, where classic dishes are reinterpreted according to new ideas. It is also a popular place for wedding parties. It would not be a bad choice for a honeymoon either; the house is secluded and extremely civilized, with large bedrooms which vary from very comfortable to extremely luxurious, and stylish bathrooms. An expensive treat.

Nearby Treviso; Padua (35 km), Venice (45 km).

Via Postumia 63, Paderno di
Ponzano, 31050 Treviso
Tel (0422) 969023
Location 10 km NW of
Treviso; in delightful park and
vineyards with private car
parking
Food & drink breakfast,
lunch, dinner
Prices rooms L235,000-
L550,000; meals L80,000-
L95,000
Rooms 10 rooms, all with
bath; all have central heating,
phone, colour TV, minibar
Facilities dining-room, 2
sitting-rooms, conference
room, swimming-pool
Credit cards AE, DC, V
Children accepted
Disabled not suitable
Pets accepted
Closed never
Manager Giorgio Zamuner

Veneto

Country villa, Dolo

Villa Ducale

Driving along the N11 highway from Padua to Venice, you follow an old canal whose banks are scattered with beautiful 18thC villas, where wealthy Venetians used to escape the heat and stench of the city in the summer months. Villa Ducale is one of them – surrounded by calm formal gardens, with statues, a fountain, ancient trees and arbours.

The entrance to the hotel is rather grand. The marble-floored reception area leads into a vast chandeliered dining-hall, with a more modest breakfast room to one side. A grand staircase leads to the bedrooms. Upstairs, the floors are the original decorative wooden parquet, overlaid with patterned rugs. In the bedrooms, much of the furniture is antique and in some the original softly painted walls and ceilings remain. The larger rooms have balconies and all are of a generous size. The bathrooms have decorative tiles and gilt fittings, which in lesser surroundings might seem pretentious. The smaller rooms at the rear overlook horse chestnut trees.

The welcome and service are not a strong point. When we last visited, no dinner was available because the chef had driven off the road. We have no complaint about that, but no attempt was made to make alternative dinner arrangements.

Nearby Venice (20 km); Padua (21 km); Treviso (33 km); Palladian villas.

Riviera Martiri della Liberta 75, Dolo 30031 Venezia
Tel (041) 420094
Location 2 km E of Dolo
Food & drink breakfast, dinner; lunch on request
Prices rooms L70,000-L105,000; DB&B L75,000 (minimum 3 days)
Rooms 14 double, 4 with bath, 10 with shower; one single; all rooms have phone, terrace
Facilities sitting-room, bar, TV room, dining-room, games room
Credit cards AE, V
Children accepted
Disabled not suitable
Pets not accepted
Closed never
Proprietors Bressan family

Veneto

Town hotel, Padua

Donatello

So-called because it overlooks Donatello's famous equestrian statue of the Venetian soldier known as Gattamelata, this hotel is easily the best-placed in the city for tourists. Inside its slightly shabby old shell the place has been simply modernized. The bright trattoria-style restaurant has a pavement terrace with a fine view of the basilica (and is therefore called the Sant' Antonio). The food is plain, unpretentious and reasonably priced. An adequate base for exploring Padua; and Venice is only 20 minutes away by coach or (less conveniently) car.

Nearby Villas of the Brenta Canal; Vicenza (35 km); Venice (37 km); Euganean hills.

Via del Santo 102-104, Padua 35100
Tel (049) 875 0634
Location on N side of Piazza del Santo, near main entrance to basilica; with private garage
Food & drink breakfast, lunch, dinner
Prices rooms L83,000-L120,000
Rooms 38 double, 37 with bath; 4 single, one with bath, 2 with shower; all rooms have

phone, minibar, TV, air-conditioning
Facilities dining-room, café, terrace, 2 bars, TV room
Credit cards AE, DC, MC, V
Children accepted
Disabled not suitable
Pets accepted
Closed mid-Dec to mid-Jan; restaurant only, Wed, and Dec to third week Jan
Proprietor Franco Moresco

Town hotel, Padua

Leon Bianco

A small lift takes you up to the public rooms of this tall terraced building in the heart of Padua. Furnishings throughout are modern, the decorations up-to-the-minute pastels; there are pink-striped sofas in the sitting-room. Modern gallery posters hang on all the walls, and fresh flowers add to the feeling of simple elegance. The bedrooms, with squeaky wooden floors, are pleasant and reasonably sized – though the concertina bathroom doors are not ideal. Breakfast can be served in the tiny roof garden when the weather permits.

Nearby Cappella degli Scrovegni (Giotto frescoes), Basilica del Santo; Venice within reach.

Piazzetta Pedrocchi 12, Padua 35100
Tel (049) 875 0814
Location in middle of town, with car parking 300 m away
Food & drink breakfast
Prices rooms L83,500-L154,000; air-conditioning L9,000 extra
Rooms 16 double, all with shower; 2 single, both with shower; 4 family rooms, all

with bath; all rooms have colour TV, phone, minibar, air-conditioning
Facilities bar, sitting-room, breakfast room, roof terrace
Credit cards AE, DC, MC, V
Children welcome
Disabled lift/elevator to some bedrooms
Pets welcome
Closed never
Proprietor Paolo Morosi

Veneto

Country villa, Oderzo

Villa Revedin

Amid open countryside just outside the little town of Gorgo al Monticano, the Villa Revedin is sheltered within its own mature, tree-screened park. Formal gardens at the front and an old fountain lead on to the park through cool tree-lined paths.

The villa dates from the 15th century, and the antique atmosphere is well preserved in the huge main salon, which has an imposing grand piano. The restaurant (which attracts local customers, particularly for its fish specialities) is more relaxed, in the familiar Italian sophisticated-rustic style, with wooden ceiling, terracotta tiled floor and cream decorations. The hotel's sitting areas have large leather sofas and chairs, and there is a pretty open fireplace for cooler evenings.

Most of the bedrooms are of generous size, and some have balconies. All have pretty views out over the park and gardens. Although most of the furniture is modern, the tall ceilings, shuttered windows, open fireplaces and tasteful decoration lend a charm to the modern competence.

This is a luxury hotel, but its setting and helpful staff make it charming and welcoming in a way that most such hotels are not.

Nearby Treviso (32 km); Venice within reach; Venetian villas.

Via Palazzi 4, Gorgo al Monticano, Oderzo 31040 Treviso
Tel (0422) 740669
Location 4 km E of Oderzo, signposted just N of Gorgo al Monticano; in private grounds with ample car parking
Food & drink breakfast, lunch, dinner
Prices rooms L58,000-L120,000
Rooms 14 double, 14 single, 4 family rooms; all with bath and shower; all rooms have TV, radio, phone
Facilities breakfast room, dining-room, function room, bar, sitting-room, conference room (30 people)
Credit cards AE, DC, MC, V
Children very welcome
Disabled not suitable **Pets** accepted by arrangement
Closed restaurant only, Jan
Proprietor Armando Salmistraro

Veneto

Locanda da Lino

The cooking at this rustic restaurant in the mountains north of Treviso is not sophisticated – a predominance of soups and pasta dishes followed by grills – but good enough to have earned a Michelin star and to have greatly impressed our inspector. The atmosphere in the beamed dining-room, its walls covered in copper and china, is delightfully friendly. The smallish but comfortable and stylish bedrooms (with smart bathrooms in the best Italian fashion) are in an ultra-modern annexe; all are on the ground floor, and each has its own small garden to the front (for privacy rather than sitting in).

Nearby Treviso (30 km); Palladian villas.

Via Brandolini 31 Solighetto, Pieve di Soligo 31050 Treviso
Tel (0438) 82150
Location 2 km N of Pieve, 12 km W of Conegliano, at Solighetto; in countryside, with private car parking
Food & drink breakfast, lunch, dinner
Prices rooms L70,000; meals L35,000

Rooms 12 double, 5 family rooms; all rooms have central heating, phone, TV, minibar
Facilities dining-room, bar
Credit cards AE, DC, MC
Children accepted
Disabled access to some rooms possible
Pets not accepted
Closed July
Proprietor Lino Toffolin

Villa Conestabile

During the 16thC, a main ambition of most of Venice's patricians was to own a country villa, not too far from the city. The Villa Conestabile was the fulfilment of one such ambition. It is not a luxury hotel, but it will cost you about half the price of a similar standard of accommodation in Venice. It still has touches of grandeur – elaborate chandeliers, grand staircases and fine period pieces of furniture, but the restaurant and bar are comparatively simple. Bedrooms are in keeping with the style of the building, and there is a spacious terrace for breakfast and for evening drinks.

Nearby Treviso; Venice (20 km), Padua (30 km).

Via Roma 1, Scorze 30037 Venezia
Tel (041) 445027
Location 13 km SW of Treviso, in village; in extensive grounds, with ample car parking
Food & drink breakfast, lunch, dinner
Prices rooms L59,000- L98,000
Rooms 18 double, 4 with bath, 12 with shower; 6 single, 3

with shower, one with bath; all rooms have central heating, phone, TV
Facilities dining-room, bar, sitting-room, TV room
Credit cards AE, MC, V
Children welcome
Disabled no special facilities
Pets small dogs only accepted
Closed restaurant only first 3 weeks in Aug
Manager Sga Martinelli

Veneto

Le Beccherie

Treviso is a charming old town, ringed by ramparts and cut through by canalized streams, and this friendly, family-run restaurant-cum-hotel lies at the heart of its intricate network of narrow one-way streets. Le Beccherie itself is a long-established, unpretentious but highly regarded restaurant on a tiny piazza, close to the splendid 13thC town hall. Above it are a few simple bedrooms, and across the piazza is a modernized annexe – known as the Albergo Campeol – containing more comfortable rooms with bathrooms.

Nearby old town of Treviso; Venice (30 km), Padua (50 km).

Piazza G Ancillotto 10, Trevisco 31100
Tel (0422) 540871
Location in historic heart of city; public car parking in front of hotel
Food & drink breakfast, lunch, dinner
Prices rooms L40,000- L74,000
Rooms 18 double, 12 with shower; 9 single, 4 with shower; all rooms have central heating; 16 rooms have radio and phone
Facilities bar, dining- room, TV room
Credit cards AE, DC, MC, V
Children accepted
Disabled no special facilities
Pets not accepted
Closed restaurant only: Thu pm Fri and 3 weeks late July
Proprietor Ado Campeol

Torcolo

This faded ochre building stands just a few steps away from the famous Arena, in the heart of Verona. Another attraction is the warm welcome of Signora Pomari and her partner Diana, both of whom speak English. Public rooms are confined to the reception (where the most interesting features are the modern Italian lithographs), a tiny TV room and an equally tiny breakfast room. But breakfast can be served outside on a terrace, in the shade of white parasols. Bedrooms are decorated in a variety of styles: Italian 18thC, art nouveau and modern. Most are not as noisy as you might expect – though street-side ones can be affected by the bar next door. The neighbouring Ristorante Torcolo is, according to Signora Pomari, 'good but expensive'.

Nearby Piazza Bra, Castelvecchio.

Vicolo Listone 3, Verona 37121
Tel (045) 800 7512
Location in middle, close to Arena; limited car parking
Food & drink breakfast
Prices rooms L46,000- L78,000
Rooms 15 double, one with bath, 14 with shower; 4 single, all with shower; all rooms have central heating, air-conditioning, phone
Facilities breakfast room, TV room, terrace
Credit cards not accepted
Children accepted
Disabled no special facilities
Pets accepted
Closed 2 weeks Jan
Proprietor Silvia Pomari

Veneto

Country villa, Ospedaletto di Pescantina

Villa Quaranta

Ospedaletto earned its name as a stopping-off point on the way to and from the Brenner pass; the Chapel of Santa Maria di Mezza Campagna was where travellers stayed. The Villa Quaranta carries on the tradition, though horses are no longer accommodated and German pilgrims come over the pass to pay homage to opera rather than Rome. The original 13thC chapel, with its Ligozzi frescos, now forms one side of the Villa Quaranta's pretty inner courtyard; the remainder of the buildings are 17thC. The main house is rather imposing, but the hotel's reception, dotted with antiques, is in the less intimidating parts behind, with the bedrooms set around the courtyard. The bedrooms are scrupulously clean, with plain carpets, polished stained-wood furniture, and bright shower rooms of pine and white ceramics. Downstairs, there is a snug little converted cellar where the splendid buffet breakfast is served. The staff are generally eager to please, and Claudio Battisti keeps an eye on things from his garden office.

The formal dining-halls in the main house form the restaurant: awe-inspiring frescoed walls, stone-arched doors and tiled floors, appropriately furnished with red leather straight- back chairs. The food here is an excellent mix of regional and international cuisine, though service can be a bit stretched at times. The only other complaint is that there are no garden chairs from which to enjoy the wonderful grounds.

Nearby Verona (minibus service to opera); Lake Garda (12 km).

Via Brennero, Ospedaletto di Pescantina 37026 Verona
Tel (0457) 156211
Location on SS12, 15 km NW of Verona
Food & drink breakfast, lunch, dinner
Prices rooms L125,000-L310,000 with breakfast; DB&B L112,000-L158,000
Rooms 25 double, 4 single, 15 family rooms, all with bath; all rooms have central heating, air-conditioning, phone, TV, radio, minibar
Facilities 4 dining-rooms, bar, TV room; swimming-pool, 2 tennis courts
Credit cards AE, DC, MC, V
Children no special facilities
Disabled lift/elevator
Pets not accepted **Closed** hotel never; restaurant Mon
Manager Claudio Battisti

Venice

Locanda Cipriani

This delightful little family-run restaurant and bar is only 40 minutes by regular boat from Venice (calling at Murano and Burano on the way), but in another, more peaceful world. Simple, country antique furniture and pretty plates decorate the hall, where arch-shaped wooden doors lead into the rooms. The double bedrooms (effectively small suites) overlook the garden, from which come the salads used in the excellent restaurant and the flowers which decorate the rooms and tables.

Depending on your mood and the seasons, you can eat in the restaurant itself, the covered terrace or in the open courtyard.
Nearby cathedral of Torcello.

Piazza S Fosca 29, Torcello, Venice 30012
Tel (041) 730757
Location on Torcello island; in gardens
Food & drink breakfast, lunch, dinner
Prices DB&B L230,000; FB L320,000
Rooms 2 double, 2 single, all with bath and shower; all rooms have phone; double rooms have sitting-room
Facilities 4 dining-areas, bar
Credit cards AE, DC, MC, V
Children welcome
Disabled not suitable
Pets accepted at proprietor's discretion
Closed early Nov to mid Mar
Proprietor Bonifacio Brass

Villa Mabapa

Despite the extensions to the original 1930s family house, the Villa Mabapa still manages to give the impression of a private home. What is more, it is good value, particularly in comparison with the large, better-known hotels on the beach at the Lido. The location may be slightly out of the way, but it does have the bonus of wonderfully peaceful rooms, a garden and a summer dining terrace – all welcome after the frenzy of visiting Venice. There are two buildings – the main hotel with the public rooms and some bedrooms (the best are on the first floor) and an annexe in the garden with more up-to-date bedrooms.
Nearby Venice (10/20 minutes by ferry).

Riviera San Nicolo' 16 – Venice Lido 30126 Venice
Tel (041) 526 0590
Location on the lagoon side of the Lido, with fine views of city; in pretty garden
Food & drink breakfast, lunch, dinner
Prices rooms L80,000-L230,000; meals about L35,000
Rooms 47 double, 15 single, all with bath or shower; all have TV, phone; 30 rooms have air-conditioning
Facilities dining-room, dining terrace, bar, sitting-room
Credit card AE, DC, MC, V
Children accepted
Disabled some rooms suitable
Pets no dogs allowed in dining-room
Closed mid-Nov to just before Christmas
Proprietor Sg Vianello

Venice

Town guest-house, close to Accademia

Accademia

Book weeks in advance and you might just be lucky enough to get a room at the Accademia – a great favourite among British and French visitors to Venice (and particularly regular visitors, whose custom is cultivated). Though it is not quite the bargain it used to be, the Accademia is still a place of immense charm and character with prices that most people can afford and a very convenient but tranquil location. But what really distinguishes the *pensione* is its gardens – the spacious patio facing the canal, where tables are scattered among potted plants and classical urns, and the grassy garden at the back where wisteria, roses and fruit trees flourish.

It is thanks to the Marzollo family, who have been here since 1955, that the aristocratic charm of the villa has been preserved. It was originally built as a private mansion, and earlier this century housed the Russian consulate. There are still touches of grandeur, and the furnishings for the most part are classically Venetian. But there is no trace whatever of formality.

Reception is a spacious hallway-cum-salon, with ample seating, stretching between two gardens. The airy breakfast room has chandeliers and a beamed ceiling supported by columns; but, weather permitting, guests will inevitably opt to start their day in the garden, and end it there with evening drinks. Most of the bedrooms are rather old-fashioned, with a haphazard collection of antiques. Some are surprisingly spartan, and those on the upper floor are quite modern in style.

Nearby Accademia gallery, Grand Canal.

Fondamenta Maravegie, Dorsoduro 1058, Venice 30123
Tel (041) 523 7846
Location on side canal just S of Grand Canal, with gardens front and back
Food & drink breakfast
Prices rooms L47,000-L160,000; extra bed L42,000
Rooms 20 double, 8 with bath, 8 with shower; 6 single, 5 with bath; all rooms have central heating, phone
Facilities breakfast room, bar, sitting-room
Credit cards AE, DC, MC, V
Children welcome
Disabled no special facilities
Pets small animals accepted
Closed never
Manager Franco Marzollo

Venice

American

This shuttered, terraced *palazzo* tucked behind the Accademia on a quiet residential canal, has in recent years been restored throughout to serve its new purpose as a hotel. The bedrooms, all of a reasonable size, were refurbished in 1989, in Venetian style. Downstairs, the little breakfast room and two adjoining sitting-rooms have old-fashioned patterned wallpapers and wood panelling; comfy chairs, some rustic wooden furniture, large paintings of Venice and Oriental-style rugs on the terrazzo floors give an air of quiet comfort. Sg Graffi and his staff are helpful and friendly, and have made the American a peaceful haven.
Nearby Accademia gallery; church of Santa Maria della Salute.

San Vio 628, Venice 30123
Tel (041) 520 4733
Location close to the Accademia, off Campo Santo
Food & drink breakfast
Prices rooms L90,000-L180,000
Rooms 24 double, 14 with bath, 10 with shower; 5 single, 3 with bath, 2 with shower; 5 family rooms, all with bath; all rooms have colour TV, minibar, phone, air-conditioning
Facilities breakfast room, sitting-room, TV room
Credit cards AE, DC, MC, V
Children babies and toddlers not welcome
Disabled some rooms on ground floor
Pets small dogs only welcome
Closed never
Proprietor Umberto Graffi

Ateneo

The Ateneo is partly an old *palazzo*, once the home of an aristocratic Venetian family. It is now a relatively simple place, but the classical Venetian style is in evidence – Murano glass chandeliers, flocked walls, fancy mirrors, carved bedheads and reproduction Venetian armchairs. Bedrooms are small but carefully and neatly furnished and reasonably quiet; and the bathrooms are spotless. The lack of a restaurant is no problem in an area liberally endowed with lively-looking trattorias. The shady courtyard in front of the hotel is no longer reserved for the plants: bar service is available.
Nearby Teatro la Fenice; Piazza San Marco.

San Marco 1876, Venice 30124
Tel (041) 520 0588
Location very close to Fenice theatre, with some rooms facing canal
Food & drink breakfast
Prices rooms L81,000-L191,000 with breakfast
Rooms 16 double, 4 with bath, 10 with shower; 3 single; 4 family rooms with bath or shower; all rooms have air-conditioning, central heating, minibar, phone, radio, colour TV
Facilities breakfast room, sitting-area, TV room, garden
Credit cards AE, V
Children accepted
Disabled no special facilities
Pets welcome
Closed never
Proprietor Massimo Maschietto

Venice

Alboretti

Enthusiastic students of Venetian painting will find this little hotel the most convenient in Venice. It lies right alongside the gallery of the Accademia and the world's finest collection of Venetian art. It is also well placed for exploration further afield: a water-bus landing-stage on the Grand Canal lies just a few steps from the entrance to the hotel.

Like many small hotels in Venice, the Alboretti occupies a building which is several centuries old, but what distinguishes it from many others is the warm welcome and the genuine family atmosphere – something of a rarity in Venice. Reception is a cosy wood-panelled room with a model of a 17thC galleon in its window; the sitting-room is small, but the upper TV room is a comfortable retreat (the TV is rarely used). The dining-room has recently been attractively extended.

The bedrooms have recently been renovated; the style is predominantly simple and modern, though a few rooms have an antique or two. Like the rest of the hotel, they are well cared for and spotlessly clean; but the bathrooms are tiny. The most peaceful are those overlooking the pretty leafy courtyard at the back of the hotel.

Nearby Accademia gallery, Zattere, Gesuati church.

Accademia 882, Venice 30123
Tel (041) 523 0058
Location between the Grand Canal and Giudecca Canal; nearest landing-stage
Food & drink breakfast, dinner
Prices rooms L57,500-L137,000 with breakfast
Rooms 12 double, 3 with bath, 9 with shower; 6 single, all with showers; one family room with bath; all rooms have central heating, phone
Facilities sitting-room, dining-room, TV room, bar
Credit cards AE, MC, V
Children welcome – cots on request
Disabled no special facilities
Pets small dogs only accepted
Closed never
Proprietor Anna Linguerri

Venice

Bel Sito

If you can't afford a room in the prestigious Gritti Palace, there are plenty of cheaper places close by. One of these is the Bel Sito, opposite the inelegantly Baroque church of Santa Maria del Giglio on the square of the same name. It is quiet despite being central – very close to one of the best shopping streets of the city. A small patio in front of the hotel, with potted plants and parasols, makes an excellent spot for watching the shoppers and tourists crossing the Campo. Bedrooms vary widely. The most inviting are those at the back, with prettily painted furniture; those overlooking the church are old-fashioned and a little dark in comparison.

Nearby Piazza San Marco, Accademia Gallery.

Campo Santa Maria del Giglio, San Marco 2517, Venice 30124
Tel (041) 522 3365
Location in square, opposite church, about 5 minutes W of San Marco
Food & drink breakfast
Prices rooms L73,000-163,000 with breakfast
Rooms 34 double, 4 single, all with bath or shower; all have phone, some minibar
Facilities 2 breakfast rooms, bar, sitting-room, terrace
Credit cards MC, V
Children accepted
Disabled no special facilities
Pets accepted by prior arrangement
Closed never
Proprietor Sg L G Serafino

Calcina

Over a hundred years ago, the great art historian Ruskin singled out the Calcina for its low prices and stunning views; the prices remain low by Venetian standards – and the view south to the Giudecca can hardly have changed at all. The *pensione*'s position on the spacious stone-flagged quay of the Zattere has other advantages too – it is out of the main tourist bustle, but not too far out. The Calcina has recently been totally renovated, happily without loss of its character. There are now many more private bathrooms, but the simple old-fashioned furnishings remain. This lack of sophistication seems only to enhance the romantic appeal of Ruskin's House, as it is known. Waterfront rooms are booked up weeks, even months ahead.

Nearby Accademia gallery, Gesuati church.

Zattere 780, Venice 30123
Tel (041) 520 6466
Location on the Zattere waterfront
Food & drink breakfast
Prices rooms L73,000-L163,000
Rooms 30 double, 10 with bath, 16 with shower; 10 single; all rooms have central heating, phone
Facilities sitting-area, TV room, terrace overlooking lagoon
Credit cards all accepted
Children welcome if under parents' control
Disabled no special facilities
Pets accepted if not too big
Closed Jan
Manager Alessandro Szemere

Venice

Casa Frollo

You are unlikely to fall upon the Casa Frollo by chance. For many years this distinguished 17thC *palazzo* on the island of Giudecca was a private residence and that is the way it likes to remain. There is no hotel sign, just a small plaque outside saying Casa Frollo. Ring the bell and the sturdy wooden door mysteriously opens revealing a cool courtyard and a quiet, sweet smelling garden beyond. A flight of stone stairs takes you up to the main salon – a beautiful big room of Renaissance furnishings, abundant flowers and a fine collection of paintings from old and modern masters. But perhaps the greatest attraction is the grand panorama the house affords across the lagoon to the church of Santa Maria della Salute and the Doges' Palace – just a five-minute ferry ride away.

Bedrooms are simpler than the grandeur of the salon might suggest and bathrooms, where they exist, are somewhat spartan. But all is crisp and clean and the rooms are tastefully furnished, with whitewashed walls, quarry-tiled floors and antique wardrobes. Casa Frollo offers none of the luxuries of hotels just across the water – no porter, no English-speaking staff – but for character and slightly eccentric charm it is hard to beat. Traditionally a favourite among the French literati, it is now becoming increasingly popular with British visitors who are looking for something entirely different.

Nearby Piazza San Marco (about five minutes across the water).

Giudecca 50, Fondamenta delle Zitelle, Venice 30133 **Tel** (041) 522 2723 **Location** on Giudecca, facing Venice; with garden; nearest landing-stage Zitelle **Food & drink** breakfast, drinks **Prices** rooms L51,900-L148,000	**Rooms** 26 rooms, 9 with bath or shower; all with telephone **Facilities** breakfast/sitting area **Credit cards** not accepted **Children** welcome **Disabled** not suitable **Pets** accepted **Closed** end Nov to mid-Mar **Manager** Marino Soldan

Venice

Ai Due Fanali

The station hotels of Venice (like those of most cities) are not usually noted for being the most salubrious, but there are of course exceptions – including the Due Fanali. It is a tiny family-run hotel, about five minutes from the station but across the Grand Canal and well away from the main concentration of station hotels. It is tucked in the corner of a quiet *campo* flanking the Grand Canal, and in front of it there is a pretty terrace with parasols and plants. The interior is compact and simple but the best things about it are the quiet, spotlessly clean modern rooms, the friendly atmosphere and the reasonable prices.

Nearby Grand Canal

Campo San Simeone Grande 946, Santa Croce, Venice 30135
Tel (041) 718490
Location on small square, close to station
Food & drink breakfast
Prices rooms L47,500-L98,000
Rooms 8 double, 4 with shower; 3 single, one with shower; 6 family rooms, one with bath, 5 with shower; all have central heating, phone
Facilities bar with TV, breakfast and sitting areas, terrace
Credit cards AE, DC, MC, V
Children accepted
Disabled no special facilities
Pets small ones only
Closed Nov
Proprietors Zanegreco family

Villa Parco

If your wish is to combine the sights of Venice with a beach holiday, the Lido is still the obvious place to stay – even if it has lost its former cachet. The problem is the price of hotels – especially those right on the waterfront. This one, however, lies a few minutes away in a quiet residential area and its prices are very reasonable.

A simple, unpretentious place, the Villa Parco's greatest asset is the garden, where you can take breakfast and evening drinks. The building is in art nouveau style, though the furnishings are mainly modern – only one bedroom has antiques. As well as breakfast, you can get snacks from the bar.

Nearby Casino; Venice (boats every ten minutes).

Via Rodi 1, Venice Lido 30126
Tel (041) 526 0015
Location about 5 minutes' walk from beach; car parking
Food & drink breakfast
Prices rooms L52,000-L145,000
Rooms 15 double, 3 with bath, 12 with shower; 2 single, all with shower; 5 family rooms, 3 with bath, 2 with shower; all rooms have central heating, phone, TV, air-conditioning, minibar
Facilities sitting-room, bar, breakfast room
Credit cards AE, DC, MC, V
Children accepted if well behaved
Disabled no special facilities
Pets small dogs and cats accepted
Closed Jan to Carnival (Feb)
Proprietors Barbaro family

Venice

Town hotel, near St Mark's

Flora

Such is the popularity of this small hotel, tucked away in a cul-de-sac close to St Mark's, that to get a room here you have to book weeks or even months in advance. You only need to glimpse the garden to understand why it is so sought after. Creepers, fountains and flowering shrubs cascading from stone urns create an enchanting setting for morning coffee and croissants, or evening drinks in summer. It is undoubtedly one of the prettiest and quietest gardens in Venice – somehow far removed from the hubbub of St Mark's.

The lobby is small and inviting, enhanced by the views of the garden through a glass arch. The atmosphere is one of friendly efficiency, reception acting as a mini tourist information bureau for the many English-speaking guests. There are some charming double bedrooms with painted carved antiques and other typically Venetian furnishings, but beware of other comparatively spartan rooms, some of which are barely big enough for one, let alone two. Prices are quite steep for a small three-star hotel but most guests agree that the setting and the intimate atmosphere make it well worth the cost.

Nearby Piazza San Marco

Calle Larga 22 Marzo 2283/a, San Marco, Venice 30124
Tel (041) 520 5844
Location 300 m from Piazza San Marco in cul-de-sac
Food & drink breakfast
Prices rooms L138,000-L190,000
Rooms 32 double, 6 single, 6 family rooms; all with bath and/or shower; all rooms have phone; air-conditioning at extra cost
Facilities breakfast room, bar, sitting-room
Credit cards AE, DC, MC, V
Children accepted
Disabled no special facilities
Pets accepted
Closed mid-Nov to Jan
Proprietors Alex and Roger Romanelli

Venice

Town hotel, west of St Mark's

Do Pozzi

In a dead-end street close to San Marco, this calm hotel enjoys one of the quietest locations of central Venice. It is also well placed for chic shopping. Bedrooms are all identical: neat, modern, in browns and beiges, and fully equipped. Public rooms consist of an elegant but tiny breakfast room and an equally tiny sitting-room with TV. Understandably more popular is the leafy courtyard at the entrance of the hotel where cats doze and guests take breakfast or evening drinks.

Ask where to lunch and dine and you will be ushered to the adjoining Raffaele restaurant. It is an inviting spot with a terrace overlooking a picturesque canal, and inside a dining-room festooned with antique weaponry.

Nearby Piazza San Marco (2-3 min walk).

Via XXII Marzo, Venice 30124
Tel (041) 520 7855
Location 200 m W of Piazza San Marco, in a dead-end street off Via XXII Marzo
Food & drink breakfast; bar service
Prices rooms L65,000-L130,000; meals L25,000
Rooms 25 double, 10 single; all with bath or shower; all rooms have central heating, air-conditioning, minibar, phone, TV
Facilities breakfast room, TV room, courtyard/patio
Credit cards AE, DC, MC, V
Children accepted
Disabled access difficult
Pets small ones only
Closed never
Proprietor Giovanna Salmaso

Town hotel, near Fenice theatre

Kette

This polished little hotel can boast an excellent position – convenient for many of the major sights, but reasonably quiet.

The building dates from the mid-18th century, and the comfortable TV room and writing-room retain a period elegance, with rugs on parquet floors, and, in the latter, Regency stripes. The breakfast room has a more modern feel, emphasized by the furniture, but retaining the parquet floor and exposed beams. Bedrooms are comfortable and restrained, with simple pieces of reproduction dark-wood furniture against light wallpapers – smarter than average for Venice.

Nearby Teatro la Fenice, Piazza San Marco, Rialto.

San Marco 2053, Venice 30124
Tel (041) 522 2730
Location close to the Fenice theatre, W of St Mark's
Food & drink breakfast
Prices rooms L75,000-L190,000 with breakfast; suites L215,000-L320,000
Rooms 38 double, 8 with bath, 30 with shower; 9 single, 3 with bath, 6 with shower; 4 family rooms, 2 with bath, 2 with shower; all have central heating, air-conditioning, TV, electronic safe, phone
Facilities TV room, reading-room, breakfast room
Credit cards AE, V
Children accepted
Disabled access difficult
Pets not accepted
Closed never
Proprietor Enzo Baessato

Venice

Nuovo Teson

This modest hotel is on a small, peaceful square in Castello, a stone's throw from the Riva degli Schiavoni, which will be your main route to Piazza San Marco, some five minutes' walk away.

By Venetian standards this is a modern building, and it has recently been renovated to a high standard. The compact breakfast room and bar feature rich fabrics, painted furniture and rugs on terrazzo floors. The lack of a dining-room is no problem, with two or three excellent restaurants to tempt you within easy walking distance.

The bedrooms are light and pretty, and all have reproduction Venetian painted furniture, from headboards to chairs and tables, and brass and glass lamps.

Nearby Piazza San Marco, Scuola di San Giorgio.

Riva degli Schiavoni 3980, Venice 30122
Tel (041) 522 9929
Location set back from the waterfront, on a small square
Food & drink breakfast
Prices rooms L80,000- L110,000 with breakfast
Rooms 29 double, one single, all with shower; all have radio, central heating, piped music
Facilities breakfast room, conference room, bar
Credit cards AE, MC, V
Children accepted
Disabled one ground-floor bedroom in annexe
Pets accepted
Closed Nov to Jan
Proprietor Nicola Caputo

Paganelli

Most of the hotels along the Riva degli Schiavoni charge notoriously high prices for the waterfront's stunning panorama across the lagoon (and proximity to St Mark's). But the Paganelli is a modest, unpretentious hotel whose best rooms, decorated in typical 18thC Venetian style, look out across the water. Elsewhere the decoration is nothing special, either in the main hotel or in the annexe in the adjoining side street, where you will also find the modern restaurant. But it is a friendly place nevertheless and, for the position, the rooms are by Venice standards not over-priced.

Nearby Piazza San Marco.

Riva degli Schiavoni 4687, Venice 30122
Tel (041) 522 4324
Location on main waterfront, close to Piazza San Marco
Food & drink breakfast, lunch, dinner
Prices rooms L77,500- L106,000; 30% reduction for young children
Rooms 12 double, 3 with bath, 7 with shower; 8 single, one with bath, 6 with shower; 3 family rooms, all with bath; all rooms have phone; 11 rooms have air-conditioning
Facilities dining-room, bar
Credit cards AE, MC, V
Children accepted
Disabled no special facilities
Pets not accepted
Closed restaurant only, mid-Nov to mid-Mar
Proprietor Francesco Paganelli

Venice

Pausania

The San Barnaba area, traditionally the home of impecunious Venetian nobility, is quiet and picturesque. The Pausania is a small hotel lying close to the last surviving floating vegetable shop in Venice – a colourful barge on the San Barnaba canal. The building is quintessentially Venetian – a faintly shabby Gothic *palazzo* with distinctive ogee windows. Inside, the staircase, the timber ceilings and the supporting stone columns of the breakfast room and the unusually spacious lobby are features of the original building. Bedrooms were refurbished not long ago, in modern and restrained traditional styles. The place's main advantages are the terrace and garden (peaceful as ever, but apparently now smartened up) and the prices, which are substantially lower than in equivalent, more central hotels.

Nearby Scuola dei Carmini, Accademia gallery.

Dorsoduro 2824, Venice 30124
Tel (041) 522 2083
Location short walk W of Grand Canal; with terrace
Food & drink breakfast
Prices rooms L90,000-L185,000
Rooms 23 double, 5 with bath, 18 with shower; 3 single, all with shower; 5 family rooms, one with bath, 4 with shower; all rooms have central heating, TV, air-conditioning, phone
Facilities breakfast room, bar, reading-room
Credit cards AE, MC, V
Children welcome
Disabled not suitable
Pets only small ones accepted
Closed never
Proprietor Guido Gatto

San Cassiano

This small Gothic *palazzo* looks across the Grand Canal to the glorious façade of the Ca d'Oro from a quiet neighbourhood where old, slightly decayed houses line narrow streets – but the tourist-thronged Rialto is only five minutes' walk away. The inside is handsomely furnished, the timbered ceilings, Murano-glass chandeliers and period pieces preserving the authentic Venetian air. Particularly impressive is the breakfast room, with canal views through ogee arches. Bedrooms are furnished with reproduction antiques and decorated with good-quality fabrics – but the smaller ones at the back tend to be a bit gloomy.

Nearby Franchetti gallery in the Ca d'Oro.

Santa Croce 2232, Venice 30135
Tel (041) 524 1768
Location on Grand Canal, facing Ca d'Oro
Food & drink breakfast
Prices L140,800-L191,000
Rooms 30 double, 3 with bath, 27 with shower; 5 single, all with shower; all rooms have air-conditioning, colour TV, radio, phone, minibar, hairdrier
Facilities breakfast room, bar, writing-room, TV room
Credit cards AE, DC, MC, V
Children welcome
Disabled special facilities
Pets accepted
Closed never
Proprietor Franco Maschietto

Venice

Town hotel, east of St Mark's

La Residenza

This grand Gothic *palazzo* dominates the square of Campo Bandiera e Moro. Just to enter is an experience: press the lion's nose on the left of the huge entrance doors and they swing open to reveal an ancient covered courtyard. A wrought-iron gate moves to one side to admit you up the ancient stone steps to the reception and sitting-room – a vast hall with mullioned windows looking out over the square, furnished with soft couches and antiques. The soft pastel shades of the plaster-painted walls add to the feeling of faded grandeur and immersion in Venice's Renaissance history.

Nearby Scuola di San Giorgio degli Schiavoni.

Campo Bandiera e Moro
3608, Castello, Venice 30122
Tel (041) 528 5315
Location on a small square,
100 m back from the main
waterfront; nearest
landing-stage Arsenale
Food & drink breakfast
Prices rooms L100,000
Rooms 14 double, 5 with bath,
9 with shower; 2 single, both
with shower; all rooms have
air- conditioning, phone, TV,
minibar
Facilities large sitting- room
Credit cards AE, DC, MC, V
Children not accepted
Disabled not suitable
Pets not accepted
Closed Jan until carnival; end
Nov to mid-Dec.
Proprietor Sg Tagliapietra

Venice

San Fantin

It is not easy to find cheap hotels in this fashionable area of Venice. The San Fantin stands in a characteristic corner, next to the ravishing little Fenice theatre, only a few minutes' walk from San Marco. You cannot mistake its façade, the lower storey dotted with cannon balls and the balcony above, where a lion stands guard, flowing with geraniums and wisteria.

The interior is distinctly modest, the bedrooms simply furnished. But it is not without character, and the breakfast room, with its profusion of pictures, has a cosy atmosphere. Also, the quiet attentiveness of Pierina and her mother makes up for a lot. There is no restaurant and the taverna opposite is overpriced; but there are plenty of cheaper alternatives in the area.

Nearby Fenice Theatre.

Campiello de la Fenice 1930/a, San Marco, Venice 30124
Tel (041) 523 1401
Location on small square in middle of city
Food & drink breakfast
Prices rooms L55,000-L106,000
Rooms 11 double, 9 with shower; 3 single; all rooms have central heating
Facilities sitting-room, breakfast room
Credit cards not accepted
Children accepted if well behaved **Disabled** no special facilities **Pets** not accepted
Closed winter
Proprietor Pierina de Ghetto

San Moisé

A couple of minutes from Piazza San Marco, bordering a quaint canal, the San Moisé has obvious attractions. Not long ago it was entirely restored and given a spruce new image. Rugs on wood-block floors, elaborate chandeliers and walnut furniture create a typically Venetian setting. Bedrooms (some rather small) are neatly furnished, in similar style to public rooms. Anyone rich enough to afford a gondola or a water-taxi can enjoy door-to-door service at the San Moisé – there is a private landing-stage just outside the hotel.

Nearby Piazza San Marco (200 m).

San Marco 2058, Venice 30124
Tel (041) 520 3755
Location between Piazza San Marco and the Fenice theatre, bordering on a canal
Food & drink breakfast
Prices rooms L81,000-L191,000
Rooms 8 double, one with bath, 7 with shower; 2 single, both with shower; 6 family rooms, all with shower; all rooms have phone, minibar, TV, radio, air-conditioning
Facilities breakfast room, sitting-room, bar
Credit cards AE, DC, MC, V
Children accepted
Disabled not very suitable
Pets accepted
Closed never
Proprietor Franco Maschietto

Venice

Town hotel, west of St Mark's

Santo Stefano

If you follow the popular route from Piazza San Marco to the Accademia gallery you will walk across the Campo Santo Stefano (which, just to confuse you, is also called the Campo Francesco Morosini). It is a large, lively and rambling square whose best-known features are the alarmingly tilted *campanile* of the church of Santo Stefano and the café/*gelateria* Paolin, whose reputation for making the best ice-creams in town is well deserved.

Close to all the activity lies the Santo Stefano, a welcoming and well-cared-for little hotel whose front rooms have views of the piazza. It is not a spacious place; downstairs there is only a modest reception area, a tiny breakfast room and an even tinier courtyard at the back; and upstairs the bedrooms are barely big enough for two. But lack of size is made up for in other ways. The decoration is exceptionally pretty – many of the bedrooms are decked out with painted furniture and pretty pink fabrics – and it is kept in immaculate condition throughout.

Finally, another bonus – for Venice the prices are low.

Nearby Accademia gallery, Grand Canal.

Campo Santo Stefano, San Marco 2957, Venice 30124
Tel (041) 520 0166
Location on large square about 500 m W of Piazza San Marco; nearest landing-stage Sant'Angelo
Food & drink breakfast
Prices rooms L55,000-L145,000; air-conditioning extra L5,000
Rooms 7 double, 3 single, 2 family rooms, all with shower; all rooms have phone, minibar, air-conditioning, TV
Facilities breakfast room, hall, tiny rear courtyard
Credit cards not accepted
Children accepted
Disabled not suitable
Pets not accepted
Closed never
Proprietor Dr Giorgio Gazzola

Venice

Scandinavia

The Campo Santa Maria Formosa is a rambling piazza with a buxom church, morning market stalls and noisy Venetian children. The Scandinavia's marble-floored breakfast room looks on to it. Despite its name, the hotel's furnishings are in 18thC Venetian style – pink Murano chandeliers, brocade chairs and floral walls, along with a mixed collection of paintings. Bedrooms are in similar style to public rooms, those on the first floor being particularly attractive, with their minibars hidden in appealing walnut cabinets. The Trattoria Pizzeria Burchiello opposite is under the same ownership, and serves both lunch and dinner; specialities are Venetian and (on request) Arab dishes.

Nearby Piazza San Marco, Rialto.

Campo Santa Maria Formosa, Castello 5240, Venice 30122
Tel (041) 522 3507
Location on square, about 5 minutes NE of San Marco
Food & drink breakfast; lunch and dinner at nearby Trattoria Al Burchiello
Prices rooms L100,000-L210,000 with breakfast
Rooms 26 double, 24 with bath; 3 single; all rooms have central heating, phone, minibar, air-conditioning, TV on request
Facilities breakfast room, sitting-room, bar, air-conditioning
Credit cards AE, MC, V
Children accepted if well-behaved
Disabled no special facilities
Pets accepted
Closed never
Proprietors Grazia and Giorgio Tinacci

Torino

An old Venetian *palazzo*, the Torino lies only a few minutes' walk from Piazza San Marco, on a popular pedestrian thoroughfare. Neither the unprepossessing exterior nor the modest official star-rating leads you to expect an interior which is extraordinarily lavish. The reception area might be small, but all the trappings of a Venetian Gothic palace are there: an elaborate ceiling, pillars, a huge chandelier. Bedrooms too have chandeliers and other touches of grandeur, along with modern comforts of private bathrooms and air-conditioning. The first-floor salon also has an air of formality, though it is softened by pretty modern sofas and water-colours of Venice. Breakfast is served only in the bedrooms.

Nearby San Marco, Accademia gallery (5 minutes).

Calle delle Ostreghe 2356, San Marco, Venice 30124
Tel (041) 520 5222
Location San Marco, 5 min
Food & drink breakfast
Prices rooms L90,000-L200,000 with breakfast
Rooms 15 double, 5 single, all with shower; all have central heating, air-conditioning, phone, radio, TV, minibar
Facilities sitting-room
Credit cards AE, DC, MC, V
Children accepted
Disabled not suitable
Pets accepted
Closed never
Proprietor Claudio Vecchiato

Venice

Town guest-house, on the Zattere

Seguso

Sitting on the wide sunny promenade of the Zattere gives you the distinct feeling of being by the seaside. The quayside is lapped by the choppy waters of the wide Guidecca canal which separates the main part of Venice from the island of Guidecca. This open setting, with a grand panorama across the lagoon, is just one of the charms of the Seguso. A *pensione* in the old tradition, it is family-run, friendly and solidly old-fashioned. And (unlike most hotels in Venice or indeed in any of the main Italian cities) it offers only half-board terms. This could be a drawback were it not for the fact that dinner, bed and breakfast combined cost no more than B&B only in hotels of similar comfort closer to the Piazza San Marco. The best bedrooms are the large ones at the front of the house, overlooking the canal – though for the privilege of the views and space you may have to forfeit the luxury of a private bathroom (only half the rooms have their own facilities). The main public rooms are the dining-room, prettily furnished in traditional style, and the modest sitting-room where you can sink into large leather chairs and peruse ancient editions of travel and guide books. Breakfast is taken on a small terrace at the front of the hotel – a prime spot for watching the ferries, launches or huge ocean-going liners plying the waters of the lagoon. Delightful.

Nearby Accademia gallery, Gesuati church.

Zattere 779, Dorsoduro, Venice 30123
Tel (041) 522 2340
Location 5 minutes S of Accademia, overlooking Guidecca canal; nearest landing-stage Zattere
Food & drink breakfast, lunch, dinner
Prices DB&B L78,000-L116,000; reductions for children

Rooms 31 double, 5 single; 9 with bath, 9 with shower; all rooms have phone
Facilities dining-room, sitting-room, terrace
Credit cards AE, MC, V
Children welcome
Disabled no special facilities
Pets accepted
Closed Dec to Feb
Proprietors Seguso family

Piedmont

Hotels in Piedmont

Piedmont does, no doubt, have its attractions, but they do not impress themselves on many foreign visitors, who tend to hurry across this large region on their way to the recognised glories of Italy to the east and south.

To the traveller, as to the resident, the region is dominated by the city lying at its heart – Turin. Although we have found a couple of recommendable hotels within easy reach of Turin, and one on the fringes of the city itself (see below), we have not found hotels in the middle of the city which deserve to be picked out in these pages. But this does not mean that the city lacks comfortable hotels: there is certainly no shortage of swish, large impersonal places right in the heart of things. Of these, the most attractive (and not quite the most expensive) is the Jolly Hotel Ligure (Tel (011) 55641). Of the more modest places, the Genio (Tel (011) 650 5771) and the Victoria (Tel (011) 553710) are smartly modern, of moderate size and central – the former particularly handy for the station. A smaller (25-room) family-run hotel near the station is the Conte Biancamano (Tel (011) 546058) which retains some traditional flavour, especially in its elegant public rooms. Only a little further away from the middle is the cheaper Piedmontese (Tel (011) 669 8101) – ideal for travellers on a tight budget who do not wish to be confined to the suburbs. None of these cheaper hotels has a restaurant, but there are plenty of eating places around, many accessible without even leaving the centre's extensively arcaded pavements.

Villa Sassi-El Toulà

The Villa Sassi is unrivalled in Turin: a noble villa, dating from the early 17th century and retaining many of the original features – marble floors, ornately carved doors, old fireplaces, 17thC candelabra and Old Master paintings on the walls – set in glorious wooded grounds, landscaped *all'inglese*. The bedrooms are furnished with antiques and look out over the park

There is also an impressive restaurant, now part of the El Toulà chain, with the option of eating on the lawns under grand parasols. The Villa Sassi, if you can afford it, is very much part of the experience of visiting Turin.

Nearby sights of Turin; basilica of Superga (3 km).

Traforo de Pino 47, Turin 10132
Tel (011) 890556
Location 2 km E of city towards Superga; in grounds, with ample car parking
Food & drink breakfast, lunch, dinner
Prices rooms L220,000-L310,000; FB L310,000
Rooms 17 bedrooms; all rooms have phone, TV, minibar
Facilities air-conditioned restaurant; sitting-rooms, bar
Credit cards AE, DC, V
Children accepted
Disabled lift/elevator
Pets dogs not accepted in public rooms
Closed Aug; restaurant only, Sun
Manager Sga R Aonzo

Piedmont

Converted monastery, Cioccaro di Penango

Locanda del Sant'Uffizio

About 20 years ago the Firato family opened a restaurant here: it now has the reputation of being one of the best places to eat in the whole region. Bedrooms were added in the late 1980s, turning the place into a hotel of style and elegance. Some original features have been preserved and chic modern furnishings added – along with a fine collection of antiques. Bedrooms are decorated in unimpeachable taste: whitewashed walls, tiled floors, fresh fabrics and antique walnut or wrought-iron beds. Our most recent visitor praises the welcome, service and food, and pronounces the hotel 'very fair value for money'.

Nearby Asti (19 km); Monferrato hills; Turin within reach.

Cioccaro di Penango
14030 Asti
Tel (0141) 91271
Location 5 km SE of Moncalvo; in private grounds with car park
Food & drink breakfast, lunch, dinner
Prices DB&B L200,000; FB L250,000
Rooms 29 double, all with shower or bath; 2 single; all rooms have central heating, minibar, TV
Facilities dining-room, billiards room, meeting-room; tennis, outdoor swimming-pool, bicycles
Credit cards AE, DC, MC, V
Children welcome
Disabled no special facilities
Pets accepted if well behaved
Closed 3 weeks in both Jan and Aug
Proprietors Giuseppe Firato and Carla Comollo

Restaurant with rooms, San Giorgio Monferrato

Castello di San Giorgio

The history of the Castello goes back to the 10th century, when it was built to ward off Saracen attacks. But the building you see today – a fine pink mansion set in extensive parkland – dates from the 16th century. Thanks to expert restoration and appropriate period furnishings, the castle is now a particularly elegant hotel; but it is the superb food – including plenty of local dishes – which attracts attention. The dining-room, with its crisp linen table-cloths, candelabras and Limoges porcelain, is the height of elegance; and bedrooms, furnished with antiques, and some with their own sitting-areas, are unlikely to disappoint.

Nearby Monferrato massif; Asti (30 km).

Via Cavalli d'Olivola 3, San Giorgio Monferrato 15020 Alessandria
Tel (0142) 806203
Location 3 km SW of Casale, in the hills, with shady park and private car parking
Food & drink breakfast, lunch, dinner
Prices rooms L100,000-L160,000; meals about L65,000
Rooms 11 rooms, all with bath; all rooms have central heating, phone, colour TV, minibar
Facilities dining-room, bar
Credit cards AE, DC, MC, V
Children accepted
Disabled no special facilities
Pets dogs not accepted
Closed Mon
Proprietor Maurizio Grossi

Piedmont

Converted convent, Ivrea

Castello San Giuseppe

This *castello* was originally a convent for Carmelite nuns before Napoleon took it over as a fort and (presumably) added the tower which now stands derelict. And although it is high on an isolated hill commanding views over the surrounding lakes, inside the walled grounds the atmosphere remains far more reflective than military. There is lots to explore. The hotel is centred around a peaceful inner garden, with ornamental pond, ancient cedars, monkey trees, magnolias and a Sicilian fig of which the proprietors are particularly proud. The open reception area oozes character, and has a sitting-area with comfortable chairs. Upstairs, the bedrooms are rustically stylish, in the best Italian tradition – wrought-iron beds, red-tiled floors, flowing curtains wafting in the breeze from the hills beyond. The best rooms have frescoed ceilings, too.

The dining-room, with its frescoed, vaulted ceiling, high-backed chairs and candles, leaves the single diner crying out for a hand to hold. Fortunately the cuisine is more than sufficiently diverting, incorporating some interesting regional dishes, and there is a limited but good choice of wines. Breakfast is served in a more informal room upstairs. Staff are friendly.

Nearby Swimming in Lake Sirio (2 km); Ivrea; local castles.

Chiaverano d'Ivrea 10010 Torino
Tel (0125) 424370
Location 3 km NE of Ivrea, near Chiaverano; in grounds, with ample car parking
Food & drink breakfast, lunch, dinner
Prices rooms L90,000-L140,000 with breakfast; meals L40,000-L60,000
Rooms 9 double, 4 with bath, 5 with shower; 7 single, 2 with bath, 5 with shower; all rooms have central heating, phone, TV
Facilities dining-room, breakfast-room, bar, TV room, banqueting hall
Credit cards AE, DC, MC, V
Children welcome
Disabled no special facilities
Pets allowed if small and quiet
Closed never
Proprietor Pasquale and Renata Naghiero

Emilia-Romagna

Town hotel, Bologna

Corona d'Oro
1890

Despite Bologna's many assets, which include fine medieval architecture and exceptional food, it is a city neglected by tourists. Most of the hotels cater for business travellers and fall far short of the 'small and charming'. The Corona d'Oro is one of the few exceptions. It lies in the historic old city, close to the two famous leaning towers, in a cobbled street which for most of the time is closed to traffic. Enticing food shops (including a wonderful delicatessen) give you some idea of why the city is nicknamed Bologna La Grassa (the Fat) – and you certainly will not find it hard to eat well in this part of town.

The Corona d'Oro became a hotel in 1890, though the original building dates back to 1300. It is here that Italy's first printing press was established and there are still a few features surviving from the original palace. In the early 1980s the hotel was bought by a packaging magnate, who elevated it from a simple hotel to four-star status, successfully combining the old features with the stylish new. The 14thC portico and Renaissance ceilings were preserved, while the plush bedrooms were provided with all modern conveniences. The showpiece was the hallway, with its fine art nouveau frieze supported on columns. Light streaming from above, fresh flowers and the central feature of lush feathery plants combined to create a cheerful, inviting entrance.

In 1989, in preparation for its centenary, the hotel went through another thorough refurbishment, which has reportedly not interfered with its existing attractions. This is not a cheap base, but in central Bologna you cannot do better.

Nearby Piazza Maggiore and Piazza del Nettuno.

Via Oberdan 12, Bologna 40126
Tel (051) 236456
Location in middle, close to the two leaning towers in Piazza di Porta Ravegnana
Food & drink breakfast
Prices rooms L110,000-L275,000
Rooms 27 double, one with bath, 27 with shower; 8 single, all with shower; all rooms have central heating, colour TV, minibar, phone, safe, air-conditioning
Facilities bar, conference room, sitting-area, TV room
Credit cards AE, DC, MC, V
Children accepted
Disabled no special facilities
Pets only small ones accepted
Closed Aug
Proprietor Mauro Orsi

Emilia-Romagna

Town hotel, Bologna

Dei Commercianti

As its name suggests, the Commercianti (in the same group as the Corona d'Oro, page 81) caters primarily for businessmen, but in a city with few tourist hotels it is a useful little place to know about, particularly since it was spruced up a couple of years ago. Bedrooms are neat and modern, apart from the occasional old beam to remind you that you are in a medieval building. There is no restaurant – just a café-like breakfast room. In a corner off reception is a little sitting-area with pretty blue flowered sofas. The hotel has an air of efficiency rather than notable character, but it is well run and for a reasonably priced base serves its purpose well.

Nearby San Petronio, Fontana and Piazza del Nettuno.

Via Pignattari 11, Bologna
40124
Tel (051) 233052
Location in middle of city, off
Piazza Maggiore, with private
car parking
Food & drink breakfast
Prices rooms L80,000-
L127,000 with breakfast
Rooms 23 double, 8 single; all
with shower; all have central

heating, colour TV, minibar,
phone, air-conditioning
Facilities bar/breakfast room,
sitting-area, TV room
Credit cards AE, DC, MC, V
Children accepted; beds and
cots available
Disabled lift/elevator available
Pets small ones only
Closed never
Proprietor Paolo Orsi

Emilia-Romagna

I Due Foscari

The Due Foscari is a mock Gothic building in a quiet corner of this charming medieval town. It is less than 30 years old, though that is hard to believe when you step into what appears to be an authentic medieval setting. There are handsome beamed ceilings, huge wrought-iron candelabras, tapestries, Gothic arches and heavy dark-wood antiques. You can try local specialities in the baronial splendour of the dining-room or, in summer, wine and dine on the elegant outdoor terrace. First and foremost the Due Foscari is a restaurant, but its spacious rooms, with modest furniture in traditional style, make a more than adequate base for exploring the area. Busseto is a charming medieval town of peeling façades, in 'the land of Verdi'.

Nearby Cremona (25 km), Piacenza (31 km), Parma (40 km).

Piazza Carlo Rossi 15, Busseto 43011 Parma
Tel (0524) 92337
Location overlooking small, grassy square in medieval town; with private car park
Food & drink breakfast, lunch, dinner
Prices rooms L50,000-L90,000; meals L35,000-L60,000

Rooms 20 rooms, all with bath or shower; all have phone
Facilities 2 dining-rooms, bar
Credit cards MC, V
Children accepted
Disabled no special facilities
Pets dogs not accepted
Closed Aug and Jan; restaurant only, Mon
Manager Marco Bergonzi

Ripagrande

Although this Renaissance *palazzo* underwent major renovations in conversion to a four-star hotel, its dignity is still preserved – at least in the public rooms. The hall, with its elegant stone columns, timbered ceiling and period furniture, makes an appropriately noble entrance. And there are two Renaissance-style courtyards – one used for eating al fresco in summer. But bedrooms are surprisingly modern and stark; some have private balconies. Staff are very friendly and helpful.

Nearby Este castle and cathedral; medieval quarter.

Via Ripagrande 21, Ferrara 44100
Tel (0532) 34733
Location in middle of city, some car parking in front
Food & drink breakfast, lunch, dinner
Prices rooms L160,000-L240,000
Rooms 20 double, 2 with bath, 18 with shower; 2 single, both with shower; 20 family rooms, 2 with bath, 18 with shower; all rooms have central heating, air-conditioning, minibar, colour TV, phone
Facilities 2 internal courtyards, dining-room, one main sitting- room and 4 smaller ones
Credit cards AE, DC, MC, V
Children welcome
Disabled access possible
Pets not accepted in restaurant
Closed restaurant only, late Jul to late Aug
Proprietors Lanfranco and Roberto Viola

Emilia-Romagna

Torino

Most of the reasonably priced hotels of Parma are the slightly seedy ones around the station. The Torino is a notable exception: it lies in the heart of the city, just a stone's throw from the main sights (and with the bonus of a private garage). Bedrooms err towards the spartan, but are clean and well-cared for. Public rooms, in art nouveau style, are confined to the foyer and some small breakfast seating areas. Breakfast, which you may take in your room, includes cakes and local specialities. In a city of high gastronomic repute, the absence of a restaurant is no real drawback. A reporter calls the staff 'astoundingly helpful'.

Nearby cathedral, baptistry and church of San Giovanni.

Via A Mazza 7, Parma 43100
Tel (0521) 281047
Location in middle of city, facing the Teatro Regio, with private garage
Food & drink breakfast
Prices rooms L78,000-L120,000
Rooms 12 double, all with shower; 15 single, all with shower; 6 family rooms, all with bath; all rooms have

central heating, piped music, TV, phone
Facilities hall, bar, conference room
Credit cards AE, DC, MC, V
Children welcome
Disabled access possible
Pets welcome
Closed first 3 weeks Aug, and Christmas
Proprietor Giulia Maria Chiri

Al Piano

The small town of Sarsina is well off the beaten tourist track, in an area of dramatic hill scenery. The Al Piano has a splendid high position, with a large grassy garden in front and a hedge hiding the industry which is beginning to encroach in the valley below. From a baronial mansion the building has been turned into a hotel with a curious mix of old and new furnishings – the bedrooms, in the annexe behind, are all very modern. For some time this has been an oasis in an area where hotels are virtually non-existent. It changed hands a couple of years ago, but to judge by an enthusiastic reader's report is now more attractive than ever: 'first-rate, with that distinctive family-run atmosphere'.

Nearby Forli (48 km), Ravenna (62 km), Rimini (66 km).

Via San Martino, Sarsina 47027 Forli
Tel (0547) 94848
Location 2 km SW of Sarsina; in own grounds with car parking
Food & drink breakfast, lunch, dinner
Prices rooms L80,000
Rooms 16 rooms, all with bath

or shower; all rooms have phone, TV, minibar
Facilities dining-room, bar, sitting-room; swimming- pool
Credit cards DC, V
Children accepted
Disabled no special facilities
Pets dogs not accepted
Closed restaurant only, Mon
Proprietor Dr Arveda

Emilia-Romagna

Gigiolè

Brisighella is a picturesque small town 13 km south-west of Faenza. A clock tower on a rocky spur, a castle with two towers and an intriguing covered alley with arcades are the main features of the old quarter. The Gigiolè stands across from the main church – a vaguely French-looking shuttered building with a shaded terrace in front.

The French style extends to the food: Tarcisio Raccagni, the chef, has been put on a par with the famous Paul Bocuse. Like Bocuse he places great stress on using seasonal local ingredients of top quality and the results are superb: succulent meats, delicious soups and imaginative use of vegetables and herbs – top quality *nouvelle cuisine* but at prices you can afford and in helpings that don't leave you hungry. The setting is late 18thC, with stone arches, ceramics and copper pots. Table-cloths are white and crisp, and glasses gleam. Service is 'grave but efficient'.

After all this, the bedrooms come as a bit of an anti-climax; but they are adequate, and give little cause for complaint. Some of the newly decorated rooms are quite pretty, with white modern furnishings and fabrics, and good new bathrooms; others are being redecorated. Ask for a room at the back if peace is a priority. 'Very friendly welcome, splendid food, excellent value; I should gladly return', says our most recent visitor.

Nearby Faenza; Florence, Ravenna, Bologna, Rimini within reach.

Piazza Carducci 5, Brisighella
48013 Ravenna
Tel (0546) 81209
Location in middle of town, 13 km SW of Faenza on S302; no private car parking, but space available in the piazza
Food & drink breakfast, lunch, dinner
Prices rooms L38,000-L51,000; meals L45,000 (excluding wine)
Rooms 7 double, 5 single, 2 family rooms; all with bath; all rooms have central heating, phone
Facilities dining-room, bar, TV room
Credit cards AE, DC, V
Children welcome
Disabled access difficult
Pets welcome if clean and well behaved **Closed** one week Feb, one week Mar; restaurant only, Mon
Proprietor Tarcisio Raccagni

Emilia-Romagna

Converted monastery, Portico di Romagna

Al Vecchio Convento

A sleepy medieval village, Portico di Romagna lies on the borders of Tuscany and Emilia-Romagna, in the valley of l'Acquacheta. It is a beautiful unspoiled region whose praises were sung by Dante in the *Divine Comedy*.

The Vecchio Convento lies in the middle of the village in the very same street as the palace which belonged to Beatrice Portinori, muse of Dante. It was built in 1840 and converted only in the mid-1980s into a hotel by the Raggi family – and, thanks to them, it still maintains the feel of an old country house. Tiles, beams and old fireplaces create a delightfully rustic setting and the warmth and hospitality of the family is part of the great charm of the place. The husband is the chef, renowned for his expertise in the kitchen, particularly his home-made pastas served with fresh herbs or *funghi* and white truffles. The ground floor is devoted mainly to the dining area – four rooms, each with the feel of a Tuscan farmhouse, ranging from a tiny vaulted room with a huge stone fireplace to the much larger old granary, with its timber ceiling and arched windows overlooking the valley.

Many of the antiques from the original buildings are still in place, and this applies even to the bedrooms. Handsome and elaborate antique beds are features of rooms that are otherwise quite plain and simple. Even the new attic rooms at the top of the house have a certain rustic charm.

Nearby walks in the valley of l'Acquacheta; Faenza (46 km).

Via Roma 7, Portico di Romagna 47010 Forli
Tel (0543) 967752
Location 30 km SE of Forli, in village; with some private parking in a garage
Food & drink breakfast, lunch, dinner
Prices rooms L45,000-L60,000; meals L25,000-L45,000
Rooms 11 double, 9 with shower; 3 single, 2 with shower; all rooms have phone
Facilities bar, dining- room, hall/sitting-room
Credit cards AE, DC, V
Children welcome
Disabled access difficult
Pets not accepted **Closed** never
Proprietors Marisa Raggi and Giovanni Cameli

Emilia-Romagna

Villa Bolis

The friendly Lucchi family have recently taken over as proprietors of this lovely country house hotel which was beautifully
restored and converted in the mid 1970s. Many of the original
17thC features have survived (high ceilings, stucco, decorations,
fireplaces) and the villa has been furnished with period antiques
plus some elegant modern additions. The modern trattoria-style
restaurant, which serves typical Romagnolo dishes, has a terrace
overlooking the main swimming-pool.

Nearby Faenza (15 km); Ravenna (30 km); Brisighella hills.

Via Corriera 5, Barbiano di
Cotignola, Lugo 48010
Ravenna
Tel (0545) 78347
Location just N of village, in
park; car parking in front of
hotel, and garaging
Food & drink breakfast,
lunch, dinner
Prices rooms L62,000-
L85,000; dinner L40,000
Rooms 8 double, all with bath,
one with bath and shower; 3
single, 2 with bath and
shower; all have radio, central
heating, phone; TV on request
Facilities dining-room, bar,
conference rooms, TV lounge;
outdoor swimming-pool and
tennis court available (charge
made)
Credit cards AE, DC, MC, V
Children welcome
Disabled no special facilities
Pets not accepted
Closed Aug; restaurant only,
Mon
Proprietor Nives Lucchi

Orologio

The Corona d'Oro (page 81), Commercianti (page 82) and the
Orologio are all under the same management; and of the three
this has in the past been the simplest and cheapest. It stands
close to the main square, flanking a pedestrianized thoroughfare
and facing the handsome Palazzo Communale. The interior has
up to now been essentially functional, with small modern bedrooms reached by a tiny lift starting from the second floor. The
main attractions have been the fresh breakfast room and the
breakfasts themselves – freshly squeezed orange juice, yoghurts
and various pastries. But in the summer of 1990 a complete
renovation was underway, designed to elevate the Orologio to
the same standard as its stablemates. We await reports.

Nearby basilica of San Petronio, Fontana del Nettuno

Via IV Novembre 10, Bologna
40123
Tel (051) 231253
Location in middle of city, on
pedestrian thoroughfare, with
private car parking
Food & drink breakfast
Prices rooms L80,000-
L127,000 with breakfast
Rooms 21 double, 8 single, all
with bath; all rooms have
central heating, phone,
air-conditioning, minibar,
colour TV
Facilities breakfast room, bar,
TV room
Credit cards AE, DC, MC, V
Children accepted
Disabled no special facilities
Pets small ones only
Closed never
Proprietor Mauro Orsi

Western Riviera

Villa Elisa

On the western side of the Italian Riviera (only 32 km from Monte Carlo), Bordighera is a popular family resort, famed for its flora and mild winter climate. The beach is no match for those of the French Riviera, and the main coastal road and railway running parallel are a distinct disadvantage, but there is a quiet and civilized area to stay at the back of the town where hotels and villas stand among sub-tropical gardens. The Villa Elisa lies in this area – an attractive old house with a lush garden of mandarins and olive trees in front. Public rooms are peaceful and civilized, bedrooms are spacious and pleasantly old-fashioned; and prices are reasonable by local standards.
Nearby San Remo (12 km), France (10 km).

Via Romana 70, Bordighera
18012 Imperia
Tel (0184) 261313
Location in residential
quarter about 10 minutes'
walk from beach; with garden
and private parking
Food & drink breakfast,
lunch, dinner
Prices DB&B L70,000- L95,000
Rooms 33 double, 16 with
bath, 17 with shower; 2 single,
both with bath; all rooms have
phone, TV
Facilities dining-room, 2
sitting-rooms, TV room,
terrace; swimming-pool
Credit cards AE, MC, V
Children accepted
Disabled not suitable
Pets not accepted in public
rooms
Closed Nov to mid-Dec
Proprietor Maurizio Oggero

La Meridiana

The Meridiana is a little oasis of peace, a short drive inland from the Riviera, among woods and vines. It has a special appeal to golfers, with 18 holes next door, but there are plenty of other sports facilities on hand, plus lovely walks. The whole place is spacious, comfortable and quiet. Bedrooms are well equipped. Food is a cut above average – particularly the pasta (try it with the local pesto sauce), the risottos and the fish.
Nearby old quarter of Albenga (12 km); Genoa (93 km).

Garlenda 17033 Savona
Tel (0182) 580271
Location one km from village
of Garlenda, 12 km inland
from Albenga; in spacious
gardens with private car
parking
Food & drink breakfast,
dinner
Prices rooms L185,000-
L300,000; suites L280,000-
L362,000
Rooms 16 double, 14 suites;
all with bath; all rooms have
phone, satellite TV
Facilities sitting-room,
dining-room, bar, bridge
room, conference room;
barbecue, swimming-pool
(Jun-Sep), sauna, massage,
bicycles
Credit cards AE, DC, MC, V
Children welcome; special
meals on request
Disabled 10 ground-floor
rooms
Pets dogs not accepted in
restaurant
Closed last 3 weeks Jan, Feb
Proprietor Edmondo Segre

Western Riviera

Splendid

The Splendid lies in the middle of Laigueglia, not far from its private beach. The building was originally a monastery – exhibits in the ground-floor showcase and the ancient well in the dining-room testify to its age, and the vaulted ceilings have been preserved. Elsewhere furnishings and style are a happy combination of old and new – antiques and tapestries in some of the public areas, with bedrooms more modern in style, particularly the fourth-floor attic rooms. A key feature is the small garden at the back of the hotel, with an inviting pool where drinks are served.

Nearby Alassio (3 km), San Remo (44 km).

Piazza Badaro 3, Laigueglia
17020 Savona
Tel (0182) 49325
Location in middle of resort, with small garden and private parking for 30 cars
Food & drink breakfast, lunch, dinner
Prices DB&B L60,000-L93,000; 20% reduction for children under 7
Rooms 35 double, 7 single, 8 family rooms; all with bath or shower; all rooms have central heating, phone
Facilities dining-room, bar; swimming-pool, beach
Credit cards AE, DC, V
Children accepted over 2
Disabled no special facilities
Pets small ones accepted, but not in dining-room, nor on beach
Closed Oct to Mar
Proprietor Angelo Marchiano

Delle Rose

One of the more secluded and peaceful hotels of Ospedaletti, the Delle Rose lies about 400 m from the beach. The resort, like so many along this coast (commonly called the Riviera dei Fiori), is famed for its flowers – and it is the garden which is perhaps the hotel's finest feature. Sandro Colombo is a cactus expert and grows (we are told) 6,000 varieties, many of which can be admired from the shady terrace. The hotel is a modest, friendly one, with essentially modern furnishings and a fine collection of post-War landscape paintings. The bedrooms are all quite simply furnished, the dining-room more elegant – a visitor notes 'silver rather than stainless steel' on the tables.

Nearby San Remo (4 km), Taggia (17 km), Baiardo (27 km).

Via De Medici 17, Ospedaletti
18014 Imperia
Tel (0184) 59016/59778
Location close to middle of resort; in gardens, with private car parking
Food & drink breakfast, lunch, dinner
Prices rooms L30,000-L69,000; dinner L25,000
Rooms 14 double, 13 with bath; 2 single; all rooms have central heating, phone
Facilities dining-room, TV room, sitting-room, bar
Credit cards MC
Children welcome
Disabled access difficult
Pets not accepted
Closed never
Proprietor Sandro Colombo

Western Riviera

Seaside villa, Finale Ligure

Punta Est

The Italian Riviera west of Genoa is for the most part disappointing: most of its resorts are dreary, and most of its hotels mediocre. Happily, both the Punta Est and Finale Ligure are exceptions. The hotel is converted from a splendid 18thC villa which stands high and proudly pink above the buzz of the main coastal road, overlooking the sea. Signor Podesta, who used to be a sculptor, has acted as resident architect since the hotel was first created in the late 1960s, and with great success. By preserving the original features of the house and adding to it in a sympathetic style, he has managed to preserve the atmosphere of a private villa. The interior is cool and elegant – all dark-wood antiques, fine stone arches, fireplaces and tiled floors. But with such an impressive setting, for most months of the year the focus is on the outdoor terraces, pool and gardens, with their pines, potted plants and lovely views.

Breakfast is taken (off Staffordshire china) in a sort of canopied greenhouse – a lovely sunny spot, surrounded by greenery. Other meals are served in a dining-room in the annexe, where stone arches and beams create a vaguely medieval setting. You can choose between international and Ligurian dishes, including bass cooked with strong aromatic local herbs.

The hotel is also very close to the beach, which is only a couple of minutes' walk down the hillside.

Nearby Finale Borgo (3 km), Alassio (26 km).

Via Aurelia 1, Finale Ligure
17024 Savona
Tel (019)
600611/600112/600513
Location E of the historic
town, in private gardens;
private car parking
Food & drink breakfast,
lunch, dinner
Prices rooms L115,000–
̇),000; meals L40,000–
̇)00
̇ s 30 double, 4 single, 5
̇ ll with bath and

shower; all rooms have central
heating, phone; minibar in 25
rooms, TV in 10
Facilities sitting-room, bar, TV
room, conference room,
piano bar; swimming-pool,
half tennis court, solarium
Credit cards AE, V
Children accepted, provided
they are under control
Disabled access difficult
Pets accepted on request
Closed Oct to Easter
Proprietors Podesta family

Eastern Riviera

Miramare

The Miramare is one of several pink shuttered houses that line the Baia del Silenzio and date from the last century. But step inside and the hotel seems anything but old. Public rooms are cool, contemporary and elegant, with white sofas, potted plants and huge arched windows making the most of the sea views. The terrace makes an idyllic spot for drinks and breakfast. A recent reporter judged the hotel very comfortable, the welcome pleasant, but the breakfasts disappointing.

Nearby Portofino (28 km); Cinqueterre, Portovenere

Via Cappellini 9, Sestri Levante 16039 Genoa
Tel (0185) 480855
Location on waterfront, above private beach; with garden and garage
Food & drink breakfast, lunch, dinner
Prices rooms L150,000-L180,000; reduction for children
Rooms 21 double, 14 apartments, all with bath or shower; all rooms have cool air system, phone, colour TV, minibar; apartments have sitting-room and kitchenette
Facilities sitting-room, bar, dining-room, conference rooms, terrace, boutique
Credit cards AE, DC, MC, V
Children welcome
Disabled not suitable
Pets not accepted
Closed never
Proprietor Sg Carmagnini

Ca' Peo

This rambling farmhouse has been in the Solari family for four generations. Franco and Melly Solari opened their attractive bay-windowed dining-room, with its magnificent views over the bay and hills, to guests in 1973. Melly produces the generous seasonal menus, while Franco provides the wine from the 350 different vintages in his cellar. Both now enjoy a high reputation, and booking for the restaurant is essential. In addition to its home-like atmosphere, the house has many delightful features including black slate fixtures of varying antiquity (a local speciality). The apartments are all modern, in an annex set into olive terraces below, but they are comfortable and airy, with new pine furniture and bright sofas. All have a kitchen and dining area, and make an ideal base for exploring the Gulf de Tigullio.

Nearby Chiavari (6 km); walks in chestnut woods.

Via dei Caduti 80, Leivi 16040 Genova
Tel (0185) 319696
Location 6 km N of Chiavari, in hills; with garden and car parking
Food & drink breakfast, lunch, dinner
Prices rooms L130,000
Rooms 5 apartments; all have phone, TV, kitchen facilities
Facilities dining-room, sitting-room, bar, wine cellar
Credit cards V
Children no special facilities
Disabled access difficult
Pets in bedrooms only
Closed November; restaurant, Mon, Tue lunch **Proprietors** Franco and Melly Solari

Eastern Riviera

Town guest-house, Portovenere

Genio

The picturesque fishing village of Portovenere, at the tip of a peninsula which flanks the western side of the Gulf of La Spezia, is one of the most popular and fashionable excursion spots along the coast. The Genio is a tiny, simple family-run hotel partially occupying an old medieval tower at the entrance to the town. Bedrooms (of which there are only seven) are basic, although all have their own bathroom. But the tower and its vine-clad terraces have character, and the rooms are, after all, the cheapest in town. The only public rooms are the modest reception/bar and a games room, popular with young locals. There is no restaurant, but plenty along the waterfront.

Nearby church of San Pietro, Byron's Grotto, castle; boat trips to the Palmaria, Tino and Tinetto islands and the Blue Grotto.

Piazza Bastrieri 8, Portovenere 19025 La Spezia
Tel (0187) 900611
Location in middle of resort, close to waterfront, with tiny garden but no private car parking
Food & drink no meals available
Prices rooms L40,000- L58,000

Rooms 6 double, one single; all with shower; all rooms have central heating
Facilities bar, games room
Credit cards MC, V
Children accepted
Disabled access difficult
Pets accepted
Closed Jan and half of Feb
Proprietor Laura Canese

Converted castle, Sestri Levante

Grand Hotel dei Castelli

Once the home of a local noble, this is now the most luxurious hotel in Sestri Levante. It is not in itself a really remarkable hotel: the decoration is not always well co-ordinated, there are some inappropriate modern furnishings, and there are signs of wear. But all may be forgiven when you sit on the balcony and enjoy glorious views of the blue seas and boats in the harbour, or when you amble through the park.

Nearby Portofino (28 km), Santa Margherita Ligure (23 km).

Via Penisola 26, Sestri Levante 16039 Genoa
Tel (0185) 41044
Location on promontory, surrounded by park with ample car parking
Food & drink breakfast, lunch, dinner
Prices rooms L129,000- L260,000; meals L80,000; 30% reduction for children under 6
Rooms 38 double, all with bath; 7 single, 3 with bath, 4 with shower; all rooms have central heating, phone; air-conditioning at extra cost
Facilities 2 restaurants (one open-air), TV room, meeting-rooms; sea-water swimming-pool, bowls
Credit cards AE, DC, MC, V
Children accepted provided they stay with parents
Disabled no special facilities
Pets accepted, but not in restaurant or on beach
Closed 2nd week Oct to 2nd week May
Manager Lino Zanotto

Eastern Riviera

Seaside hotel, Sestri Levante

Helvetia

The Helvetia's claim that it has 'the quietest and most enchanting position of Sestri Levante' is no exaggeration. It stands at one end of the appropriately named Baia del Silenzio, a peaceful crescent of sands lined by mellow pink and ochre houses. The hotel is distinguished by its spotless white façade, and the yellow and white canopies that shade its balconies and terrace. Lorenzo Pernigotti devotes himself wholeheartedly to making his guests as content as possible. He provides the sort of extras – including 15 gleaming yellow bikes – that you might expect to find in a four-star hotel; but the special charm of the Helvetia is that it is small and personal.

The sitting-room/bar has the air of a private home – antiques, coffee-table books, newspapers, potted plants – and the breakfast room is lovely and light, with bird's-eye views of the bay. Bedrooms are light and airy, overlooking either the bay – there are six with their own balconies – or the gardens. The day starts on the delightful terrace, with an unusually liberal help-yourself breakfast of croissants, cheese, fruit, coffee and rolls. Behind the terrace luxuriant gardens climb up the hillside, with tables in the shade of palm trees. Serious sunbathers can take to sunbeds. And there is a tiny pebble beach with private changing cabins just across the road.

There is now no restaurant at the Helvetia, but Lorenzo's son can be persuaded to serve prosciutto and salad on the beach; and guests may get discounts at neighbouring eateries.

Nearby Beauty spots of the eastern Riviera; eg Portofino (28 km); Cinqueterre and Portovenere within easy reach.

Via Cappuccini 43, Sestri Levante 16039 Genova
Tel (0185) 41175
Location on the Baia del Silenzio, overlooking small beach, with private paying garage
Food & drink breakfast
Prices rooms L90,000-L110,000; 30% reduction for children under 6 sharing parents' room
Rooms 28 double, 14 with bath, 14 with shower; all rooms have central heating, phone, hairdrier, radio, colour TV, video, minibar
Facilities sitting-room, TV/video room, dining-room, bar, terrace; solarium, ping-pong, free bicycles
Credit cards not accepted
Children welcome; small beds provided
Disabled no special facilities
Pets dogs accepted but not in dining-room
Closed Nov to Feb
Proprietor Lorenzo Pernigotti

Eastern Riviera

Town guest-house, Portofino

Eden

Such is the popularity of Portofino – small, chic and enchanting – that you can spend two hours waiting for car parking space in peak season; its charms are invariably spoiled by the onslaught of day-trippers. But stay the night and you see a different Portofino: you can dine on the waterfront in relative peace, and watch the early-morning fishing activities before the tourist crowds arrive.

Hotel rooms are at a premium. There is the grand (and expensive) Hotel Splendid, and a handful of much smaller, more modest hotels. The Eden is one of these – a tiny place tucked away down a narrow street a couple of minutes from the waterfront. The garden, shaded by a large palm and a mass of greenery, is a quiet enclave in the middle of the resort – all meals can be taken on the terrace here in summer. On cooler days meals are taken in the trattoria-style dining-room which over-looks the garden. The only other public area is the entrance hallway, with a bar, prints of Portofino and Genoa and, at the end, a reception desk tucked under the stairs.

Bedrooms range from the spruce, newly whitewashed rooms on the upper floors to the larger doubles downstairs with floral walls; all are light and fresh, with spotless bathrooms, and we are assured that the 'signs of wear' originally noted by our inspector have been remedied.

Nearby walk to lighthouse (half-hour); fishing village of San Fruttuoso (reached by boat or 2 hr walk); Santa Margherita Ligure (5 km).

Portofino 16034 Genoa
Tel (0185) 269091
Location in middle of resort, with private garden in front; public car park only (very expensive)
Food & drink breakfast, lunch, dinner
Prices rooms L120,000-L160,000; meals L40,000-L60,000
Rooms 12 double, 6 with bath, 6 with shower; all have central heating, phone; some have air-conditioning and TV
Facilities dining-room with outdoor terrace, bar
Credit cards AE, DC, MC, V
Children welcome if well behaved
Disabled no special facilities
Pets accepted, but not in restaurant **Closed** never
Proprietor Osta Ferruccio

94

Tuscany

Hotels in Tuscany

No other region of Italy is as rich in good small hotels as Tuscany. The greatest concentrations of hotels are naturally around the tourist highlights of Florence, Siena and San Gimignano. But on recent visits we have been struck by the momentum that tourism is gaining in the countryside between Florence and Siena – the Chianti wine region. There have been good hotels in this area for many years; but alongside the old favourites there are some new discoveries, and the area also contains other promising hotels which the visitor may wish to look out for.

We have heard flattering comments about the Albergo del Chianti (Tel (055) 853763), a spick-and-span little hotel (16 rooms) close to the middle of Greve, entirely refurbished in 1986 'with great care and taste' (according to another Chianti hotelier); it has a fair-sized swimming-pool in the back garden, and offers attractively modest prices. A little way outside Gaiole, on the western side of Chianti, is the Cavarchione Toscanum (Tel (0577) 749550) – a highly individual old farmhouse with pool and gardens, in an elevated spot with good views, run with characteristic care by charming German owners.

Further south, a reader of the French edition recommends the Castiglion del Bosco (Tel (0577) 807078) near Montalcino. The hotel consists of a hilltop complex – mansion, apartments, a 13thC tower, and chapel in acres of woodland.

An acceptable alternative to our recommendation in Volterra is the more central San Lino (Tel (0588) 85250).

Paggeria Medicea

Ferdinand I of Medici was so impressed by the beauty of the hilltop village of Artimino that he built a grand villa there in the 16th century. The villa still stands, and a few years back the smaller simpler building which used to be the servants' quarters was converted into this smart, well equipped hotel. The furnishings are a stylish mix of new and old. Features such as old sloping wood beams, chimneys and ceilings have where possible been retained in the bedrooms and the public areas. Tuscan dishes 'with a Renaissance flavour' are served in the rustic restaurant just a couple of minutes away, along with wines from the estate.

Nearby an Etruscan museum; a medieval village; Prato (18 km), Florence (22 km).

Viale Papa Giovanni XXIII, Artimino 50040 Firenze
Tel (055) 871 8081
Location 22 km NW of Florence, close to village, with ample car parking
Food & drink breakfast, lunch, dinner
Prices rooms L95,000-L160,000; DB&B L100,000-L120,000
Rooms 34 double, 8 with bath, 26 with shower; 3 single, all with shower; all have central heating, minibar, TV, phone
Facilities dining-room, reading-room, TV room; 2 tennis courts, jogging, swimming-pool
Credit cards AE, DC, MC, V
Children accepted
Disabled no special fa
Pets accepted, but no dining-room **Closed**
Manager Alessandro

Tuscany

Country hotel, Camaiore

Peralta

Skiers who are used to the chalet holiday may find echoes in the way Peralta is run – at least in the summer months, when it is taken over by a London-based company. They organise it informally along house-party lines, with set meals which may now be taken around big shared tables or at smaller tables for two. As in a chalet, much of the success of a holiday at Peralta depends on how you get on with fellow inmates – particularly if (as is likely) you go with the idea of spending much of your time at base.

Peralta is a tiny hamlet, high in the Tuscan hills but within sight of the sea, dating from Etruscan times and restored from ruin by the sculptress Fiore de Henriquez, who still lives there (and – if she is at home – welcomes guests herself when the place reverts to her control out of season). Its great attractions are simplicity (rough walls, beams, country furniture), peaceful seclusion (you have to walk the last few hundred yards from the end of the narrow, winding access road) and superb views from flowery terraces across woods and olive groves. Lucca, with its wealth of churches and flower market, is only a short drive away.
Nearby coastal resorts; Lucca (30 km).

Pieve di Camaiore 55043
Lucca
Tel (0584) 951230; London
office 071-736 5094
Location 10 minutes' drive SE
of Camaiore
Food & drink breakfast; buffet
lunch, dinner (except Thu)
Prices DB&B £32-£37; single
supplement £6 (prices apply
for UK bookings)
Rooms 16 double, all with
shower; rooms spread over 5
buildings

Facilities bar, sitting-room,
dining-room, terrace;
swimming- pool, boule
Credit cards not accepted
Children welcome over 16
Disabled access difficult
Pets not advised
Closed early Oct to May –
though rooms available by
arrangement
Managers Philip Harrison
Stanton and Humphrey
Haslam

Tuscany

Country inn, Pieve Santo Stéfano

Locanda Sari

The upper Tiber valley is an unjustly neglected corner of Tuscany – slightly awkward to get to from Florence, but worth the effort if you fancy an Alpine change of scene, and not without cultural interest either.

Locanda Sari has long been run by Carmen Pierangeli's family as a local inn and convenient port of call on the road over to Ravenna; but the traffic which once passed within feet of the front door now whizzes up a neo-motorway on the other side of the narrow valley, and Carmen has seized the opportunity to turn the Locanda into a place worth travelling to find. The house has been restored with real panache in classy country style. In the bedrooms, rustic antiques and painted reproduction wardrobes sit on glistening tiled floors, with creamy rugs and bedspreads woven to a special pattern; old iron bedheads are fixed to the walls, but the beds themselves are new (and splendidly firm); the shower rooms are compact but smart. The dining-room shows the same simple good taste, but the real attraction here is Carmen's exquisite country cooking, of the kind that tourists rarely taste; the daily batch of ravioli, made with local ricotta, for example, is superb.

The new road was something of an eyesore when we visited, but husband Pio has been planting screening trees, and we did not find noise a problem even in front rooms. Plans are afoot to create a swimming-pool on the hillside behind the house.

Nearby Sansepolcro (16 km); La Verna (20 km).

Via Tiberina km 177, Pieve
Santo Stéfano, Arezzo
Tel (0575) 799129
Location in countryside 3 km
N of village, on minor road;
car parking across the road
Food & drink breakfast,
lunch, dinner
Prices rooms L42,500; meals
L28,000-L32,000
Rooms 8 double, one with

bath, 7 with shower; all rooms
have central heating
Facilities dining-room, lobby,
bar; small terrace
Credit cards AE, MC, V
Children welcome
Disabled access difficult
Pets not accepted
Closed never
Proprietor Carmen Pierangeli

Tuscany

Belvedere di San Leonino

San Leonino is equidistant between Siena and Castellina, in a true Tuscan countryside dotted with stone farmhouses, vineyards and olive groves. The Belvedere is one such farmhouse, built around 1400 and recently (and carefully) converted into a stylishly simple family-run hotel. All its original features have been retained. The spacious bedrooms have sloping beamed ceilings, tiled floors, small windows, and dark wood furniture. There is a comfortable sitting-room-cum-bar lined with modern chairs under brick arches and crossed beams. Another old out-building makes a delightfully rustic breakfast (or snack dinner) setting. Copper pans and vessels decorate white walls.

Nearby Castellina; Siena (9 km); Monteriggioni (10 km).

Castellina in Chianti 53011
Siena
Tel (0577) 741034
Location in rural setting, 8 km
S of Castellina off Siena road;
with garden and car parking
Food & drink breakfast,
dinner
Prices rooms L85,000; dinner
L25,000
Rooms 28 double, all with
bath; all rooms have central
heating, phone
Facilities dining-room, bar/
sitting-room; swimming-pool
Credit cards AE, V
Children welcome;
baby-sitting on request
Disabled no special facilities
Pets not accepted
Closed never
Proprietor Giovanni Falassi

Casetta delle Selve

Yet another Tuscan farmhouse – but this one has a personality all its own. The gleaming white house, the peaceful surroundings, the flower-filled garden and the terrace with wonderful views are all there as you would hope – but the interior is stunningly different. Not only is the whole house lovingly maintained, with varnished beams standing out against immaculate white paintwork, but also the bedrooms, in particular, are furnished in bold, bright colour schemes, involving bedheads, rugs, bedspreads and pictures (lots of them) – all happily rubbing along with the antique furniture. The public areas are more sober, but still full of pictures and ornaments. Nicla Menchi is no ordinary hostess either – many visitors leave as her friend.

Nearby Lucca (10 km); Pisa (12 km).

Pugnano 56010 Pisa
Tel (050) 850105
Location in countryside 2 km
off SS12, E of Pugnano, 10 km
SW of Lucca; with ample car
parking
Food & drink breakfast
Prices rooms L60,000;
breakfast L10,000
Rooms 5 double, one family
room, all with bath; all rooms
have central heating, hairdrier
Facilities breakfast room,
terrace
Credit cards none
Children accepted
Disabled no special facilities
Pets accepted
Closed never
Proprietor Nicla Menchi

Tuscany

Country villa, Castellina in Chianti

Villa Casalecchi

It is not difficult to find fault with this unassuming villa immersed in woods and vineyards in the heart of Chianti. It does not set particularly high standards of decoration, house-keeping or cuisine, and not all of those involved in its running are notably welcoming. But Casalecchi is one of those places it is always comfortable to be going back to; perhaps the fact that it does not feel the need to try too hard is part of its charm.

The house sits high on a steepish slope. There is no clearly defined front and back, but you approach from above, and below is the fair-sized pool. Bedrooms fall into two categories: the old ones in the main house, which are lofty, fairly spacious and full of lovely antique furniture; and the ones added on to the downhill side of the house overlooking the pool, which are rather cramped but which have the undeniable attraction of a terrace immediately outside where you can take breakfast. This last is a pleasant setting, with nothing but trees and vines in view, and a great advance on the dreary breakfast room. The sitting-areas – one a sort of lobby and the other a more rustic affair looking out over the vineyards – are no more than adequately comfortable. The dining-room, in welcome contrast, boasts splendid old wood-panelled walls.

Nearby Florence, Siena, San Gimignano, Volterra, Perugia.

Castellina in Chianti 53011 Siena
Tel (0577) 740240
Location one km S of Castellina, in countryside, with adequate car parking
Food & drink breakfast, lunch, dinner
Prices DB&B L198,000; FB L230,000; 20% reduction for children under 6
Rooms 19 double, 16 with bath, 3 with shower; all rooms have central heating, phone
Facilities dining-room, breakfast room, bar, 2 sitting-rooms, open-air swimming-pool
Credit cards AE, DC, MC, V
Children accepted
Disabled access difficult
Pets accepted, but not in public rooms
Closed Oct to Mar
Proprietor Elvira Lecchini-Giovannoni

Tuscany

Country hotel, Castellina in Chianti

Tenuta di Ricavo

If away from it all is where you want to get – while retaining the possibility of doing some serious sightseeing – Ricavo is hard to beat. The hotel occupies an entire hamlet, deserted in the 1950s when people left the land for the cities in search of work. The charming family who took it over then are there still: day-to-day running is in the hands of the third generation.

The grouping of houses along a wooded ridge in the depth of the countryside might have been conceived as a film-set replica of a medieval hamlet. The main house, facing a little square of other mellow stone cottages, houses some of the bedrooms, the no-smoking dining-room – smart and restrained, with plain white walls, brick arches and tiled floor – and the several sitting-rooms, which are comfortably furnished with a pleasant jumble of antique chairs and sofas (one of them with a small library of English, Italian, French and German books).

Breakfast can be had in several spots outdoors – perhaps in the shade of linden trees. At the right time of the year the gardens are bright with flowers – one of the highlights is a grand old wisteria – and there are plenty of secluded corners, with the result that the place seems calm and quiet even when the hotel is full. The small garden pool is ideal for quiet cooling off, the larger one out of the way so that lively children are no problem.

We lack recent reports of the food, which in some eyes has not matched the hotel's appeal in the past.

Nearby Siena (22 km); San Gimignano and Florence within a day's drive.

Localita Ricavo, Castellina in Chianti 53011 Siena
Tel (0577) 740221
Location isolated in countryside, about 3 km N of Castellina in gardens, with ample car parking
Food & drink breakfast, lunch, dinner
Prices DB&B L150,000-L210,000 (min stay 3 days)
Rooms 13 double, 2 single, 10 family rooms; all with bath; all have central heating, phone
Facilities 3 sitting-rooms, bar, dining-room; 2 swimming-pools, table tennis, 2 *boccia* courts
Credit cards not accepted
Children welcome
Disabled some ground-floor rooms
Pets not accepted
Closed Nov to Easter; dining-room Wed lunch-time
Proprietor Dr Scotoni

Tuscany

Country guest-house, Castellina in Chianti

Salivolpi

This welcome addition to the Castellina hotel establishment – open since 1983 – offers a much cheaper alternative to its two illustrious neighbours. It occupies two well-restored farm buildings and one new bungalow in an open position on the edge of the village. There is a Spanish feel to the older of the houses – iron fittings, exposed beams, white walls, ochre tiles – and the spacious rooms are both neat and stylish. The garden is well cared for, with plenty of space. Breakfast (*"molto abbondante,"* claims the boss) is served in a crisp little room in the smaller of the houses.

Nearby Siena (18 km); Florence, San Gimignano and other attractions within reach.

Via Fiorentina, Castellina in Chianti 53011 Siena
Tel (0577) 740484
Location 500 m from middle of village, on the road to San Donato, with gardens and ample open-air car parking
Food & drink breakfast
Prices rooms L55,000-L75,000 with breakfast
Rooms 18 double, 16 with bath; one single with bath; all rooms have central heating, phone
Facilities hall, breakfast room, bar; swimming-pool
Credit cards accepted
Children accepted
Disabled no special facilities
Pets not accepted
Closed never
Manager Cristina O Agnese

Country inn, Certaldo

Osteria del Vicario

This simple inn was a monastery in the 13th century and has retained its basic structure, with a garden enclosed in a Romanesque cloister. It is a delightful place; bedrooms, with leaded windows and old terracotta floors, have plenty of old-fashioned charm. A summer bonus is the lovely flowered terrace; but game and wild mushrooms are autumnal attractions. Sadly, we have a report from an American couple of an inexplicably hostile reception from the English-speaking lady of the house.

Nearby House of Boccaccio; San Gimignano (13 km).

Via Rivellino 3, Certaldo Alto 50052 Firenze
Tel (0571) 668228
Location at top of main street of upper town; in garden, with car parking in front of hotel
Food & drink breakfast, dinner; vegetarian meals
Prices DB&B L75,000 (3 nights' stay preferred)
Rooms 10 double, 2 single, 2 family rooms, all with shower; all rooms have small TV on request
Facilities bar, 3 sitting- rooms (one with TV), 2 dining-rooms; terrace, small swimming-pool
Credit cards AE, DC, V
Children welcome if well behaved
Disabled not suitable
Pets small ones only accepted
Closed mid-Jan to end Feb
Proprietors Ferdinando and Linda Steyn Ulivieri

Tuscany

Town guest-house, Fiesole

Villa Bonelli

The friendly and helpful Boninsegni brothers have run this appealing little hotel since 1972. Bedrooms are simple but pleasant, public rooms rather cramped, except for the restaurant – a beamed room on the top floor which enjoys marvellous picture-window views of the countryside, especially when candle-lit at night. There is also a pleasant terrace. Regional specialities and local wines are served and you are expected to take at least half-board, except in low season; this is no disadvantage, as the food is excellent and varied. The approach to the hotel is narrow and steep, but well signed.

Nearby cathedral, Roman theatre; Florence (10 km).

Via Francesco Poeti 1, Fiesole, Florence 50014
Tel (055) 59513
Location 10 km N of Florence; ample car parking, and garaging for 8 cars
Food & drink breakfast, dinner
Prices rooms L47,500-L89,000; DB&B L85,000-L165,000
Rooms 15 double, one with bath, 12 with shower; 7 single; one family room, with shower; all rooms have central heating, phone
Facilities dining-room, bar/TV room, terrace
Credit cards AE, DC, MC, V
Children welcome
Disabled bedrooms on ground floor
Pets dogs accepted in bedrooms
Closed restaurant only, Nov, to mid-Mar
Proprietors Andrea and Silvano Boninsegni

Country villa, Colle di Val d'Elsa

Villa Belvedere

Though it calls itself a hotel, this handsome, weathered villa standing in open countryside a few miles from Siena is perhaps better thought of as an elegant restaurant with rooms; although there is a grand first-floor salon, it is often taken over as a function room, and the stylish dining-room – with its bentwood café chairs, white walls and low, vaulted ceiling – is very much the heart of the place. The food here enjoys a high reputation in the locality. Bedrooms are similarly restrained in decoration, but some do contain amusingly ornate antique furniture.

Nearby San Gimignano (14 km), Siena (25 km); Florence and other Tuscan attractions within reach.

Localita Belvedere, Colle di Val d'Elsa 53034 Siena
Tel (0577) 920966
Location 2 km E of Colle di Val d'Elsa, in countryside, with large garden and ample car parking
Food & drink breakfast, lunch, dinner
Prices rooms L115,000; DB&B L100,000; FB L140,000
Rooms 15 double, all with bath; all rooms have phone
Facilities 2 sitting-rooms, TV room, bar, dining-room
Credit cards AE, DC, MC, V
Children welcome if not too noisy
Disabled no special facilities
Pets not accepted
Closed never
Proprietor Daniele Conti

Tuscany

Country guest-house, Fiesole

Bencista

'Don't send us too many tourists,' the smooth Simone Simoni begged our inspector – and he genuinely meant it. It is easy to see why the Bencista is so popular. The *pensione* stands on a hillside overlooking Florence and the Tuscan hills; views from the terrace and many of the bedrooms are unforgettable. Added to this are the charms of the building, once a monastery: a handsome hallway, three salons almost entirely furnished with antiques (including a little reading-room with shelves of old books and a cosy fire), plus plenty of fascinating nooks and crannies.

No two bedrooms are alike, and each one has some captivating feature – perhaps a beautiful view, a fine piece of furniture, a huge bathroom or, in some, a private terrace. They are nearly all old-fashioned, with plain whitewashed walls and solid antiques, and the accent is more on character than luxury.

The dining-room is simple, light and spacious, overlooking gardens where olives, roses and magnolia flourish. Breakfast is taken *al fresco* on the terrace – a glorious spot to start (and end) the day. Meals offer no choice, but are well cooked, puddings are 'superbly wicked', and the house wine excellent.

Nearby Roman theatre, cathedral and monastery of San Francesco, all at Fiesole.

Via B da Maiano 4, Fiesole 50014
Tel (055) 59163
Location 2.5 km S of Fiesole on Florence road, set in private park overlooking city; garage and ample open-air car parking
Food & drink breakfast, lunch, dinner
Prices DB&B L62,700-L81,400; FB L78,100- L96,800

Rooms 27 double, 15 with bath, 9 with shower; 8 single, 2 with bath; all rooms have central heating
Facilities 3 sitting-rooms, dining-room
Credit cards not accepted
Children accepted
Disabled no special facilities
Pets no dogs in restaurant
Closed never
Proprietor Simone Simoni

Tuscany

Country villa, Fiesole

Villa San Michele

According to its brochure the Villa San Michele was designed by Michelangelo – which perhaps accounts in part for the high prices. Rooms are among the most expensive in Italy – only a fraction less than at the hotel's more swanky sister, the Cipriani in Venice – and beyond the reach of most readers; but the guide would be incomplete without this little gem on the peaceful hillside of Fiesole – originally a monastery, built in the early part of the 15th century and enlarged towards the end of it.

What you get for your money is not extravagant decoration or ostentatious luxury but restrained good taste and an expertly preserved aura of the past. The furniture is mostly solid antiques including 17thC masterpieces (religiously maintained every winter, we are told); many of the bedrooms have tiled floors which are themselves of notable antiquity. The bathrooms, on the other hand, are impressively contemporary.

The views from the villa are exceptional. One of the great delights of the place is to lunch or dine *al fresco* in the loggia, gazing down slopes of olives and cypresses to the city below. The pool terraces share this glorious view.

Breakfast is an American buffet feast; the DB&B prices we quote include an *à la carte* meal, lunch or dinner.

Nearby Roman theatre, cathedral and monastery of San Francesco at Fiesole.

Via Doccia 4, Fiesole 50014
Tel (055) 59451
Location on Florence- Fiesole road, in private grounds with car parking available
Food & drink breakfast, lunch, dinner
Prices DB&B L375,000-L610,000; suites more
Rooms 24 double, 2 single, and 2 suites; all with bath and shower; all rooms have central heating, air- conditioning, music, phone; TV and minibar on request
Facilities reading- room/bar, piano bar, dining-room with loggia/terrace; heated swimming-pool (closed winter)
Credit cards AE, DC, MC, V
Children accepted
Disabled access difficult
Pets small dogs accepted, but not in dining-room or in pool area
Closed mid-Nov to mid-Mar
Manager Maurizio Saccani

Tuscany

Country villa, Candeli

Grand Hotel Villa la Massa

The three villas making up this sumptuous (and expensive) hotel date from the 17th century – and the old dungeons now serve as the piano bar and discothèque. Bedrooms are the height of luxury, combining antique-style furniture with modern high-quality fabrics. Public rooms have a formal atmosphere, particularly the rather grand room beyond reception, with its lofty ceiling, pillars and arches, and the ornate bar to one side. More relaxing is the riverside restaurant, where you can dine outside at elegantly laid tables.

Nearby Florence (7 km).

Via La Massa 6, Candeli, Florence 50010
Tel (055) 630051
Location 7 km E of Florence, on Arno in extensive grounds with abundant car parking
Food & drink breakfast, lunch, dinner
Prices rooms L262,000-L474,000 (suites L610,000); DB&B L290,000-L342,000 (suites L730,000)
Rooms 32 double, 3 single, 5 suites; all with bath; all have central heating, phone, air-conditioning, TV, minibar
Facilities dining-room, bar, piano bar, sitting- room; tennis, swimming-pool
Credit cards AE, DC, MC, V
Children accepted
Disabled no special facilities
Pets not accepted in dining-room
Closed never
Manager Arturo Secchi

Converted castle, Gaiole in Chianti

Castello di Spaltenna

The Castello sits romantically at the top of a hill above Gaiole, a group of ancient rustic buildings in green surroundings. Beyond a grassy courtyard is the high-ceilinged dining-room – impressively medieval, with huge beams and gallery. Candles and a log fire at one end contribute further to the atmosphere. The bedrooms are spacious, with exposed beams, tiled floors and simple antique furniture. The new British proprietor has refurbished the whole place (it is now centrally heated, springtime visitors will be pleased to note); he has also raised prices considerably – and introduced ambitious but Tuscan-based cuisine.

Nearby Siena (28 km), Arezzo (56 km), Florence (69 km).

Gaiole in Chianti 53013 Siena
Tel (0577) 749483
Location on hilltop close to middle of Gaiole, 28 km NE of Siena
Food & drink breakfast, lunch, dinner
Prices rooms L130,000-L200,000 with breakfast; meals L40,000- L60,000
Rooms 15 double (2 twin), all with bath and shower; all rooms have phone, central heating, TV, minibar
Facilities dining-room, 2 sitting-rooms, wine bar, terrace bar; swimming-pool
Credit cards AE, DC, MC, V
Children welcome
Disabled no special facilities
Pets accepted, with small charge
Closed mid-Jan to Feb; main restaurant, Wed dinner
Proprietor Seamus de Pentheny O'Kelly

Tuscany

Converted castle, Leccio

Castello di Sammezzano

Once a princely Renaissance residence, the Castello was rebuilt in the mid-1850s by the eccentric Marquis of Aragona. The exotic first-floor apartments and hallways are stunning: every inch of wall and ceiling is decorated with Saracen, Arabic or Indian motifs. Bedrooms are less lavish and the downstairs public rooms are restrained and simple in comparison. The main area is the dining-room, which is cool, trattoria-style. Meals draw on the produce of the castle farm. The huge park, planted with exotic shrubs and trees, is open to the public.
Nearby walks in the park; Florence (half-hour drive); Arezzo, Siena within reach.

Leccio, 50066 Reggello, Florence
Tel (055) 865 7911
Location in town, 10 km S of Pontassieve, 30 km SE of Florence; in huge park with ample car parking space
Food & drink breakfast, lunch, dinner
Prices rooms L145,000-L185,000
Rooms 15 double, 5 with bath, 10 with shower; all rooms have central heating, minibar, TV, sitting-room, phone
Facilities dining-room, sitting area, bar
Credit cards AE, DC, MC, V
Children accepted
Disabled access difficult
Pets not accepted
Closed never
Proprietor Sammezzano Sp.A

Country villa, Lucca

Villa la Principessa

La Principessa was once occupied by the last Dukes of Bourbon-Parma and still has a somewhat French feel in the furnishings and the formal park. The bedrooms have bold colour schemes and modern comforts, the public rooms rather more character – notably the grand central sitting-room, with its painted beams, and rugs on a marble floor. The restaurant is elegant but relatively informal, the food excellent. The pool, behind the house is a pleasant place to relax. With easy access from Pisa airport, La Principessa makes a comfortable base, ideal for those who want to be looked after by English-speaking staff.
Nearby Pisa (18 km)

Massa Pisana, Lucca 55050
Tel (0583) 370037
Location 4 km S of Lucca on SS12r towards Pisa
Food & drink breakfast, lunch, dinner
Prices rooms L200,000-L360,000; suites L500,000; meals from L45,000
Rooms 32 double, 5 single, 5 suites; all with bath or shower; all rooms have phone, air-conditioning, TV
Facilities sitting-room, bar, TV room, breakfast room, dining-room, banquet and congress room; outdoor swimming-pool
Credit cards AE, DC, MC, V
Children accepted
Disabled no special facilities
Pets small dogs accepted, but not allowed in restaurant
Closed early Jan to mid-Feb; restaurant only, Wed
Proprietor Sg M G Mugnani

Tuscany

San Sano

Heidi and Giancarlo Matarazzo, a German/Italian combination, have converted this 13thC fortress (basically just a solidly built farmhouse) into a rather special 'hotel residence'. 'Our concept,' they say 'is to keep small (just 10 rooms) for peace and comfort'. You can be assured of both. Between the 'bountiful' buffet breakfasts and typical Tuscan dinners (served in a delightful rustic dining-room under an old stone arch), there is plenty to do – walks in the vineyards, sightseeing in nearby cities. In winter you come back to a blazing log fire in the tiled sitting-room. Bedrooms are stylishly simple – cream woven bedspreads, painted iron bedsteads, plain walls – with individual features; several have stunning views across the Chianti hillsides.

Nearby Lecchi; Siena (25 km); Florence (65 km).

Loc. San Sano 21, Lecchi in Chianti 53010 Siena
Tel (0577) 746130
Location in country, 2 km SW of Lecchi (25 km NE of Siena); with garden and car parking
Food & drink breakfast, dinner
Prices rooms L120,000 with breakfast; dinner L25,000

Rooms 10 double, all with bath; all rooms have central heating, phone
Facilities dining-room, sitting-room, bar
Credit cards AE, MC, V
Children not accepted
Disabled no special facilities
Pets not encouraged
Closed Nov to mid-Mar
Proprietor Giancarlo

Villa Rucellai

This rambling red-roofed villa, nestling among terraced olive groves, has mellowed beautifully. A formal garden leads to the door; inside, floors gleam with polish, and the cavernous rooms show the care and attention of a dedicated family. The furnishings are a mixture of the antique and the comfortable, with something of the style of an English country house. The core of the villa is 16thC; later additions include a chapel, farm buildings, formal gardens and a swimming-pool. Bedrooms are large and simply furnished, often with antiques. Breakfast is served at large dining-tables in another high-ceilinged room.

Nearby Prato; Florence (20 km).

Via di Canneto 16, Prato 50047 Florence
Tel (0574) 460392
Location in Bisenzio river valley, 4 km NE of Prato; with car parking and grounds
Food & drink breakfast
Prices rooms L60,000-L80,000
Rooms 10 double, one single, one family room; 3 rooms have bath; all have central heating; some have phone

Facilities dining-room, sitting-room, TV room, gymnasium, terrace; swimming-pool
Credit cards not accepted
Children welcome; cots and high chairs by arrangement
Disabled no special facilities
Pets accepted on payment of supplement
Closed never
Proprietor Giovanna Rucellai Piqué

Tuscany

Country villa, Panzano in Chianti

Villa le Barone

Le Barone, the attractive 16thC country house of the della Robbia family, became a hotel in 1976, but still feels very much like a private home. The bedrooms mostly contain antique furniture. There are always fresh flower arrangements in the elegant little sitting-rooms, and guests who are not out on sightseeing excursions have plenty of space to themselves in the peaceful garden or by the lovely pool. The minimum stay of three nights contributes to a low-key house-party atmosphere.
Nearby Siena (31 km), Florence (31 km).

Via San Leolino 19, Panzano in Chianti 50020 Siena
Tel (055) 852215
Location 31 km S of Florence off SS222; covered car parking
Food & drink breakfast, lunch, dinner
Prices DB&B L140,000-L160,000 (min 3 nights); reductions for children
Rooms 25 double, 20 with bath, 5 with shower; one single, with shower; 5 rooms have air- conditioning, 5 rooms have tea-makers
Facilities self-service bar, TV room, 3 sitting- rooms, dining-room, breakfast room; ping-pong, swimming-pool
Credit cards AE
Children welcome
Disabled not suitable
Pets not accepted
Closed Nov to Mar
Proprietor Marchesa Franca Viviani della Robbia

Converted monastery, Pistoia

Il Convento

A converted monastery in the verdant hills of Pistoia sounds like quite a find. Inside, Il Convento is not all that you might expect – bedrooms are uncompromisingly modern, with the emphasis firmly on efficient facilities rather than on individual character. But the public rooms are more in sympathy with their surroundings – particularly the restaurant, where the cells have been converted into tiny, intimate dining-rooms, and the food and wines (many of them vintage) are above average. Service is always smiling and professional, but what impresses visitors most is the delightfully peaceful setting, and the glorious views down to Pistoia from the lush garden.
Nearby sights of Pistoia; Prato, Florence within reach.

Via San Quirico 33, Pontenuovo, Pistoia 51100
Tel (0573) 452652
Location 4 km E of Pistoia in Pontenuovo area, on hillside overlooking city; with car parking space
Food & drink breakfast, lunch, dinner
Prices rooms L69,000-L104,000
Rooms 20 double, 4 single; all with bath; all rooms have central heating, phone
Facilities dining-room, sitting-area, bar, games room; swimming-pool
Credit cards MC, V
Children accepted
Disabled access difficult
Pets not accepted
Closed restaurant only, Mon
Proprietor Paozo Petrini

Tuscany

Country villa, Pistoia

Villa Vannini

Here is a real gem, lying in an area which has surprisingly few small, charming places to stay – in a remote and delightfully quiet setting, high on a hill about 2 km above the small village of Piteccio and not far from the lively little city of Pistoia. To get there, you wind your way up a narrow, roughly surfaced road through unspoiled countryside. The congenial Signora Vannini offers a particularly warm welcome, and looks after her house with loving care. There are various little sitting areas with large vases of flowers, chintz or chunky modern seats, prints and water-colours, and the sort of antiques that complete an elegant family home. The dining-room, with its whitewashed walls, polished parquet floor and marble fireplace, makes an elegant setting for the excellent Tuscan specialities that are served here ('the best we had on our travels,' says a recent report).

Bedrooms are beautifully and individually furnished – many of them in flowery fabrics and with fine antiques.

In front of the house a simple terrace provides a haven after a hard day's sightseeing in Florence, Lucca or even Bologna.

In the last edition, we had a report of double-booking by Signora Vannini. No such blemishes on this year's record.

Nearby cathedral, Ospedale del Ceppo and church of Sant'Andrea at Pistoia

Villa di Piteccio, Pistoia 51030 Pistoia
Tel (0573) 42031
Location 6 km N of Pistoia on hillside, in private garden, with car parking
Food & drink breakfast, lunch, dinner
Prices rooms L60,000; DB&B L55,000 (minimum 3 days)
Rooms 6 double, 3 with bath, one with shower; 3 single, all with bath
Facilities 2 sitting-rooms, games room, 2 dining-rooms
Credit cards AE (5% surcharge)
Children not very suitable
Disabled no special facilities
Pets not accepted
Closed never
Proprietor Maria-Rosa Vannini

Tuscany

Country hotel, Radda in Chianti

Relais Fattoria Vignale

This is a rare example of the hotel-guide editor's dream: an exquisite new establishment, entirely undiscovered by rival publications when, in 1987, our inspector came upon it by chance. He was immediately captivated by the taste and style with which this manor-house has been converted to a hotel. Subsequent visits have not dimmed our enthusiasm.

The house is built on a slope down from the middle of the village. On the main 'ground' floor are four interconnecting sitting-rooms, each on a domestic scale and beautifully furnished with comfy sofas, antiques, muted rugs on polished terracotta floors, walls either white and dotted with paintings or covered by murals – and one or two grand stone fireplaces. The bedrooms above are similarly classy, with waxed wooden doors, white walls, antique beds.

There is a neat breakfast-room in a brick vault beneath the hotel, where an excellent buffet is set out, and coffee and extras are served by friendly waitresses. The proprietors have arranged for the best-known local restaurant (300 m away) to operate under the Vignale name, and will make reservations for you.

The sitting-rooms, the back bedrooms and the moderate- sized pool all share a grand view across the Radda valley.
Nearby Siena, Florence, Arezzo all within reach.

Via Pianigiani 15, Radda in Chianti 53017 Siena
Tel (0577) 738300
Location in middle of village, 31 km N of Siena, with private gardens and ample car parking
Food & drink breakfast, snacks
Prices rooms L125,000-L220,000
Rooms 17 double, 2 with bath, '5 with shower; 4 single, all 'h shower; 3 family rooms, 2 with bath, one with shower; all rooms have central heating, phone, minibar
Facilities 3 sitting-rooms, breakfast room, indoor and pool bars, 2 conference rooms
Credit cards AE, V
Children accepted, but prefer quiet ones **Disabled** access difficult
Pets not accepted
Closed Jan to mid-Mar
Manager Silvia Kummer

Tuscany

Villa di Corliano

A sweeping, tree-lined drive leading through lawns with lofty palms to a fine late Renaissance mansion set against thickly wooded hills; then, an interior no less splendid – frescoes embellishing every inch of wall and ceiling, handsome classical busts on ornate stands, antiques, chandeliers and, from the 16thC salon and its balcony, a beautiful view of the sloping lawns below. Ruinously expensive? For once, no: all this comes for less than you pay for a room in some seedy station hotel in Pisa.

The bedrooms are not quite so grand, which accounts for the strikingly low prices. In fact the cheapest are bordering on the basic, with a basin and portable bidet (hidden discreetly behind decorative screens), creaky beds and possibly a long walk to the public bathroom. But there is compensation in the sheer size of the bedrooms (most are huge, with big 1920s wardrobes). The best doubles have touches of grandeur, and their own bathrooms; and the only rooms that could be described as small are the three in the 'tower' at the top.

The old cellars serve as the breakfast room, where framed awards and the colossal terracotta urn are clues to the basis of the 19thC success of the estate: top-quality olive oil.

Nearby Pisa (10 km); Lucca (15 km).

Rigoli, San Giuliano Terme 56010 Pisa
Tel (050) 818193
Location 2.5 km NW of San Giuliano Terme at Rigoli; in large park with ample car parking
Food & drink breakfast
Prices rooms L65,000-L78,000; suite L150,000
Rooms 18 double, 6 with bath, 4 with shower; all rooms have central heating; 6 rooms have phone
Facilities sitting-rooms, bar, breakfast room, conference room
Credit cards V
Children acccepted
Disabled no special facilities
Pets accepted **Closed** never
Proprietor Conte Ferdinando Agostini della Seta

Tuscany

Country hotel, San Gimignano

Pescille

Until recently the Pescille was difficult to recommend wholeheartedly. It is a rambling hilltop manor house a couple of miles out of San Gimignano, converted with great taste and care, and with sufficient diversions to keep you there all day if sightseeing seems too strenuous – and yet until 1987 it lacked a restaurant. This problem was then remedied in no uncertain fashion by the creation of a big, spanking-new dining-room, decorated in a cool, modern, grey-and-white style with cane chairs on a tiled floor. We saw it the day before it opened, and have not yet eaten here – but the food is reported to be 'excellent' and 'highly ambitious, perhaps sometimes over-creative', and service impeccable; breakfast has traditionally been good.

Meanwhile, the hotel in general remains a peaceful and relaxing haven. The rustic terraced garden leading down to the vineyards beyond has plenty of secluded spots, while indoors there are several little sitting areas, trendily mixing smart modern furniture and antique agricultural clutter. Bedrooms are simple, stylish and moderately spacious, with enchanting views of open countryside or towards the distinctive skyline of San Gimignano. The pool is less than ideal – it has a raised lip about a foot high, which makes it seem utilitarian.

Nearby San Gimignano; Florence, Siena, Pisa all within reach.

Localita Pescille, San Gimignano 53037 Siena
Tel (0577) 940186
Location 3 km SW of San Gimignano, in large gardens with private car parking
Food & drink breakfast, lunch, dinner
Prices rooms L80,000-L100,000
Rooms 28 double, 4 single, one family room; all with bath; all rooms have central heating, phone
Facilities sitting-room, TV room, breakfast room, 2 bars, dining-room; swimming-pool, tennis, bowls
Credit cards AE, DC, MC, V
Children accepted, provided they are quiet
Disabled access difficult
Pets not accepted
Closed Jan and Feb
Proprietors Gigli brothers

Tuscany

Bel Soggiorno

Just inside the walls of the extraordinary town of San Gimignano, the Bel Soggiorno is a simple hotel in a 13thC house. Inside it has mostly been unimaginatively modernized and there is little space or comfort, although on our last visit there were some improvements in progress. But, despite these disadvantages, one major feature makes this the best-value base in town: the excellent food served in the attractive restaurant, with a wall of windows overlooking the hills and olive groves. The menu varies little; constant favourites are a creamy risotto and pasta *alla lepre* (with hare sauce, a Tuscan speciality). Many of the ingredients come from a farm belonging to the owners, perhaps a factor in the modest prices.

Nearby sights of San Gimignano; Siena, Florence within reach.

Via San Giovanni 91, San Gimignano 53037 Siena
Tel (0577) 940375
Location inside Porto S Giovanni, at S end of town; park outside town gates
Food & drink breakfast, lunch, dinner
Prices rooms L80,250-L133,750; DB&B L74,900
Rooms 21 double, 2 mini-suites; 2 single; all with bath; all rooms have central heating, phone
Facilities TV/sitting-room, bar, dining-room
Credit cards AE, DC, MC, V
Children accepted
Disabled not suitable
Pets not accepted
Closed restaurant only, Mon and mid-Jan to mid-Feb
Proprietors Gigli brothers

Leon Bianco

Directly opposite the Cisterna (page 107) in the main square of San Gimignano, the Leon Bianco is not so well known and has fewer pretensions, but it offers considerably better value. The visitor's eye may be caught first by the fresco on the wall behind reception; other pictures and antiques are dotted around the corridors. Rooms are generally spacious, decorated with restraint and furnished with a bit of panache, and everything is spick and span; side rooms have good views of the countryside. A recent highly satisfied reporter speaks of 'copious' buffet breakfasts on the enclosed terrace.

Nearby Piazza del Duomo, civic museum, church of Sant'Agostino; Florence, Pisa, Volterra, Siena all within reach.

Piazza del Cisterna 13, San Gimignano 53037 Siena
Tel (0577) 941294
Location in main square
Food & drink breakfast
Prices rooms L68,000- L74,000
Rooms 20 double, 8 with bath, 12 with shower; 2 single with shower; 3 family rooms with shower; all rooms have phone
Facilities bar/breakfast room, sitting-room, TV room, lecture/conference room, terrace
Credit cards AE, DC, MC, V
Children accepted
Disabled no special facilities
Pets not accepted
Closed Jan and Feb
Proprietor Sg. Galgani

Tuscany

Country hotel, San Gimignano

Le Renaie

A simple, well-run country hotel – built up over the years by the present owners from a simple bar and restaurant – which makes a respectable base within a short drive of San Gimignano. Outside, Le Renaie looks fairly unprepossessing: just a modern villa set back from a rural lane. Inside, it is cool and pretty with freshly painted walls, rattan furniture and traditional polished brick floors; bedrooms are spacious and immaculate, some with individual terraces. The restaurant, Da Leonetto, is popular with locals but gets mixed notices from reporters; on fine days you can eat outside on the veranda. For most holidaymakers the chief attractions are the small swimming-pool, the tranquil location ('a guest can live peaceful hours of repose', promises the brochure) and the reasonable prices.

Nearby sights of San Gimignano; hills and vineyards of Chianti; Volterra, Siena, Florence within reach.

Localita Pancole, San Gimignano 53037 Siena
Tel (0577) 955044
Location 6 km N of San Gimignano off road to Certaldo; private car parking
Food & drink breakfast, lunch, dinner
Prices rooms L58,000-L85,000; meals L35,000-L50,000
Rooms 24 double, 2 single; all with bath; all rooms have phone

Facilities hall, TV room, dining-room, bar; swimming-pool, tennis
Credit cards AE, DC, MC, V
Children accepted, but must be accompanied by parents at swimming-pool
Disabled access difficult
Pets accepted in bedrooms
Closed last 3 weeks Nov
Proprietor Leonetto Sabatini

Tuscany

La Cisterna

This very well-known and indeed long-established hotel has three enduring things in its favour: its position on the (virtually) car-free central square, the views away from the town shared by the two dining-rooms and some of the better bedrooms, and a splendid stone-arched sitting-room just off reception. In some respects it seemed to our inspector to be over-rated; but we have enthusiastic reports this year of both the 'friendly and efficient' service and of the cooking. The famous 14thC Loggia Rustica dining-room is certainly rustic but is crammed with too many tables. And the worst bedrooms are very ordinary indeed.

Nearby Piazza del Duomo, civic museum, church of Sant'Agostino; Florence, Pisa, Volterra, Siena all within reach.

Piazza della Cisterna 24, San Gimignano 53037 Siena
Tel (0577) 940328
Location in middle of town, on main square; car park 200 m away
Food & drink breakfast, lunch, dinner
Prices rooms L56,000-L99,000 with breakfast; DB&B L75,500- L86,000
Rooms 40 double, 19 with bath, 21 with shower; 6 single, 2 with bath, 4 with shower; all have central heating, phone
Facilities 2 dining-rooms, bar, 2 TV/reading-rooms
Credit cards AE, DC, MC, V
Children accepted
Disabled no special facilities
Pets accepted, but not in restaurant
Closed 10 Nov to 10 Mar; restaurant only, Tue and midday Wed
Proprietors Salvestrini family

Villa Patrizia

We can imagine this plain-looking villa just to the north of central Siena making a truly excellent small hotel one day – the house has just a bit of aristocratic style, its setting in a small wooded garden (although uncomfortably close to the main road northwards) is relaxed and dignified, and the dining-room is pleasantly light, overlooking the garden along its length. (We're told another restaurant has been created in the 'Limonaia', too.) What it lacks is an appropriate sitting-room, and some character in the bedrooms, which are quite plush but sadly routine in their furnishings. Breakfast is an adequate self-service buffet.

Nearby sights of Siena, Chianti wine country.

Via Fiorentina 58, Siena 53100
Tel (0577) 50431
Location on N fringe of city, on road to Florence; private car parking
Food & drink breakfast, lunch, dinner
Prices rooms L200,000-L300,000
Rooms 32 double, all with bath and shower; all rooms have central heating, phone, minibar, TV
Facilities restaurant, dining-room/bar, sitting-room; outdoor swimming-pool, tennis
Credit cards AE, DC, MC, V
Children welcome
Disabled no special facilities
Pets small ones only and not accepted in dining-room
Closed never
Manager Sg. Righi

Tuscany

Town villa, Siena

Villa Scacciapensieri

This modest hilltop villa dating from the early 1900s has been in the Nardi family since it ceased to be a private house in the 1930s. In that time the tentacles of suburban Siena have reached out to surround it; but if the villa can no longer claim to be in the country it is certainly on the edge of it, and it is still a calm and gracious retreat from the bustle of the city.

The garden is a great asset – a neat, formal, flowery area in front of the house, and a more rustic area to the side including the swimming-pool and a leafy terrace where meals are served in summer. Inside, beyond the cool entrance hall, the dining-room is smartly traditional in style; the sitting-room is something of a disappointment, with modern furniture which is neither stylish nor comfortable – though in cooler weather there is the attraction of a roaring log fire in the grand modern fireplace.

Bedrooms are spacious and solidly furnished, with views either of the roof-tops and towers of Siena or, in the opposite direction, of vineyards, olive groves and the hills beyond. Reports of the Tuscan and international cooking are few, but consistently encouraging.

Nearby sights of Siena; Florence within reach.

Via di Scacciapensieri 10, Siena 53100
Tel (0577) 41442
Location 2 km NE of middle of city, on hill; in private gardens with car parking
Food & drink breakfast, lunch, dinner
Prices rooms L162,500-L300,000; suites L330,000; 20% reduction for children under 6
Rooms 22 double, 15 with bath, 7 with shower; 4 single, 2 with bath, 2 with shower; 2 suites, both with bath; all rooms have central heating, minibar, colour TV, phone, 10 rooms have air-conditioning
Facilities dining-room, hall, bar, TV room; open air swimming-pool, tennis
Credit cards AE, DC, MC, V
Children welcome **Disabled** lift/elevator
Pets small ones only accepted, but not allowed in public rooms or at pool
Closed Nov to Mar; restaurant only, Wed
Proprietors Emma, Riccardo and Emanuele Nardi

Tuscany

Converted monastery, Siena

Certosa di Maggiano

If you are looking for an exclusive but unostentatious hotel in Siena, this is probably it: a former Carthusian monastery – the oldest in Tuscany – secluded in a large park (yet only minutes from the enchanting old city) with just 14 bedrooms of which the majority are suites. Although it is extremely expensive, this is not a swanky place: the calm good taste, the atmosphere of a delightful country house and the discreet service appeal mainly to those in search of peace and privacy.

Meals are served in an exquisite dining-room, in the tranquil 14thC cloisters or under the arcades by the swimming-pool. Guests can help themselves to drinks in the book-lined library, play backgammon or chess in a little ante-room, or relax in the lovely sitting-room. Flower arrangements are just about everywhere and bowls of fresh fruit in the bedrooms add a personal touch. Bear in mind that exploration of Siena will have to be by taxi or bus – it's too far to walk, and parking is almost impossible in the centre. You may, however, wish to stay put and enjoy the beauty of this place – you will have paid for the privilege after all. **Nearby** sights of Siena; hills and vineyards of Chianti; San Gimignano, Florence, Arezzo within reach.

Via Certosa 82, Siena 53100
Tel (0577) 288180
Location 1 km SE of middle of city and Porta Romana; in gardens, with car parking opposite entrance and garage available
Food & drink breakfast, lunch, dinner
Prices rooms L350,000-L400,000 with breakfast; suites L540,000-L650,000; meals about L100,000
Rooms 5 double, 9 suites; all with bath; all have central heating, TV, phone, radio
Facilities dining-room, bar, library, sitting-room; tennis, heated outdoor swimming-pool, heliport
Credit cards AE, DC, V
Children accepted
Disabled access possible – 3 rooms on ground floor
Pets small dogs accepted, but not in dining-room
Closed restaurant only, Tue
Manager Anna Recordati

Tuscany

Town guest-house, Siena

Palazzo Ravizza

We found the welcome here *sotto* to say the least, but when you see your room and begin to let the Ravizza's atmosphere sink in, even the deadpan nature of the staff seems in keeping – and a more recent visitor was received 'with great charm and good humour'. Owned by the same noble Siennese family for the past 200 years, it has been a hotel for most of this century (the card table was their undoing) and it positively oozes that elusive, faded charm which makes for a memorable stay.

Bedrooms vary – all are rather sombre – but the best have views over the Tuscan countryside, quirky pieces of period furniture, comfy beds and huge modern bathrooms. (The thin bath towels, like table-cloths, apparently suit many guests though they don't suit us.) Downstairs there is a little sitting-area with bookshelves or the leather-bound visitors' books to browse through, as well as a large shady terrace (with a magnolia which is magnificent in spring) and a well-kept dining-room with a ravishingly pretty ceiling. The food fits exactly – unpretentious but perfect home cooking (*pasta in brodo*, roast veal with artichokes and so on). For breakfast there are croissants filled with apricot jam, a welcome change from the usual hard rolls.

Nearby cathedral, Piazza del Campo.

Pian dei Mantellini 34, Siena 53100
Tel (0577) 280462
Location inside city walls, close to heart of city; public car parking opposite
Food & drink breakfast, optional picnic lunch, dinner
Prices DB&B L97,500
Rooms 25 double, 15 with bath, 3 with shower; 2 single; 3 family rooms; all rooms have central heating, phone
Facilities dining-room, library, bar, garden terrace; sightseeing mini-bus
Credit cards AE, DC, MC, V
Children welcome
Disabled level access to ground floor, small lift/elevator to bedrooms
Pets small dogs and cats only accepted
Closed restaurant only, Jan and Feb
Proprietor Giovanni Iannone

Tuscany

Town hotel, Siena

Santa Caterina

Owned by the same family as the Palazzo Ravizza (facing page), the Santa Caterina appears on the strong recommendation of two readers; one judges it 'a truly great little hotel – friendly staff, breakfast a cut above anywhere else we stayed'. The 18thC house, ten minutes' walk from the heart of Siena, has been carefully converted, and furnished in rustic style in keeping with its age. Bedrooms vary in size and style; all have pleasant furniture (some antiques) and fresh or dried flowers. A French reporter approved of a split-level room with the bed on a mezzanine under a wooden sloping roof. Breakfast is served in a glassed-in room overlooking the garden (where drinks can be served).
Nearby Porto Romana, sights of Siena.

Via E S Piccolomini 7, Siena 53100
Tel (0577) 221105
Location on corner of two streets, by Porto Romana; with limited private car parking and garden
Food & drink breakfast
Prices rooms L120,000
Rooms 11 double, 3 with bath, 8 with shower; 8 family rooms, 4 with bath, 4 with shower; all rooms have central heating, air-conditioning, phone
Facilities breakfast room, bar, TV room
Credit cards AE, DC, MC, V
Children accepted
Disabled 2 ground-floor rooms
Pets well-behaved pets by prior arrangement
Closed 15 Nov to 3 Mar
Proprietor M Stefania Stasi

Hilltop villa, Regello

Villa Rigacci

This creeper-covered 16thC farmhouse is in a beautiful secluded spot – on a hilltop surrounded by olive groves, pines, chestnut trees and meadows – yet only a short drive away from Florence and Arezzo. Many of the original features of the house have been preserved – arched doorways, beamed bedrooms, open fires, stone-flagged floors. The bedrooms are vast, full of antiques, and overlook the gardens or pleasant swimming-pool and the woods beyond. If you are after complete relaxation, there are no end of quiet shady spots in the park.
Nearby Florence (45 km); Arezzo (55 km).

Vággio 76, Reggello 50066
Tel (055) 865671
Location in rural setting, 1 km N of Vággio, 30 km SE of Florence; exit Incisa from A1; with car parking and gardens
Food & drink breakfast, lunch, dinner
Prices DB&B L128,000-L160,000
Rooms 16 double, 13 with bath, 3 with shower; 2 single with bath; all rooms have central heating, phone, TV, radio, minibar
Facilities dining-room, sitting-rooms, library; swimming-pool, golf practice, horse-riding available
Credit cards AE, DC, V
Children tolerated
Disabled access difficult
Pets accepted if small and well-behaved **Closed** Jan to Feb
Proprietors Frederic and Odette Pierazzi

Tuscany

Converted castle, Monte San Savino

Castello di Gargonza

Gargonza is not so much a castle as a whole village, perfectly preserved in a typically Tuscan landscape, surrounded by cypresses. The various houses, each with its own character and name (the farmer's house, the guard's house, Lucia's house) are let individually, some on a long-term basis, but usually by the week. Mostly dating from the 13th century, they have been restored and comfortably furnished. All have kitchens but there is also a restaurant just outside the walls (specialities include spinach and ricotta roulade and wild boar) and you can take breakfast in the old oil-pressing house ('il fantoio'). In the main guest-house ('la forestiera') you can stay for a few nights on bed-and-breakfast terms.

The English-speaking Count is both efficient administrator and charming host. Keen to preserve the sense of community in his village, he organizes concerts and other evening entertainment from time to time.

Nearby Arezzo (25 km); hills and vineyards of Chianti, Val di Chiana.

Gargonza, Monte San Savino 52048 Arezzo
Tel (0575) 847021
Location 35 km E of Siena on SS73, 7 km W of Monte San Savino; walled village of 18 houses with garden; ample car parking outside village walls
Food & drink breakfast, lunch, dinner
Prices rooms L93,000-L120,000 with breakfast, in main guest-house; meals L28,000-L35,000
Rooms 7 double in main guest-house; 30 double in 18 self-catering houses; all rooms have phone, central heating; main guest-house rooms have minibar
Facilities 4 sitting-rooms (2 available for meetings), TV room; ping-pong, bowls
Credit cards AE
Children accepted
Disabled not suitable
Pets small dogs only accepted
Closed Jan
Proprietor Conte Roberto Guicciardini

Tuscany

Casalta

Only a couple of miles from the San Luigi (below), but far removed in style and atmosphere, this tiny and intimate hotel is tucked away in the middle of the sleepy hilltop village of Strove. It is categorized as a restaurant with rooms by Michelin despite its civilized first-floor sitting-room. The restaurant is cool and relaxed – arches, white walls, tiled floor – and specializes in fish dishes, though we can also recommend the spicy *pasta Strovese* and the *gnochetti*. Bedrooms, reached via corridors off the sitting-room, are confidently simple: bare floors, brass bedsteads, smart little bathrooms. The gently good-humoured *padrone* oversees the whole operation with an eagle eye.

Nearby Colle Val d'Elsa (7 km); Siena (16 km); San Gimignanao (15 km); Volterra (37 km); Florence (45 km).

Strove 53035 Siena
Tel (0577) 301002
Location 4 km SW of Monteriggioni
Food & drink breakfast, lunch (Sun only), dinner
Prices rooms L47,000-L84,000 with breakfast; DB&B L70,000
Rooms 10 double, one single, one family room, all with bath and shower; all rooms have central heating
Facilities dining-room, sitting-room; tennis **Credit cards** not accepted **Children** accepted **Disabled** no special facilities **Pets** not accepted **Closed** mid-Nov to Feb; restaurant Wed **Proprietor** Sg Cellerai

San Luigi Residence

The San Luigi earns its place here by offering a formula which suits families who want access both to the sights of Tuscany and to the kind of outdoor activities which appeal to children. It is a polished conversion of a sizeable old house and its outbuildings, which are separated by expansive lawns from a very big pool. With its adjacent restaurant, this can be a hubbub of activity – though there is plenty of space in which to escape from the fun and games if you want. Food is limited ('steak is the highlight').

Nearby Siena (25 km); Florence (52 km).

Via della Cerreta 38, Strove, Monteriggioni 53030 Siena
Tel (0577) 301055
Location 2 km W of Strove; in large park with private car parking
Food & drink breakfast, lunch, dinner
Prices DB&B L120,000-L160,000
Rooms 10 rooms, 34 apartments (for 2, 2-4, 2-5 people), all with bath or shower; all have central heating, kitchenette, fridge, dishwasher, phone, radio, TV
Facilities dining-room, bar, sitting areas; volley and basket ball, swimming- pool, tennis, sauna, *boccia*, table tennis
Credit cards AE, MC, V
Children welcome; separate pool and games
Disabled ground-floor bedrooms
Pets small animals accepte
Closed Nov to mid-Mar
Manager Francesco Palla

Tuscany

Town villa, Sesto Fiorentino

Villa Villoresi

The aristocratic Villa Villoresi looks rather out of place in what is now an industrial suburb of Florence, but once in the house and gardens you suddenly feel a million miles away from modern, bustling Florence.

Contessa Cristina Villoresi is a warm hostess who has captured the hearts of many transatlantic and other guests. It is thanks to her that the villa still has the feel of a private home – all rather grand, if a little faded.

You could spend hours just exploring the house. As you make your way through the building, each room seems to have some curiosity or feature of the past. The entrance hall is a superb gallery of massive chandeliers, frescoed walls, antiques and lofty potted plants. Then there are the beautiful frescoes on the first-floor landing, the family tree in reception, the sober looking Tuscan nobility in the dining-room, the leather-bound novels and back numbers of National Geographic magazine in the sitting-room. Bedrooms are remarkably varied – from the small and quite plain to grand apartments with frescoes and Venetian chandeliers. Some overlook an inner courtyard, others look out on to the pool and garden.

Half- or full-board terms at the Villa Villoresi are still quite reasonable; and we are assured that the food is now better than it once was.

Nearby Florence (8 km).

Via Ciampi 2, Colonnata di Sesto Fiorentino, Florence 50019
Tel (055) 443692
Location 8 km NW of Florence; adequate car parking; from motorway exit Prato-Calenzano, follow signs to Sesto Fiorentino, then to Villa Villoresi/Colonnata
Food & drink breakfast, lunch, dinner
Prices rooms L120,000-L270,000; DB&B L140,000-L215,000; dinner L45,000

Rooms 18 double, 3 single, 7 suites, all with bath or shower; all rooms have central heating, phone
Facilities sitting-rooms, bar, dining-room, veranda; swimming-pool, ping-pong
Credit cards AE, DC, MC, V
Children welcome
Disabled no special facilities
Pets not accepted in public rooms
Closed never
Proprietor Contessa Cristina Villoresi

Tuscany

Country hotel, Volterra

Villa Nencini

Volterra is a severely impressive hilltop town in glorious, sweeping hill country to the west of Chianti. The Villa Nencini, in contrast, is a captivating, mellow stone house not far outside the town walls, with a jolly garden and long views. Bedrooms are small but simply smart and light, and there is a neat breakfast room. The *padrone* likes to play it cool, but is easily disarmed by smiles or any sign of interest in his house, of which he is naturally proud. Readers report favourably, though one complains of cleaners noisily at work at too early an hour.
Nearby Siena and San Gimignano within easy reach.

Borgo Santo Stefano 55,
Volterra 56048 Pisa
Tel (0588) 86386
Location outside city walls, in small park about 500 m from heart of city, with private car parking
Food & drink breakfast
Prices rooms L48,000- L90,000
Rooms 13 double, 10 with shower; one single, with shower; all rooms have central heating, phone; TV on request
Facilities sitting-room with bar, TV room, hall, terrace, breakfast room, piscina
Credit cards MC, V
Children welcome
Disabled no special facilities
Pets small ones only
Closed never
Proprietor Mario Nencini

Country villa, Trespiano

Villa le Rondini

The great attraction of this villa is its secluded grounds and their beautiful views of the city and Arno valley. The hotel dates back to the 16th century though it looks quite new. There are three buildings; some of the rooms in the main house are exceptionally spacious and beautifully furnished in traditional style, some in the annexes rather simpler. The main sitting-room is split-level, providing two comfortable areas where beams and an antique fireplace lend an old-fashioned atmosphere. We lack recent reports on the food, not a strong point when we visited.
Nearby walks in the park.

Via Bolognese Vecchia 224,
Florence 50139
Tel (055) 400081
Location 7 km N of Florence; in park with ample car parking
Food & drink breakfast, lunch, dinner, snacks
Prices rooms L90,000- L117,500; suites L199,100
Rooms 39 double, 2 suites, all with bath or shower; 4 single, one with bath, one with shower; all rooms have central heating, minibar, phone
Facilities 4 sitting-rooms, 2 bars, piano bar, restaurant, TV room, 4 conference rooms; fashion shows, illuminated tennis courts, swimming-pool, sauna, gym
Credit cards AE, MC, V
Children accepted if well behaved
Disabled no special fa
Pets accepted
Closed never
Proprietor Franc

Tuscany

Country inn, Sinalunga

Locanda dell'Amorosa

The Locanda dell'Amorosa is as romantic as it sounds. An elegant Renaissance villa-cum-village, within the remains of 14thC walls, has been converted into a charming country inn. The old stables, beamed and brick-walled, have been transformed into a delightful rustic restaurant serving refined versions of traditional Tuscan recipes, using ingredients from the estate, which also produces wine. The restaurant, which has earned the coveted array of chefs' hats in several Italian guides, can serve up to 80 people and is often full.

Only a fortunate few can actually stay at the Locanda – either in apartments in the houses where peasants and farmworkers once lived, or in ordinary bedrooms in the old family residence. The bedrooms we saw were cool, airy and pretty, with whitewashed walls, wood-block floors, wrought-iron beds and flowery cotton curtains and bedspreads – and immaculate modern bathrooms. To complete the village there is a little parish church with lovely 15thC frescoes of the Sienese school. The Locanda is a paradise for connoisseurs of Tuscany, for gourmets and for all romantics.

Nearby Siena (45 km); Arezzo (45 km); Chianti wine country.

Sinalunga 53048 Siena
Tel (0577) 679497
Location 2 km S of Sinalunga; ample car parking
Food & drink breakfast, lunch, dinner
Prices rooms L190,000-L290,000; suites L355,000-L420,000; meals from L60,000
Rooms 8 double, all with bathroom; 7 suites; all rooms with central heating, phone, colour TV, minibar
Facilities dining-room, sitting-room
Credit cards AE, DC, MC, V
Children accepted
Disabled access difficult
Pets not accepted
Closed mid-Jan to end Feb; restaurant only, Mon, Tue (but a hot buffet is provided for hotel guests)
Proprietor Carlo Citterio

Florence

Alba

A complete renovation in 1985 transformed the Alba into a spruce new hotel. The Via della Scala is not one of the most desirable streets of the city but it is handy for the station and only a few minutes' walk from the heart of the city. The bedrooms have all been entirely modernized and equipped with bathrooms and double glazing. Downstairs the main public area is the prettily decorated breakfast room. The building may be short on charm, but the reception is smiling and friendly – which is more than can be said for many nearby hotels.

Nearby church of Santa Maria Novella (3 minutes' walk); *Duomo* (10 minutes' walk).

Via della Scala 22-38, Florence 50123
Tel (055) 211469
Location on busy street, about 2 minutes from station; car parking awkward
Food & drink breakfast
Prices rooms L85,500-L135,000 with breakfast
Rooms 20 double, 4 single; all with bath or shower; all rooms have air-conditioning, central heating, double glazing, phone, TV, minibar
Facilities breakfast room/bar, TV room
Credit cards MC, V
Children accepted
Disabled not suitable
Pets not accepted
Closed never
Proprietors Caridi family

Annalena

This 15thC *palazzo* is one of those typically Florentine places where you ring a bell and a large creaky door slowly opens to let you in to a courtyard. A wide flight of stone stairs brings you to the first floor where reception, breakfast room and sitting-room are all combined in a huge, high-ceilinged hall filled with fine antiques, paintings and sculpture. Bedrooms lead off white-washed galleries of drawings and prints; the majority are spacious and handsomely furnished with solid antiques or painted furniture, but otherwise quite simple.

Nearby Pitti Palace, Boboli Gardens, church of Santo Spirito

Via Romana 34, Florence 50125
Tel (055) 222402
Location S of the Arno, on fairly busy street; several paying garages in the vicinity
Food & drink breakfast
Prices rooms L87,000-L136,000
Rooms 17 double, 3 single; all with bath or shower; all rooms have central heating, phone
Facilities breakfast and sitting area, bar
Credit cards AE, DC, MC, V
Children accepted
Disabled no special facilities
Pets dogs and small animals accepted
Closed never
Proprietors Salvestrini and Salimbeni families

Florence

Town hotel, south of the station

Aprile

The station area of Florence is liberally endowed with hotels but there are few with any charm. The Aprile is one of the exceptions, converted from a 15thC Medici palace and retaining original, well preserved features such as frescoes and vaulted and painted ceilings. Downstairs there are chandeliers and a few Old Master reproductions, but the hotel as a whole is unpretentious, and some of its bedrooms are surprisingly simple and in need of decoration. They vary from large (sometimes rather gloomy) rooms with antiques, through light, flowery rooms with painted furniture to simple modern ones with basic fittings. Back rooms away from the busy street are definitely to be preferred.

Nearby church of Santa Maria Novella.

Via della Scala 6, Florence 50123
Tel (055) 216237
Location close to Piazza Santa Maria Novella and station, on fairly busy street with no car parking facilities
Food & drink breakfast
Prices rooms L65,500-L126,000 with breakfast
Rooms 25 double, 21 with bath or shower; 4 single, one with bath; all have central heating, phone, some have minibar
Facilities breakfast room, bar/sitting-room, patio
Credit cards AE, MC, V
Children accepted
Disabled access difficult
Pets accepted **Closed** never
Proprietor Valeria Cantini

Town guest-house, near Piazza della Signoria

Cestelli

Only a tiny plaque on the front door reveals that this typically Florentine *palazzo* contains a hotel. Once inside, first impressions are not good. But, after you have climbed two rather gloomy flights of stone stairs, confidence is restored by the delightful little entrance hall, furnished with immaculate small antiques and a few lovingly kept curiosities. This is a family hotel, run with great pride like a home by Signora Ada Cestelli.

The bedrooms range from a huge high-ceilinged room with big antiques, candelabra and sofa, down to the simple and slightly shabby – but none is without character. There is only one private bathroom, but prices are remarkably low. Book six months ahead to be sure of a room.

Nearby Ponte Vecchio, Uffizi Gallery, Palazzo Strozzi, *Duomo*.

Borgo SS Apostoli 25, Florence 50123
Tel (055) 214213
Location in heart of city, close to Piazza della Signoria; car parking awkward
Food & drink breakfast
Prices rooms L37,000- L58,800
Rooms 7 rooms, one with bath
Facilities tiny breakfast room
Credit cards not accepted
Children not very suitable
Disabled not suitable
Pets accepted
Closed never
Proprietor Ada Cestelli

Florence

Town hotel, north of the *Duomo*

Loggiato dei Serviti

One of Florence's newest charming hotels is in one of its loveliest Renaissance buildings, designed (around 1527) by Sangallo the Elder to match Brunelleschi's famous Hospital of the Innocenti, which stands opposite. Until a few years ago the arcades were dilapidated, the building housed a modest *pensione* and the beautiful square was a giant car park. But, thanks to the loving restoration of the Budini-Gattai family, the Loggiato is now an elegant place to stay and, thanks to the city council's change of heart, it is also one of the most tranquil in Florence.

The decoration is a skilful blend of old and new, all designed to complement the original vaulting and other features with a minimum of frill and fuss. Floors are terracotta tiled, walls rag painted in pastel colours. Furniture and paintings are mostly, but not exclusively, old. There is a small, bright breakfast room in which to start the day (with fruit juice, cheese and ham, brioches, fruit and coffee) and a little bar where you can recover from it, browsing glossy Italian magazines and sipping a Campari and soda.

Sadly, one visitor felt misled by our description, complaining of dirty rooms and unhelpful staff. Others have been quite happy. More reports, please.

Nearby church of Santissima Annunziata and Foundlings' Hospital; *Duomo*, church of San Marco, Accademia gallery.

Piazza SS Annunziata 3, Florence 50122
Tel (055) 219165
Location a few minutes' walk N of the *Duomo*, on W side of Piazza SS Annunziata; garage service on request
Food & drink breakfast
Prices rooms L110,000-L170,000
Rooms 19 double, 9 with bath, 10 with shower; 6 single, all with shower; 4 suites, all with bath; all rooms have phone, minibar, piped music; colour TV on request
Facilities breakfast room, bar
Credit cards AE, DC, MC, V
Children welcome
Disabled not suitable
Pets accepted
Closed never
Proprietor Rodolfo Budini-Gattai

Florence

Ariele

Lovers of music are likely to appreciate the location of this pleasant small hotel: it lies just a stone's throw from the Teatro Communale – main Florentine venue for concerts, opera and ballet. It is so close, in fact, that you can sometimes hear the music when you are sitting in the small garden of the hotel. Inside, the Ariele has the charm of a private Florentine home, with modestly elegant public rooms and a friendly, distinctly Italian atmosphere. Bedrooms are somewhat spartan, but any lack of furnishings is outweighed by more than ample space and very reasonable prices.

Nearby Teatro Communale (concerts, opera etc), banks of river Arno; historic heart of city about 15 minutes' walk.

Via Magenta 11, Florence 50123
Tel (055) 211509
Location between station and the Arno, about one km W of *Duomo*; with private garden and car parking
Food & drink breakfast
Prices rooms L75,000-L110,000
Rooms 36 double, 4 single, all with bath or shower; all rooms have central heating
Facilities breakfast room, 4 sitting-rooms, bar, terrace
Credit cards AE, MC, V
Children accepted
Disabled lift-elevator
Pets accepted
Closed never
Proprietors Bartelloni family

Hermitage

Everything about the Hermitage is small-scale, like a doll's house – only upside down, with the old-fashioned bedrooms on the lower floors while the reception desk and public rooms are on the fifth floor, with views of the Arno. Right at the top is the charming roof terrace, with more wonderful views and overflowing with greenery and flowers. The place does not have a period look, but it has a definitely Forsterian feel, and the owners are charming. The one drawback (common to many Florentine hotels) is noise from the night-time traffic on the Lungarno, though front bedrooms do have double glazing.

Nearby Uffizi gallery, Ponte Vecchio

Vicolo Marzio 1, Piazza del Pesce, Florence 50122
Tel (055) 287216
Location in heart of city, facing the river; car parking difficult
Food & drink breakfast, snacks
Prices rooms L96,000-L135,000
Rooms 20 double, 15 with bath, 3 with shower; 2 single with shower; all rooms have central heating, phone
Facilities breakfast room, sitting-room with bar, roof terrace
Credit cards not accepted
Children welcome
Disabled access difficult
Pets small dogs only
Closed never
Proprietors Vincenzo Scarcelli and Paolo Pietro

Florence

Photo: Ariele (facing page)

Town villa, east of the *Duomo*

Monna Lisa

Despite other challengers, the Monna Lisa remains Florence's most charming small hotel – an unusual combination of comfort without pretension. Five minutes' walk from the *Duomo*, the Monna Lisa is an elegant Renaissance *palazzo* around a small courtyard set back from the unprepossessing street façade. The main rooms, on the ground floor, have polished brick floors with Oriental carpets and beamed or vaulted ceilings, plus a very individual collection of antique furniture, paintings and sculpture. In the cosy little salon is the first model for Giambologna's famous Rape of the Sabines, and there is also a collection of drawings and statues by Giovanni Dupre, the neo- classical sculptor, from whom the owner's family is descended. The best bedrooms are huge and high-ceilinged, with old furniture, although when we visited (a few years ago) some others seemed rather dark. The quietest rooms overlook the lovely garden, a rare bonus in Florence. The Monna Lisa is not cheap, but it is both a polished and a relaxing place to stay.

Nearby *Duomo* (about five minutes' walk), Santa Croce, Bargello, Uffizi all within easy walking distance.

Borgo Pinti 27, Florence 50121
Tel (055) 247 9751
Location about 5 minutes' walk E of the *Duomo*; with garden and private car parking
Food & drink breakfast
Prices rooms L160,000-L230,000
Rooms 15 double, 5 single; all with bath or shower; all rooms have central heating, air-conditioning, phone, minibar, colour TV
Facilities sitting-rooms, bar
Credit cards AE, DC, V
Children accepted
Disabled no special facilities
Pets accepted
Closed never
Manager Riccardo Sardei

Florence

Town guest-house, on the Arno

Rigatti

With its stone-arched entrance and heavy wooden doors, the Rigatti looks a cut above your average *pensione*, and so it is. It occupies the two upper floors of the 15thC Palazzo Alberti, and is furnished in sympathetically Florentine style throughout. Polished antiques stand on wood-block floors, gilt mirrors and portraits in oils hang on whitewashed walls, and the atmosphere is civilized without being formal: like her parents and grandparents before her, the charming Signora di Benedetti and her brother-in-law (both of them now getting on in years) manage to preserve that desirable but elusive private-home feeling, despite the comings and goings of their international (largely English-speaking) clientele.

The bedrooms are comfortably but simply furnished; most are fair-sized, but some are on the small side. Most visitors, whether Forster fans or not, prefer A Room With A View, despite the noise from the traffic roaring along the riverside Lungarno (an undeniable drawback common to many central hotels in Florence). But the quieter rooms at the back overlook the courtyard garden, and you can always enjoy the views from the roof-top terrace and from the tiny side terrace.

The Rigatti won't last forever: catch it while you can.

Nearby Uffizi gallery, Santa Croce, Ponte Vecchio, *Duomo* – all within easy walking distance.

Lungarno Generale Diaz 2, Florence 50122
Tel (055) 213022
Location on the Arno, a few minutes' walk E of the Ponte Vecchio; with river-view roof garden
Food & drink breakfast
Prices rooms L56,000- L74,500
Rooms 28 rooms, 14 with bath or shower
Facilities 3 sitting-rooms, breakfast room, terrace
Credit cards not accepted
Children accepted
Disabled no special facilities
Pets not accepted
Closed never
Proprietor Sga di Benedetti

Photo: Residenza (facing page)

Florence

Town hotel, east of the *Duomo*

Liana

Via Alfieri lies a good 15 minutes' walk from the *Duomo* and it is not one of the most interesting parts of the city. But prices at the Liana are low in comparison to more central hotels, and the rooms are quieter. For a brief period in the late 19th century the building served as the British Embassy and there are still a few touches of grandeur about it, such as the painted ceiling in the breakfast room. Bedrooms are a little gloomy and faded, though the biggest rooms at the back (which include the Consul's Room) overlook a small garden belonging to the hotel. Breakfasts at the Liana are rather better than you expect from a simple hotel: you get ham, cheese and juice in addition to the usual coffee and rolls.

Nearby *Duomo* (15 minutes' walk).

Via Alfieri 18, Florence 50121
Tel (055) 245303
Location 15 minutes E of *Duomo*; car parking
Food & drink breakfast
Prices rooms L48,000- L95,000
Rooms 19 double, 8 with bath, 4 with shower; one single; 2 suites, one with bath, one with shower; all rooms have central heating, phone
Facilities breakfast room, reading-room
Credit cards AE, MC, V
Children accepted
Disabled no special facilities
Pets small ones only accepted
Closed never
Proprietor Sg. Spina

Town hotel, in shopping district

Residenza

The Residenza still occupies the top four floors of an old *palazzo* – reached by a charmingly old-fashioned lift up the stone stairwell – but has been renovated and improved. The sitting-room has blue velour sofas and potted plants, the simple dining-room a cheerful array of wine bottles, carafes and ceramics. There are pictures everywhere, some of them the work of guests. Bedrooms range from the rustically antique to the modern in style. Some of the upper ones have their own balcony, and on the top floor there is also a panoramic sitting- room and a delightful roof-terrace with a cluster of plants and flowers.

Nearby Palazzo Strozzi, Palazzo Rucellai and the church of Santa Trinita.

Via Tornabuoni 8, Florence 50123
Tel (055) 284197
Location on smart central shopping street; private paying garage nearby
Food & drink breakfast, dinner
Prices rooms L70,250- L186,000 with breakfast; DB&B L95,000- L127,500; 50% off for children 0-4 years
Rooms 18 double, 11 with bath, 6 with shower; 7 single, one with bath, 3 with shower; all have central heating, phone; 7 have air-conditioning
Facilities sitting-room, bar, dining-room, roof terrace
Credit cards AE, DC, V
Children accepted
Disabled no special facilities
Pets small, friendly ones accepted **Closed** never
Proprietor Giovanna Vasile

Florence

Town guest-house, south of the Ponte alle Grazie

Silla

Set back from the south bank of the Arno in a relatively quiet position, the Silla is a solid Florentine *palazzo* with a handsome inner courtyard. But what really distinguishes it from other *pensioni* is its spacious terrace, where you can take drinks under the shade of gaily coloured parasols and enjoy river views. Reception (where recent visitors have had a 'very friendly' welcome) has some pretty Venetian 18thC furnishings, while the breakfast room is simply decorated with copper pots and ceramics. Bedrooms, with dark walnut furniture and flowery tapestries, provide adequate comfort and good value.

Nearby Santa Croce, Uffizi, Ponte Vecchio, Pitti Palace all within walking distance.

Via dei Renai 5, Florence 50125
Tel (055) 234 2888/2889
Location on left bank of Arno, near Ponte alle Grazie; small private garage
Food & drink breakfast
Prices rooms L80,000-L122,000 with breakfast
Rooms 18 double, 6 with bath, 8 with shower; 4 single, 3 with shower; 10 family rooms, 6 with bath, 3 with shower; all rooms have central heating, TV, phone
Facilities breakfast room, reading-room, bar, large terrace
Credit cards AE, DC, MC, V
Children accepted if under supervision of parents
Disabled no special facilities
Pets small ones only accepted
Closed 2 weeks Dec
Proprietor Avellino Silla

Town guest-house, south of Ponte Vecchio

Pitti Palace

A popular Florentine *pensione*, run by the very helpful Amedeo Pinto and his friendly American wife. The main attractions are the pretty roof terrace (with views) and the elegant sitting-room. Bedrooms vary from light and bright to plain and rather spartan (especially the singles) and almost all suffer from traffic noise – the price you pay for the convenient location just south of the Ponte Vecchio. In the entrance hall the English-speaking staff are always on hand to book taxis or lend guide-books; on the walls are signed photographs of famous guests and current lists of museum opening hours, and so on.

Nearby Pitti Palace and Boboli gardens, Ponte Vecchio, Uffizi.

Via Barbadori 2, Florence 50125
Tel (055) 282257
Location just beyond the S end of the Ponte Vecchio
Food & drink breakfast
Prices rooms L65,000-L125,000 with breakfast
Rooms 28 double, 22 with bath; 12 single, 6 with bath, one with shower; all rooms have central heating, phone
Facilities sitting-room, breakfast room, TV room
Credit cards AE, V
Children accepted
Disabled no special facilities
Pets accepted if well behaved
Closed never
Manager Amedeo Pinto

Florence

Town guest-house, in shopping district

Tornabuoni Beacci

Via Tornabuoni is one of the most desirable streets of Florence, renowned for the elegance of its shops, and the Tornabuoni Beacci is one of the most desirable hotels in the area.

The hotel used to be a *de luxe pensione* and it still has the feel of a family home rather than a hotel – largely due to the warm personality of Signora Beacci, who has run the place since 1954. In fact there has been a Beacci here since 1900, when her mother first established the hotel at a nearby location. The present hotel occupies the third and fourth floors of a fine old *palazzo*.

The rather gloomy ground-floor entrance gives no hint of the charming interior of the hotel, where prints and paintings, patterned carpets on wood block floors and classical antiques all create an elegant, yet welcoming atmosphere. The sitting-room is exceptionally comfortable and well furnished – the sort you rarely find in a small central city hotel. The bedrooms are comfortable and classically furnished. And there is a delightful roof-top terrace, cluttered with potted plants, flowers and creepers, and equipped with several tables where you can have breakfast or evening drinks.

The volumes of visitors' books, which date back to the 1920s, are full of glowing praise from famous travellers who have been captivated by this little 'home from home' hotel.

Nearby Palazzo Strozzi, Palazzo Rucellai, church of Santa Trinita.

Via Tornabuoni 3, Florence 50123
Tel (055) 268377
Location at N end of busy central street, with car parking in paying garage
Food & drink breakfast, lunch, dinner
Prices DB&B L101,000-L130,000
Rooms 20 double, 18 with bath or shower; 10 single, 7 with bath or shower; all have central heating, minibar, air-conditioning, phone; colour TV in some rooms
Facilities sitting-room, bar, restaurant, roof terrace
Credit cards AE, DC, V
Children accepted
Disabled lift/elevator
Pets accepted
Closed never
Proprietor Sga Beacci

Florence

Country villa, south of the Boboli gardens

Villa Belvedere

This modern house with modern furnishings might be anywhere in Europe – except that it stands on a peaceful hillside giving unsurpassed views across Florence. Everything is spotlessly clean and well cared for, with light, sunny rooms and plenty of potted plants and freshly cut flowers. All bedrooms except two have a full-size bath, and breakfast is taken in a glassed-in room overlooking the immaculate garden. The Ceschi-Perotto family extend a warm welcome.

Nearby Pitti Palace, Boboli gardens.

Via Benedetto Castelli 3,
Florence 50124
Tel (055) 222501
Location 3 km S of city, in
gardens with some private car
parking
Food & drink breakfast, snacks
Prices rooms L150,000-
L220,000
Rooms 24 double, 22 with
bath, 2 with shower; 3 single, 2
with bath, one with shower; all
rooms have central heating,

air- conditioning, phone,
colour TV, safe
Facilities breakfast room, 2
sitting-rooms, bar, TV room,
veranda; swimming- pool,
tennis
Credit cards AE, DC, MC, V
Children welcome
Disabled no special facilities
Pets not accepted
Closed Dec to Feb
Proprietors Ceschi-Perotto
family

Town guest-house, north of the *Duomo*

Splendor

Many of the *pensioni* in central Florence have become so expensive that they are now beyond the means of the average tourist. The Splendor, north of the *Duomo* and close to the Accademia, is a happy exception. It occupies part of a typically Florentine countrified building. Painted ceilings, frescoes and antiques are part of its appeal, though modern seating and other newer additions are not altogether sympathetic to their surroundings. Perhaps the most charming feature of all is the sunny terrace, with its cluster of potted plants; sadly, breakfast is apparently not available there. The bedrooms are remarkably varied – some with chandeliers and painted furniture, others with modern vinyl and no atmosphere – but the majority are large.

Nearby church of San Marco, Accademia gallery.

Via San Gallo 30, Florence
50129
Tel (055) 483427
Location 50 m from Piazza
San Marco; car parking in
paying garage or on street
Food & drink breakfast buffet
Prices rooms L60,000-
L90,000 with breakfast
Rooms 25 double, 16 with
bath or shower; 6 single, all

with bath or shower; all rooms
have central heating
Facilities sitting-room, 2
breakfast rooms, terrace
Credit cards MC, V
Children accepted
Disabled access difficult
Pets accepted if small and well
behaved
Closed never
Proprietor Masoero Vincenzo

Florence

Town villa, south of Boboli gardens

Villa Carlotta

A gracious 19thC patrician house, the Villa Carlotta was one of several mansions built on the south-east slopes of Florence in the days when they were almost open countryside. Today the villa stands on a quiet tree-lined street in a residential area.

The hotel has recently been upgraded to four stars and rooms have been revamped – but without sacrificing the oldest and finest features of the building. Moulded ceilings and stucco bas-reliefs in the forms of garlands and flower-filled baskets still embellish the public rooms. Oriental rugs and Tuscan furnishings (mainly reproduction antiques) create an elegant and impeccable setting. Bedrooms are furnished in sophisticated style with silk-like wall fabrics in blue or pink, wall-to-wall carpeting, woven floral bedspreads and linen sheets – plus of course all the extras you would expect in a four-star hotel. The rooms are delightfully quiet, overlooking the hills or the hotel's small garden.

Breakfast is copious, with fruit juice, yoghurts, porridge, cereal, eggs, bacon, cheese and ham – in addition to coffee, rolls and croissants. It is served in a glazed veranda – or in fine weather outside on the terrace, around the stone fountain.

Nearby Pitti Palace, Boboli Gardens, Piazzale Michelangelo.

Via Michele di Lando 3, Florence 50125
Tel (055) 220530
Location on SE side of city, close to Porta Romana on quiet street, with small garden and private garage
Food & drink breakfast, dinner
Prices rooms L127,000-L294,000
Rooms 17 double, 6 with bath, 11 with shower; 7 single, all with shower; 3 family rooms, all with bath; all rooms have central heating, air-conditioning, minibar, room safe, colour TV, phone
Facilities bar, sitting-rooms, 2 dining-rooms, breakfast room, conference room
Credit cards AE, DC, MC, V
Children accepted
Disabled access difficult
Pets small, clean ones accepted, except in dining-rooms
Closed never
Proprietor Evelina Pagni

Florence

Torre de Bellosguardo

'We like to think of Torre di Bellosguardo as a sort of peaceful oasis where travellers can feel as comfortable as in their own homes' says Giovanni Franchetti, who with his French wife Michele began renovating his beautiful 16thC family home in 1980. He created thirteen luxurious guest rooms, using (as far as possible) original materials and furniture. The rooms are spacious, with beamed or arched ceilings, shuttered windows and fabulous views of the city (especially the two magnificent tower rooms). There are five sitting-rooms; one domed and bordered by frescoes, another with a huge fireplace, another in an arched corridor, flanked by ferns and lemon trees. Salad lunches are served by the swimming-pool in the shady gardens in summer.

Nearby Ponte Vecchio, Pitti Palace, Passeggiata ai Colli (hills).

Via Roti Michelozzi 2, Florence 50124
Tel (0552) 298145
Location on hill overlooking city, just S of Porta Romana; with garden and car parking
Food & drink breakfast, lunch (by swimming-pool)
Prices rooms L210,000-L280,000
Rooms 8 double, 2 single, 3 suites, all with bath; all rooms have central heating, phone; 2 rooms have air-conditioning
Facilities dining-room, sitting-rooms, bar; swimming-pool
Credit cards AE, DC, MC, V
Children accepted
Disabled lift/elevator
Pets accepted **Closed** never
Proprietor Giovanni Franchetti

Morandi alla Crocetta

An American family holidaying in Florence brought this converted convent to our attention. They were particularly impressed with its blend of modern comfort and traditional style. So are we. Kathleen Doyle (an Englishwoman who moved here in the 1920s) and her son Paolo have decorated the white interior of the house thoughtfully. Antique Tuscan furniture, beautiful patterned rugs, interesting pictures and fresh flowers abound. The sitting-room (in contrast to the small, neat bedrooms) is large and lofty, with floral armchairs scattered among potted plants. Breakfast is served in bedrooms or the 'breakfast nook'.

Nearby *Duomo*, archaeological museum, Academy of Fine Art.

Via Laura 50, Florence 50121
Tel (0552) 344747
Location in quiet street, NW of Piazza del Duomo; car parking on street problematic
Food & drink breakfast
Prices rooms L63,000-L135,000
Rooms 4 double, 2 single, 3 family rooms, all with shower; all have central heating, air-conditioning, phone, TV, hairdrier, radio, minibar
Facilities breakfast room, sitting-room
Credit cards AE, DC, MC, V
Children welcome; baby-sitting on request
Disabled no special facilities
Pets small well-behaved dogs accepted **Closed** never
Proprietor Kathleen Doyle

Tuscan Coast

Hotels on the Tuscan coast

The Versilian Riviera begins its long sweep of resorts only a little way north-west of Lucca and Pisa, so the visitor to Tuscany should have no difficulty in combining sightseeing with seaside sunbathing. Finding notably welcoming places to stay is not so easy – although many of the better hotels in resorts such as Forte dei Marmi and Marina di Pietrasanta have attractive shady gardens, few have any other distinguishing features. At the north end of this coastline at Montignoso is the Bottacio, a highly-praised (Michelin-starred) restaurant with just five rooms in a converted olive-mill. Its style, service and prices are all impressive. At Livorno is the Villa Godilonda (Tel (0586) 752032), a spotless, modest seaside hotel near two sandy beaches. Further south and just off the coast (but within easy reach of the long sandy beach at Marina de Castagneto) is an old stone villa, La Torre at Castagneto Carducci (Tel (0565) 775268), which, as its name suggests, stands next to a ruined tower. It has been converted into a simple hotel offering B&B and basic evening meals.

The Tuscan island of Elba is big enough to absorb the many summer visitors it attracts without being swamped in the way that some of the smaller and more southerly islands have been. We have one clear recommendation on the island (p 138), but in general Elba presents us with a problem, which is that its small hotels are, to be honest, less attractive than many of the bigger ones which cannot properly be given full entries here. There is a handful of charming and comfortable (but not cheap) hotels with 60 to 100 rooms within a few miles of the port of arrival, Portoferraio. High in the hills to the south, with wonderful views from its terraces and pool, is the Picchiaie (Tel (0565) 933072). Across the bay from Portoferraio, in leafy grounds close to the sea, is the polished Villa Ottone (Tel (0565) 933042). Nearby at Magazzini is the smart and expensive Fabricia (Tel (0565) 933181) with its own beach facilities. In the opposite direction, to the west, is the excellent sandy beach of Biodola, shared by the delightful but expensive Hermitage (Tel (0565) 969932), with most of its rooms in bungalows dotted among pines, and the more modest Biodola (Tel (0565) 969966). Both have extensive leisure activities on offer. On the south side of the island are a couple of places worth mentioning; the 43-room Montecristo at Marino di Campo (modern and pleasant, on sandy beach, good big swimming-pool, Tel (0565) 976861) and the Bahia at Cavoli (new, 60 rooms in houses, gardens of olives and cacti, Tel (0565) 987055).

We mention two hotels on the island of Giglio in greater detail (pp 138-139). Also worth considering is the Arenella (quiet and comfortable, with great views of the coast, Tel (0564) 809340).

Hotel prices
As we explain in the Introduction, many hotels did not know their 1991 prices when we were preparing this edition, so it will not be surprising if some prices have increased by now. But in any case it is always wise to check room prices when making a booking or taking a room: hotels can and do sometimes change their prices by much more than inflationary amounts.

Tuscan Coast

Seaside villa, Giglio

Pardini's Hermitage

A real get-away-from-it-all place, perched on the edge of a cliff above the sea, and accessible only by boat (unless you can face the hour's walk). Federigo Pardini's white villa – surrounded by wooded hills, flower-filled meadows and rocky paths to an aqua-marine cove – is a paradise for nature-lovers. It is also a very friendly hotel; guests are treated as old friends. There are a couple of modern sitting-rooms and a smart white dining-room, but you will probably spend more time outside, enjoying a meal (often fresh fish on the barbecue) or a drink on one of the shady terraces, or sunbathing and swimming from the rocks in the cove. Bedrooms have balconies and panoramic sea views.

Nearby Giglio Porto; Giglio Castello.

Isola del Giglio 58013 Grosseto
Tel (0564) 809034
Location in isolated spot overlooking sea, reached by hotel boat from Giglio Porto; with grounds
Food & drink breakfast, lunch
Prices FB L80,000-L130,000;
Rooms 8 double, 5 with bath, 2 with shower; 2 single; all rooms have phone; some rooms hairdrier, TV
Facilities dining-room, 2 sitting-rooms; outdoor bar, barbecue; water-skiing available
Credit cards not accepted
Children welcome
Disabled access very difficult
Pets accepted
Closed Oct to Mar
Proprietor Federigo Pardini

Resort village, Elba

Capo Sud

More of a village than a hotel, the Capo Sud is a complex of little villas in a quiet, rather remote spot with plenty of activities on hand. Rooms are modern and quite simple, scattered among trees and *macchia*, none of them very far away from the focal area of the restaurant, bar, sitting-room and open-air terrace with fine views of the bay. The hotel has its own vineyard, and most fruit served here comes straight from the private orchards. There is a special weekly menu of dishes which are supposedly exclusive to the island.

Nearby Portoferraio (14 km).

Lacona, Portoferraio 57037 Livorno
Tel (0565) 964021
Location 11 km NW of Capoliveri on Golfo Stella, in grounds sloping down to sea; ample car parking.
Food & drink breakfast, lunch, dinner
Prices DB&B L57,200-L93,500 (minimum 3 days)
Rooms 37 double, 2 with bath, 35 with shower; 2 single, both with shower; all rooms have phone; 20 rooms have minibar
Facilities TV room, bar, dining-room; beach, tennis, bowls, rowing, sailing, windsurfing
Credit cards DC
Children accepted
Disabled no special facilities
Pets not accepted
Closed Oct to Apr
Proprietor Enzo di Puccio

Tuscan Coast

Castello Monticello

The pretty little island of Giglio (particularly its smart little port) attracts many day-trippers; but the island is also an attractive place to stay if good beaches are not your priority. Built as a private house in the style of a castle, the Castello Monticello lies on an unspoilt hillside. Perhaps it looks austere, but inside it is cosy and welcoming – more like a villa than a castle. Furnishings are relatively simple but any lack of luxury here is more than outweighed by the fine location. From the shady gardens, the terrace and most of the bedrooms there are splendid views of sea and coast.

Nearby Giglio Porto; Giglio Castello (4 km).

Via Provinciale per il Castello Giglio Porto, Isola del Giglio 58013 Grosseto
Tel (0564) 809252
Location about 2 km from port on hillside, with car park
Food & drink breakfast, lunch, dinner
Prices rooms L40,000-L76,000; DB&B L69,000-L87,000
Rooms 27 double, 4 single and 6 family rooms, all with shower; all rooms have central heating, phone
Facilities dining-room, breakfast room, bar, TV room, terrace
Credit cards MC, V
Children accepted
Disabled no special facilities
Pets not in dining-room
Closed mid-Nov to mid-Mar
Manager Sergio Chiucini

Piccolo Hotel Alleluja

Fine white sands bordered by pine woods, a variety of sports (including riding and an excellent 18-hole golf course) and a marina lure the wealthy from Florence, Milan and Rome to Punta Ala, to stay in second homes or in one of the four prestigious hotels. Of these, the Piccolo Alleluja is perhaps the most inviting. It is small, stylish and intimate, in surroundings of Mediterranean *macchia*, aromatic herbs, lawns, and flowering shrubs. Inside, rustic chic prevails. Designs and furnishings are simple, colours are light and the atmosphere cheerful. Bedrooms are elegant, some with their own sitting-rooms.

Nearby Grosseto (41 km).

Punta Ala 58040 Grosseto
Tel (0564) 922050
Location near middle of resort, 7 minutes from private beach; with large park and ample car parking
Food & drink breakfast, lunch, dinner
Prices rooms L265,000-L300,000; DB&B L175,000-L345,000
Rooms 42 rooms, all with bath or shower; all rooms have air-conditioning, phone, TV, minibar, radio
Facilities bar, 2 sitting-rooms, bridge room; swimming-pool, tennis; beach restaurant
Credit cards AE, DC, MC, V
Children accepted
Disabled lift to first-floor, but not wide enough for some wheelchairs
Pets not accepted
Closed never
Proprietor Paolo Moretti

Tuscan Coast

Seaside hotel, Porto Ercole

Il Pellicano

Porto Ercole is one of those fashionable little harbours where wealthy Romans moor their boats at weekends. Il Pellicano is a russet-coloured vine-clad villa with gardens tumbling down to the rocky shoreline, where the flat rocks have been designated the hotel's 'private beach'. It was built in the mid-1960s with only nine rooms. Today it has grown to over three times the size, and provides all the luxuries you might expect from a very expensive four-star seaside hotel. However, it manages at the same time to preserve the style of a private Tuscan villa – and the exposed beams, stone arches and antique features make it feel much older than it really is. Antique country-house furnishings are offset by whitewashed walls, brightly coloured stylish sofas and large vases of flowers.

Fish and seafood are the best things in the restaurant – if you can stomach the prices. Meals in summer are served on the delightful open-air terrace in the garden, or beside the pool where the spread of *antipasti* is a feast for the eyes.

Peaceful bedrooms, many of them in two- or three-storey cottages, combine antiques and modern fabrics. The majority are cool and spacious, and all of them have a terrace or balcony.
Nearby Orbetello (16 km).

Cala dei Santi, Porto Ercole 58018 Grosseto
Tel (0564) 833801
Location 4 km from middle of resort, in own gardens overlooking the sea; private car parking
Food & drink breakfast, lunch, dinner
Prices rooms L190,000-L520,000; DB&B L195,000-L360,000; suites L470,000-L950,000; extra bed in room L90,000-L110,000
Rooms 30 double, 4 suites, all with bath and shower; all rooms have central heating, air-conditioning, minibar, phone
Facilities indoor and outdoor restaurants and bars, sitting area, terrace; swimming-pool, private beach, tennis, riding, water-skiing, clay-pigeon shooting
Credit cards AE, DC, V
Children accepted over 14
Disabled access difficult
Pets not accepted
Closed Nov to Mar
Managers Sg. and Sga. Emili

Umbria

Hotels in Umbria

Visitors are increasingly discovering that there is more to Umbria than Assisi; but it remains the main tourist highlight of the region. Choice of hotel is tricky: there are many that are mediocre, and some of the more comfortable hotels are too big for a full entry here; of these, the Subasio (Tel (075) 812206) is a polished, rather formal place, but notable for the views from its better bedrooms and beautiful flowery terraces.

One other out-of-town hotel is worth bearing in mind in addition to those we have featured. The Castel San Gregorio (Tel (075) 803 8009) is about 10 km north-west of Assisi, up a winding dead-end track; it enjoys a splendid secluded position in gardens on a hilltop, with glorious views across a broad valley.

Perugia is not nearly so well known as Assisi, but well worth a visit if you can penetrate the infuriating defences of its traffic system. The Brufani (page 149) lies at one end of it, and just along it is another hotel worth knowing about – La Rosetta (Tel (075) 20841); it is much bigger, but not worryingly impersonal, and indisputably better value.

In the north-eastern extremity of Umbria is Gubbio – an unusual little town with plenty to interest the visitor for a day or two, but a scarcity of outstanding small hotels. The Bosone (page 147) is an acceptable overnight stop. The Grand Hotel at Cappuccini – housed in a 16thC monastery about one km out of town – is still in the process of being restored to its former glory.

Dei Priori

Originally the palace of Assisi's lord mayor, this well-presented hotel is in the heart of the tourist-thronged town, close to all the sights – which means that guests here can easily do their sightseeing before the trippers arrive, or after they have gone. Bedrooms are tastefully and comfortably furnished, with antique or reproduction beds, the sitting-room cool and polished – a place to perch for minutes rather than relax for hours – the bar and reception rather overdone with modern wood panelling and plastic seating. The restaurant offers a wide variety of food; local, regional and international.

Nearby Cathedral of San Rufino, basilica of Santa Chiara.

Corso Mazzini 15, Assisi 06081 Perugia
Tel (075) 812237
Location in middle of city, just E of Piazza del Commune; with car parking behind the hotel
Food & drink breakfast, lunch, dinner
Prices rooms L62,000-L87,000; lunch/dinner L25,000-L35,000
Rooms 20 double, 11 with bath, 9 with shower; 7 single, 3 with bath, 4 with shower; 5 family rooms with bath; 2 suites; all rooms have central heating, phone
Facilities dining-room, sitting-room, TV room, bar
Credit cards AE, DC, MC, V
Children accepted
Disabled lift/elevator
Pets not accepted
Closed mid-Nov to mid-Mar
Manager Maria Stella Laudenzi

Umbria

Country House

An unassuming guest-house standing amid fields and orchards, yet within walking distance of the main westerly gates of Assisi. Silvana Ciammarughi has had the brilliant idea of running two complementary businesses in one small and beautifully restored little country house – really little more than a cottage. From the ground-floor rooms she sells antiques, and in the upper rooms (furnished with pieces borrowed from below) she accommodates guests. Extra rooms on a lower level have recently been added, with doors opening on to the garden. Ms Ciammarughi is a charming hostess and speaks excellent English.

Nearby the sights of Assisi.

San Pietro Campagna 178, Assisi 06081 Perugia
Tel (075) 816363
Location in countryside, about 10 minutes' walk from Assisi; with extensive garden and private car park
Food & drink breakfast
Prices rooms L65,000- L90,000
Rooms 10 double, all with bath; 5 family rooms, all with bath; all rooms have central heating
Facilities Sitting-room with bar, sitting-room; large terrace, solarium
Credit cards AE, V
Children accepted
Disabled 2 rooms accessible
Pets accepted
Closed never
Proprietor Silvana Ciammarughi

Fontebella

There is certainly no reason to prefer the Fontebella to the Umbra (page 143), but it is worth knowing about in case the Umbra is full. The hotel occupies an old *palazzo* lying on one of the well-worn routes from the central piazza to the basilica of St Francis, and its chief merit is the immaculate condition in which everything is kept – elegant dining-chairs stand on dangerously shiny marble floors in the sitting-room. There are good reports of the proprietors, but we (and others) have encountered a dour receptionist. Some bedrooms are reported to be 'incredibly small', and late-night noise can be a problem in those rooms on the street side of the hotel.

Nearby basilica of San Francesco, cathedral, church of San Pietro.

Via Fontebella 25, Assisi 06081 Perugia
Tel (075) 812883
Location within city walls, with private garden; car parking in front of hotel
Food & drink breakfast, lunch, dinner
Prices rooms L85,000- L221,000 with breakfast; 30% reduction for children under 6
Rooms 23 double, 7 single, 8 family rooms, all with bath or shower; all rooms have central heating, phone, TV
Facilities dining-room, TV room, bar, reading-room
Credit cards AE, DC, MC, V
Children accepted
Disabled no special facilities
Pets accepted
Closed never
Proprietor Giovanni Angeletti

Umbria

Umbra

Assisi, a place of pilgrimage for hundreds of years, is surprisingly not well endowed with places to stay. The largest and least charming are concentrated close to the Basilica which is the town's main attraction. But tucked away down a little alley off the main square is this delightful little family-run hotel, with a restaurant worth a visit in its own right.

The Umbra consists of several small houses – parts date back to the 13th century – with a small gravelled courtyard garden shaded by a pergola. The interior is comfortable and in parts more like a private home than a hotel; there is a bright little sitting-room with Mediterranean-style tiles and brocaded wing armchairs, and a series of bedrooms, mostly quite simply furnished but each with its own character and some with lovely views over the Umbrian plain. We like the elegant dining-room, where imaginative regional dishes triumph over the bland cooking you so often find in hotel restaurants. Reporters generally agree, but one complains of a sombre atmosphere and poor food. In fine weather, meals are served outside. The Umbra offers all the peace and tranquillity which you might hope to find in Assisi, and nothing is too much trouble for Alberto Laudenzi, whose family has run the hotel for more than 50 years.

Nearby basilica of St Francis, church of Santa Chiara, medieval castle, cathedral

Via degli Archi 6, Assisi
06081 Perugia
Tel (075) 812240
Location in middle, off
Piazza del Comune, with
small garden; nearest car
park some distance away
Food & drink breakfast,
lunch, dinner
Prices rooms L65,000-
L100,000 with breakfast;
suites L138,000
Rooms 23 double, 16 with
bath, 5 with shower; 4 single,
2 with bath, 2 with shower; all
rooms have phone, central
heating
Facilities 3 sitting-rooms, bar,
dining-room
Credit cards AE, DC
Children tolerated
Disabled access difficult
Pets not accepted
Closed mid-Nov to mid-Dec,
mid-Jan to mid-Mar
Proprietor Alberto Laudenzi

Umbria

Le Casaline

Here is one of those restaurants out in the country which attract families from miles around on holidays; no further testimony to the quality of the food (especially the charcoal grills) is necessary. The bedrooms are very much a sideline – so much so that the *padrone* has been known to throw a room in with the price of a good meal (in the days before he realised that he could charge substantial amounts for them). The simply furnished bedrooms are in converted outbuildings a little way from the delightfully rustic restaurant.

Nearby Spoleto (14 km); Assisi (35 km).

Località Poreta, Campello sul Clitunno 06042 Perugia
Tel (0743) 520811
Location 3 km E of Campello, isolated in countryside; in gardens, with ample car parking
Food & drink breakfast, lunch, dinner
Prices rooms L45,000-L70,000; meals from L30,000

Rooms 7 rooms, 2 with bath, 5 with shower
Facilities dining-room terrace, TV room
Credit cards AE, DC, V
Children welcome
Disabled access to 2 bedrooms possible **Pets** accepted
Closed restaurant only, Mon
Proprietor Benedetto Zeppadoro

Umbria

Nel Castello

Deruta is a valley town famous for its long-established ceramics industry; high above it is the walled village of Castelleone, and higher still stands this little castle. It could be a modern folly, so neat are its warm-stone crenellations, but it is apparently of 11thC origin.

The food here is dependable although unexciting, the rooms quite pretty, with colourful tiled floors. There is only a small sitting area off the stone-walled dining-room, but there are also a number of chairs outside in the shady garden – a lovely place to sit and watch the sun go down across the broad valley below.

Nearby Assisi (38 km); Perugia (25 km).

Castelleone, Deruta 06053 Perugia
Tel (075) 971 1302
Location 5 km SE of Deruta, on hilltop; surrounded by gardens, with car parking
Food & drink breakfast, lunch, dinner
Prices DB&B L95,000
Rooms 9 double, one family room; all with bath and

shower; all rooms have phone; some rooms have TV, minibar
Facilities dining-room, sitting-room; swimming- pool
Credit cards AE, DC, V
Children accepted
Disabled no special facilities
Pets not accepted
Closed Nov to Mar
Proprietor Sg. Carlo Mari

Villa Roncalli

Few drivers on the main road south from Assisi to Terni deviate into Foligno. But this smart little restaurant with rooms is one good reason to pause. It is a neat little villa in a woody garden, its light, vaulted dining-room (with huge paintings on the walls) occupying much of the ground floor. Above this, a grand central hall gives access to the high-ceilinged, sparely furnished first-floor bedrooms; those on the top floor are more compact, but still comfortable. A knowledgeable reporter pronounces the cooking exceptional, the housekeeping impeccable.

Nearby Assisi (18 km); Perugia (35 km); Terni (59 km).

Via Roma 25, Foligno 06034 Perugia
Tel (0742) 670291
Location 1 km S of middle of Foligno; with private car parking
Food & drink breakfast, lunch, dinner
Prices rooms L80,000; meals L50,000
Rooms 10 rooms, all with bath or shower; all rooms have TV,

phone
Facilities dining-room, hall, TV room; shady terrace
Credit cards AE, DC, V
Children accepted
Disabled no special facilities
Pets not accepted
Closed 2 weeks Aug; restaurant only, Mon
Proprietors Angelo and Sandra Scolastra

Umbria

Castello di Monte Vibiano

This handsome hilltop castle, rebuilt in the 17th century and renovated earlier this century, has been a hotel only since 1988. Despite its size, it accommodates only 12 guests, so there is no danger of tripping over one another in the vaulted public rooms of the house or on the beautifully kept lawns of the grounds (which enjoy grand views of the Umbrian hills). You share the elegantly furnished house with the proprietors, who have novel ideas about hotel-keeping; all drinks are included in the prices.

Nearby Perugia, Lago Trasimeno (25 km).

Monte Vibiano, Mercatello 06050 Perugia
Tel (075) 878 3371; Florence booking office (055) 218112
Location in hills SW of village, 25 km SW of Perugia – take road through Pila and turn off after Spina; ample car parking space
Food & drink breakfast, lunch, dinner
Prices DB&B L200,000-L240,000; FB L230,000-L270,000; includes all wine; (min stay 3 days)

Rooms 6 double, all with bath; all rooms have central heating
Facilities dining-room, 3 sitting-rooms; swimming-pool, tennis court
Credit cards not accepted
Children accepted, but children under 8 must eat separately
Disabled no special facilities
Pets not accepted
Closed Nov to Easter
Proprietor Dr Andrea Fasola Bologna

Le Silve

Here is a rustic gem, close enough to Assisi for sightseeing expeditions but remote enough for complete seclusion – and with good sports facilities immediately on hand. It is an old farmhouse (parts of it very old indeed – 10th century) converted to its new purpose with great sympathy and charm – all tiled floors, stone or white walls and beamed ceilings, and furnished with country antiques. The hotel is virtually self- sufficient, the farm producing its own oil, cheese and meat. The self-contained suites are in villas about 1.5 km from the main house.

Nearby sights of Assisi.

Località Armenzano, Assisi 06081 Perugia
Tel (075) 801 9000
Location in countryside 12 km E of Assisi, between S444 and S3; ample car parking space
Food & drink breakfast, lunch, dinner
Prices rooms L130,000-L200,000; DB&B L140,000-L170,000; reductions for children
Rooms 11 double, 3 single, 4

self-contained suites; all with bath; all rooms have central heating, phone, TV
Facilities dining-room, 2 sitting-rooms, bar; swimming-pool, tennis, sauna, riding, archery, mini-golf, motor-bike
Credit cards AE, DC, V
Children welcome
Disabled no special facilities
Pets not accepted
Closed mid-Jan to mid-Feb
Manager Daniela Taddia

Umbria

Bosone

While the Cappuccini is out of action, the Bosone rates as best in town. It occupies a *palazzo* which is as old as some of the sights you visit Gubbio to see, but its antiquity is not much in evidence. Most of the bedrooms are furnished in anonymous modern style, and the public areas mainly look worn rather than antique. But there are two remarkably grand bedrooms decorated in a highly flamboyant Renaissance style: staying in them could be entertaining (and costs little or nothing more than routine rooms). There is no restaurant, but meals may be taken at the nearby Taverna del Lupo, which is quite jolly.

Nearby historic sights of Gubbio.

Via XX Settembre 22, Gubbio 06024 Perugia
Tel (075) 927 2008
Location in heart of historic city; access and parking difficult, but private garage available
Food & drink breakfast, lunch, dinner; meals taken in nearby Taverna del Lupo
Prices rooms L52,000-L88,000; DB&B L71,000

Rooms 16 double, 2 single, 16 family rooms; all with bath; all rooms have phone
Facilities bar, sitting-room with TV
Credit cards AE, DC, MC, V
Children accepted
Disabled access possible; lift/elevator to bedrooms
Pets accepted
Closed Jan or Feb
Manager Mario Cannevali

Villa Ciconia

In a modest leafy park watered by three streams that meet nearby, the Villa Ciconia was until recently mainly a restaurant, with just a few simple rooms above. Now, the Petrangeli family have repossessed their 16thC home, and re-established it as a country hotel. The bedrooms are simply but tastefully furnished, with elegant iron-framed canopy beds; the old granary on the first floor has become a comfortable sitting-room. The lofty dining-room is as splendid as ever, with its coffered ceiling and surrounding murals. Cooking is distinctly Umbrian, using oil and wine from the adjacent family farm.

Nearby Cathedral at Orvieto; Todi (40 km); Lake Bolsena.

Via dei Tigli 69, 05019 Orvieto
Tel (0763) 92982
Location set in its own park, about 3 km from Florence-Rome motorway; with private car parking
Food & drink breakfast, lunch, dinner
Prices rooms L70,000-L120,000; DB&B L85,000-L108,000; FB L115,000-L138,000 (min stay 3 days)

Rooms 8 double, one single, all with bath; all have central heating, TV, phone, minibar
Facilities dining-room, sitting-room, bar, conference room
Credit cards AE, DC, MC, V
Children accepted
Disabled no special facilities
Pets not encouraged **Closed** mid-Jan to mid-Feb; restaurant only, Mon **Proprietor** Dr Valentino Petrangeli

Umbria

Converted monastery, Orvieto

La Badia

This marvellously preserved former Benedictine abbey (*badia*) dating from the 12th century is probably the best place from which to visit Orvieto, with its splendid cathedral. It is a sight worth seeing in its own right, with its 12-sided tower and beautifully harmonious Romanesque arches. The mellow stone buildings, the view across to the dramatically sited town, and the swimming-pool are powerful attractions.

In the first edition of the guide we were critical of some aspects, but more recent reports have been entirely favourable – 'I particularly enjoyed its quiet, modest luxury, and regional cooking,' says a discerning American reader. An inspection visit confirms this view; rooms are thoroughly comfortable, the suites notably spacious and restful; excellent Umbrian food is served (grills on an open fire the speciality); and service is courteous and efficient, with English, French, German and Spanish spoken.
Nearby Cathedral in Orvieto; Lake of Bolsena; Todi (40 km).

La Badia, Orvieto Scalo 05019 Terni
Tel (0763) 90359
Location 1 km S of Orvieto, off Viale 1 Maggio towards Viterbo; in large park with parking for 200 cars
Food & drink breakfast, lunch, dinner
Prices rooms L140,000-L188,000 (suite L300,000); FB L210,000- L269,000 (suite L558,000)
Rooms 15 double, 14 with bath, one with shower; 3 single, 2 with bath, one with shower; 4 suites, 2 with bath, 2 with shower; all rooms have phone, air- conditioning, central heating
Facilities dining-room, bar, sitting-room with TV, conference hall; swimming-pool, 2 tennis courts
Credit cards AE, V
Children welcome
Disabled access difficult
Pets no dogs **Closed** Jan and Feb; restaurant only, Wed
Proprietor Luisa Fiumi

Umbria

Virgilio

Piazza del Duomo 5/6,
Orvieto 05018 Terni
Tel (0763) 41882
Location in heart of city –
follow signs to Piazza Duomo;
2 public car parks 100 m away
Food & drink breakfast
Prices rooms L77,000-
L120,000
Rooms 14 double, 2 with bath,
12 with shower; 2 single, both
with shower; all rooms have
phone
Facilities bar, breakfast room,
TV room
Credit cards not accepted
Children accepted
Disabled one ground-floor
room; lift/elevator
Pets cats and dogs accepted
Closed 20 days Jan-Feb
Proprietor Virgilio Pedetti

Orvieto is probably best known outside Italy for the crisp white wines of the surrounding region, but the city itself also has much to offer. Without doubt, the centrepiece is the astonishing, glistening façade of the *duomo*, more of a work of art than of architecture. Look left as you confront it and you will see the engagingly shabby-looking Virgilio. As you do so you will already have appreciated this hotel's prime virtue: its position right at the heart of things. Inside, sadly, it has been left shiny but soulless by modernization; but it is comfortable, and prices are moderate.
Nearby cathedral, Etruscan and medieval museums; Rome, Perugia, Siena all within reach.

Brufani

This is included especially for disciples of Conrad Hilton, who, according to legend, asserted that 'only three things matter about a hotel: location, location and location'. The Brufani stands at the south-west extremity of the *corso*, on top of one of the cliffs which circumscribe central Perugia – so you get great views south to Assisi and west to the setting sun. It is a polished little hotel, with a refined lobby (reception is at the back, beyond it), a smart restaurant, a glossy and fashionable 'American' bar, and bedrooms which are comfortable enough, but of no great charm – especially considering their prices.
Nearby old town of Perugia.

Piazza Italia 12, Perugia 06100
Tel (075) 62541
Location at southern end of
central *corso*; garage (L20,000
a night)
Food & drink breakfast,
lunch, dinner
Prices rooms L249,900-
L499,800; meals from L40,000
Rooms 22 double, 2 suites, all
with bath; all rooms have
central heating, phone, TV,
hairdrier, minibar
Facilities bar, sitting- room,
dining-room
Credit cards AE, DC, MC, V
Children accepted
Disabled access possible –
lift/elevator to bedrooms
Pets small dogs only accepted
Closed never
Manager Sg. G Carturan

Umbria

Medieval manor, Ospedalicchio de Bastia

Lo Spedalicchio

Despite the attractions of Assisi and of a sound central hotel such as the Umbra (page 131), for the touring motorist there is much to be said for staying out of town in an hotel easily accessible by car. This one is the best around: a four-square manor house on the road to Perugia.

The ground-floor public rooms have high, vaulted brick ceilings and tiled floors with the occasional rug – whether you approach from the 'back' door as most drivers do or from the 'front' door opening on to the village square, the immediate impression is of centuries of calm living. The restaurant (which enjoys a high local reputation) is on one side – stylishly set out with bentwood chairs and pink napery; sadly, the sitting-room bar area which occupies much of the ground floor is less welcoming. Bedrooms vary widely – some high-ceilinged, some two-level affairs with sitting space (an attractive possibility, given the poor public sitting area) – but all those we have seen are spacious and inviting. The staff are courteous and helpful. Most recent visitors endorse our recommendation, but one complains of intrusive church bells until 10pm and reckons the food high-priced.

Nearby Assisi (10 km); Perugia (10 km); Gubbio, Orvieto, Todi and Spoleto all within reach.

Piazza Bruno Buozzi 3, Ospedalicchio di Bastia 06080 Perugia
Tel (075) 801 0323
Location between Assisi and Perugia on S147; in garden with ample car parking
Food & drink breakfast, lunch, dinner
Prices rooms L59,000-L86,000; meals from L34,000-L48,000
Rooms 20 double, 2 single, 3 family rooms; all with shower; all rooms have central heating, phone, colour TV
Facilities dining-room, American bar, TV room, conference rooms
Credit cards AE, DC, V
Children welcome; special meals, baby-sitter, small beds on request
Disabled no special facilities
Pets small ones only
Closed never
Manager Sg. G Costarelli

Umbria

Gattapone

Although chiefly known for its summer Festival of Two Worlds, Spoleto has interesting year-round sights too – among them the 14thC Bridge of Towers, a tremendously high crossing of the steep-sided Tessino valley, of which the Gattapone has a grand-stand view. The house was converted into a hotel in the 1960s, and much of it is evocative of Italian style of that era – notably the split-level bar/sitting-room; but there are also old-fashioned rooms in the older part of the house, and all the rooms we saw were admirably spacious.

Nearby Ponte delle Torri, *Duomo.*

Via del Ponte 6, Spoleto 06049 Perugia	bath, 3 with shower; all rooms have minibar, TV
Tel (0743) 36147	**Facilities** American bar, hall, meeting-room
Location on W fringe of town, with garden and private car parking	**Credit cards** AE, DC, MC, V
Food & drink breakfast	**Children** accepted
Prices rooms L150,000-L230,000 with breakfast	**Disabled** no special facilities
Rooms 13 double, 10 with	**Pets** accepted
	Closed never
	Proprietor Filippo Hanke

Bramante

In a more competitive part of the country, the Bramante would frankly not rate an entry here: it is a little too big and impersonal for comfort. But applying our acid test – would we or would we not wish to know about it while touring in this area? – we get a positive result. The most important things in its favour are an amiable old stone house at the core of the hotel, restrained modern decoration and furnishings, and a splendid position on the hillside just along from Todi's most distinctive building – the church of Santa Maria, which looks like the work of the celebrated Bramante, but is not.

Nearby church of Santa Maria della Consolazione.

Via Orvietana, Todi 06059 Perugia	air-conditioning, TV; some rooms have minibar
Tel (075) 894 8381	**Facilities** sitting-rooms (one with TV), dining-room, conference room, terrace, piano bar; fitness room, tennis
Location just outside town on Orvieto road; in gardens, with ample car parking	
Food & drink breakfast, lunch, dinner	**Credit cards** AE, DC, MC, V
Prices rooms L120,000-L180,000	**Children** welcome
	Disabled access possible
Rooms 43 double, 2 family rooms, all with bath and shower; all rooms have phone,	**Pets** accepted
	Closed never
	Proprietor Sg. M Montori

Umbria

Town hotel, Torgiano

Le Tre Vaselle

On paper, the Tre Vaselle sounds disturbingly impersonal – it has 50 bedrooms (above our usual limit) and several conference rooms. But the hotel is entirely without ostentation, its modest entrance on a narrow street scarcely detectable. Friendly and courteous staff make you feel instantly at home, while the maze of ground-floor sitting-rooms – with its massive arches, white walls, rustic beams, terracotta floors, shabby but colourful armchairs and sofas, card-table and stone fireplaces – is immediately captivating.

Bedrooms, some in a more modern building behind the main one, do not have such character, but are smart and civilized. The cavernous main dining-room is also a weak spot. Breakfast is served in a much more atmospheric room on the main ground floor. The food at the Tre Vaselle is excellent, and well complemented by the wines for which the owner, Dr Lungarotti, has made Torgiano well known (don't miss the fascinating wine museum a street away from the hotel).

This is the sort of place which the touring visitor hesitates to leave, knowing for sure that the next night's hotel will be inferior. Console yourself in this case with the thought that it is also pretty certain to be cheaper.

Nearby Perugia; Assisi (25 km).

Via Garibaldi 48, Torgiano
06089 Perugia
Tel (075) 982447
Location in side street of
village, 12 km SE of Perugia;
ample car parking nearby
Food & drink breakfast,
lunch, dinner
Prices rooms L200,000-
L280,000
Rooms 50 double, most with
bath, some with shower; all
rooms have central heating,
phone, minibar
Facilities sitting-rooms,
dining-room, breakfast room,
bar, conference rooms
Credit cards AE, DC, MC, V
Children accepted
Disabled access possible –
lift/elevator to bedrooms
Pets not accepted
Closed never
Manager Romano Sartore

Marche

O'Viv

This beautifully restored medieval palace is set on a hill-top a little way inland from the Adriatic coast, and makes a good base for exploring this lesser-known but historical area of Italy. The O'Viv (which means 'Acquaviva' in one of the ancient dialects) was restored and converted into a hotel in 1976 but did not really take off until 1984 when Piero Cinciripini and wife took over. All the bedrooms are well furnished, some with remarkable decorated ceilings, some with breathtaking views across the surrounding countryside. The restaurant has established a reputation for rich local dishes – you can eat on the terrace in summer.

Nearby Ascoli Piceno (42 km); coast (7 km).

Via Marziale 43, Acquaviva
Piceno 63030 Ascoli Piceno
Tel (0735) 764649
Location in the middle of
town; with parking on road
Food & drink breakfast,
lunch, dinner
Prices rooms L75,000; meals
L30,000
Rooms 10 double, one single,
one family room, all with
bath; all rooms have central

heating, phone, TV
Facilities dining-room,
sitting-room, bar, terrace,
sauna, jacuzzi
Credit cards AE, DC, MC, V
Children welcome;
baby-sitting on request
Disabled no special facilities
Pets accepted if well-behaved
Closed 3 weeks in Oct
Proprietor Piero Cinciripini

Villa Pigna

This substantial pink villa must once have been surrounded by fields and vineyards; now it is enveloped by a prosperous dormitory of Ascoli Piceno (though once inside its tiny grounds the surroundings are not intrusive – the dawn chorus is more so). It is very much a business hotel – breakfast when we visited consisted of pastries and coffee from the bar – and the comfortable bedrooms lack character. But the ground-floor sitting areas are exceptionally welcoming, and satisfactory food is served in the smooth modern dining-room.

Nearby old quarter of Ascoli Piceno (4 km).

Viale Assisi 33, Folignano
63040
Tel (0736) 491868
Location 4 km N of
Folignano; in private grounds,
with garage and car parking
Food & drink breakfast,
lunch, dinner
Prices rooms L92,000-
L138,000; suites L160,000;
meals about L25,000
Rooms 46 double, 8 single, 4
suites, all with bath; all rooms

have phone, TV, minibar,
balcony
Facilities dining-room, bar,
conference room, private
chapel
Credit cards AE, DC, V
Children accepted
Disabled no special facilities
Pets accepted
Closed restaurant only, 3
weeks July-Aug
Proprietor Anna Maria Rozzi

Marche

Country villa, Montecassiano

Villa Quiete

Macerata is a sizeable hilltop town a few miles inland from the Adriatic, and remarkable mainly for its huge 19thC arena, the Sferisterio, scene of a major opera festival in the summer. The Villa Quiete, across the valley at Montecassiano, is a substantial house of mixed merits: dreary sitting-rooms, smart café-style dining-room, bedrooms varying widely – some ordinary, some grand and furnished with antiques. Its key asset, perhaps, is the moderate-sized garden with its pines, palms and geraniums.

Nearby Porto Recanati – Adriatic coast (30 km); Ancona (40 km).

Vallecascia di Montecassiano, 62010 Macerata
Tel (0733) 599559
Location 3 km S of Montecassiano; in large shady park, with car parking
Food & drink breakfast, lunch, dinner
Prices rooms L65,000-L120,000
Rooms 30 double, 8 single; all with bath or shower; all rooms have central heating, phone, TV
Facilities 2 dining-rooms, 2 bars, sitting-rooms; conference facilities
Credit cards AE, DC, V
Children accepted
Disabled some rooms suitable
Pets dogs not accepted
Closed never
Proprietor Mario Palmucci

Seaside hotel, Portonovo

Fortino Napoleonico

And now for something completely different: a single-storey fortress, apparently dating as the name suggests from the early 19th century, right on the sea next to the popular beach of Portonovo. Bedrooms, contained within the ramparts, are simple and somewhat gloomy, but spacious – many can accommodate three or four – and real value for the families who make up the bulk of the clientele. The restaurant and bar/sitting-room are also simple, clean and roomy.

Nearby Monte Conero; Ancona.

Portonovo 60020 Ancona
Tel (071) 801124
Location 12 km SE of Ancona, on promontory near beach; with ample car parking
Food & drink breakfast, lunch, dinner
Prices rooms L100,000; suites L160,000-L200,000
Rooms 26 double, 4 with bath, 22 with shower; 4 suites; all rooms have central heating, phone
Facilities dining-room, sitting-room, bar, terrace
Credit cards AE, DC, MC, V
Children welcome
Disabled access possible – single-storey building
Pets accepted
Closed never
Manager Sg. Roscioni

Marche

Country villa, Pesaro

Villa Serena

The Adriatic coast south of Rimini is not short of hotels, but it is very short of our kind of hotel – which makes this one a real find. It is a handsome 17thC mansion with some token castellations, standing in a wooded park high above the hubbub of the coast. In this oasis the Villa Serena lives up to its name.

The villa has always belonged to one family – the counts Pinto de Franca y Vergaes, who used it as a summer residence until, in 1950, they turned it into a small hotel to be run like a family home. Renata Pinto does the cooking and serves up some better-than-average dishes; Mario sees to guests and reception; while their mother, Signora Laura, busies herself in the house and garden. All three are reassuringly down-to-earth, and the emphasis in their house is on character, simplicity and tranquillity, rather than luxury. There are salons of baronial splendour, antiques and curiosities wherever you go, and corridors delightfully cluttered with ceramics and potted plants. A few faded corners reinforce the villa's appealing air of impoverished aristocracy. No two bedrooms are exactly alike but antiques and fireplaces feature in most of them.

In the last edition we had a report from an unimpressed reader who was offered only biscuits for breakfast, and no other meals. Our most recent reporter was much happier.

Nearby municipal museum, Ducal Palace at Pesaro; Gabicce Mare corniche road (NW 27 km) starting from Pesaro.

Via San Nicola 6/3, 61100 Pesaro
Tel (0721) 55211
Location 4 km from Pesaro and beach, in a large wooded park on hillside with private car parking
Food & drink breakfast, lunch, dinner
Prices rooms L60,000- L90,000
Rooms 10 double, all with bath or shower; all rooms have central heating, phone
Facilities 4 sitting-rooms, dining-room, bar, terrace
Credit cards AE
Children accepted
Disabled access difficult
Pets accepted
Closed never
Proprietor Renato Pinto

Marche

Farfense

San Vittoria is an out-of-the-way little hilltop town midway between the Adriatic coast and the Sibillini mountains. The surrounding countryside is distinctive and pretty – a delightful patchwork of tiny fields covering the steep slopes of little valleys cut by streams in the soft soil. The Farfense is a very simple, old-fashioned, family-run hotel with spotless bedrooms and a charming little restaurant down in the brick vaults (as well as a bigger room upstairs, brought into action to feed the locals for weddings and feast days). Good views from a tiny terrace and some of the rooms.

Nearby Sibillini mountains.

Corso Matteotti 41, Santa Vittoria in Matenano 63028 Ascoli Piceno
Tel (0734) 780171
Location 35 km SW of Fermo, in middle of town; car parking on street
Food & drink breakfast, lunch, dinner
Prices rooms L28,000-L50,000; meals from L18,000
Rooms 8 double, 2 single, all with bath or shower; all have central heating; 4 have balconies
Facilities sitting-room, bar, dining-room, garden
Credit cards MC, V
Children accepted
Disabled no special facilities
Pets dogs not accepted
Closed 2 weeks end Sep/early Oct; restaurant only, Mon
Proprietor Eva Pettinelli

Monteconero

Yet another example of a religious house in a prime position – on the very summit of Monte Conero, 500 metres above the nearby sea, with superb views south-east along the coast. The bedrooms give no sign of historic origins – they are simple, adequate, modern – but there is an atmospheric little stone-vaulted restaurant on the lower floor (as well as a bigger, more anonymous one), and some pleasantly polished sitting areas. The big bar is another asset, with a terrace giving splendid views along the coast.

Nearby Sirolo; Ancona (21 km).

Monte Conero, Sirolo 60020 Ancona
Tel (071) 936122
Location 3 km N of Sirolo, in woods on shoulder of Monte Conero; with ample car parking
Food & drink breakfast, lunch, dinner
Prices rooms L50,000- L85,000
Rooms 43 double, 4 single; all with shower; all rooms have phone
Facilities sitting-room, bar, 2 dining-rooms; outdoor swimming-pool, tennis
Credit cards AE, DC, V
Children welcome
Disabled access difficult
Pets small dogs only accepted
Closed Nov to Easter
Proprietor Augusto Melappioni

Marche

Seaside hotel, Portonovo

Emilia

Although the Emilia is a seaside hotel, it stands aloof from the beaches south of Ancona, on the flanks of Monte Conero above the little resort of Portonovo (which is a car-journey away for all but the most energetic). It is a modern building of no great architectural merit. But its proprietors some years ago hit on a clever way of giving the hotel a distinctive appeal: they invited artists to come and stay, and to pay their way in kind. The results continue to accumulate on the walls: score upon score of paintings (none, we are assured, has ever been sold). Among the Italian signatures, our inspector spotted the artist Graham Sutherland's.

Even without the extraordinary wall-covering, the hotel would have an attractive air. A long, low sitting-room with clusters of chunky modern armchairs links reception to the large, light, simply furnished dining-room, which has big windows looking on to a passable imitation of a *prato inglese* (a lawn). Bedrooms are thoroughly modern and snazzy. Most are in the older part of the hotel, ranged at an angle so as to give each room a sea-view and a small balcony,.

Food is taken seriously, although it no longer earns a Michelin star. Fish dominates the menu, and is competently cooked, though expensive.

Nearby church of Santa Maria (at Portonovo), Monte Conero; Ancona (12 km).

Via Poggio, 149/A Portonovo, Ancona 60020
Tel (071) 801145
Location 2 km W of Portonovo on cliffs; ample private car parking
Food & drink breakfast, lunch, dinner
Prices rooms L90,000-L150,000
Rooms 23 double, 2 with bath, 21 with shower; 2 single, both with shower; 5 family rooms, one with bath, 4 with shower; all rooms have central heating, phone, colour TV, minibar
Facilities dining-room, TV room, conference room, bar, gazebo-bar; swimming-pool, tennis
Credit cards AE, V
Children accepted
Disabled some ground-floor rooms
Pets not accepted
Closed Dec and Jan
Proprietor Lamberto Fiorini

Lazio

Hotels in Lazio

Rome is a city of grand hotels rather than small and charming ones. Suggestions from readers for additional entries would be gratefully received. Among the hotels we have looked at but not given an entry to are a trio of simple but adequately comfortable places in the peaceful residential area of Aventino – the Domus Maximi (Tel (06) 578 2565), the Sant'Anselmo (Tel (06) 574 3547) and the San Pio (Tel (06) 575 5231).

A reader has recommended the Pensione Parlamento (Tel (06) 678 7880), another budget place run by a charming multi-lingual Indian family in the heart of the city – 'polished floors, prints, etchings and contemporary lithographs raise it above the ordinary'. Nearby, the Condotti (Tel (06) 679 4661) is an intimate hotel which by now will probably have been refurbished. At the opposite extreme of the market (and of the Spanish Steps) is the luxurious 50-room Lord Byron (Tel (06) 322 0404) – certainly less impersonal than most smart Rome hotels, but still impressively ritzy.

Palestrina (birthplace of the 16thC composer) and Tivoli (villas of Emperor Hadrian and the 16thC Cardinal d'Este) are within day-trip range of Rome, but if you want to stay overnight, go for the Stella (Tel (06) 955 8172) in Palestrina (modern, excellent restaurant, clean spacious bedrooms) or the Torre Sant'Angelo (Tel (0774) 23292) outside Tivoli. North of the capital is the pretty wooded countryside around Viterbo and Lago di Vico. The Rio Vicano (Tel (0761) 612339) is a modern 50-room hotel in a picturesque setting near the clifftop medieval village of Ronciglione. An average town hotel in the heart of Viterbo is the Leon d'Oro (Tel (0761) 344444).

Gregoriana

An unprepossessing building in a narrow street running away from the top of the Spanish Steps, the Gregoriana is distinguished by its friendly and personal atmosphere and its highly individual decor. There is something for everyone – leopard-skin wallpaper on one landing, raffia on another, Liberty prints on a third. Rooms are uniform in style, modern and slightly glamorous, but vary appreciably in size; some have a little terrace. There is no public room apart from the tiny reception area, and breakfast is served ('with commendable speed') in your bedroom.
Nearby Spanish Steps, Villa Borghese, Fontana di Trevi.

Via Gregoriana 18, Rome 00187
Tel (06) 679 7988
Location 100 m from top of Spanish Steps, with car parking on street or garage 50 m away
Food & drink breakfast
Prices rooms L120,000-L185,000
Rooms 15 double, 12 with bath, 3 with shower; 4 single, all with shower; all rooms have central heating, air-conditioning, TV, phone
Facilities tiny lobby; bar service in rooms
Credit cards not accepted
Children welcome **Disabled** no special facilities **Pets** small ones only **Closed** never
Proprietor Ernesto Bagat

Lazio

Town hotel, Rome

La Residenza

The Via Vittorio Veneto is one of Rome's most fashionable addresses, and the location of some of its grandest hotels. The Residenza is not one of them, but its position only a block away from this sweeping tree-lined avenue gives it a head start. The Spanish Steps and the Villa Borghese are about equidistant, to the west and north respectively.

The Residenza is part of the small Giannetti chain of hotels, concentrated in dreary Lido di Jesolo – not a good sign. But Signor d'Arezzo does a sound job as manager and the front desk staff are friendly and helpful.

Another key aspect of the hotel's appeal is its bar and sitting areas on the elevated ground floor, which are comfortable and welcoming, with a mixture of modern and antique furniture. (An attractive area in which to relax over a drink is a rarity in modest Rome hotels.) A better-than-average help-yourself breakfast is served in a more ordinary, windowless room at the back of the hotel, with bright red café-style chairs.

Bedrooms are comfortable and well equipped, but uniformly furnished with no great flair or character. Those at the back are quieter than those at the front, which despite their double glazing suffer from noise from a nearby nightclub. Some have fair-sized terraces, and there is also a communal roof-top terrace with interesting views.

Nearby Spanish Steps, Villa Borghese.

Via Emilia 22, Rome 00187
Tel (06) 460789
Location in side-street off Via Veneto; limited car parking
Food & drink breakfast
Prices rooms L95,000-L190,000
Rooms 24 double, all with bath; 3 single, all with shower; all rooms have central heating, minibar, satellite TV, air-conditioning, hairdrier, phone
Facilities sitting-rooms, bar, breakfast room, patio, terrace
Credit cards not accepted
Children accepted
Disabled access difficult
Pets not accepted
Closed never
Manager Adriano d'Arezzo

Lazio

Town villa, Rome

Villa Florence

On the broad Via Nomentana to the north-east of the middle of Rome, this well-run hotel has particular attractions for motorists reluctant to tangle with the worst of Rome's traffic (in addition to a convenient location, it has private parking in the garden behind the house).

The villa's other chief merit is the welcoming ambience of its public areas. Great efforts have been made to give the little sitting area (off reception) and the adjacent café-style breakfast room some interest and warmth. Dotted around all the public areas are interesting archaeological fragments which have been discovered on the site of the hotel.

There is a small, secluded terrace behind the house, with sun-beds as well as tables and chairs. The bedrooms (some of them in outbuildings, with doors opening on to the garden) are comfortable, and we are told that the characterless melamine unit furniture has been replaced.

The cheerful proprietor makes an effort to see that breakfast is more than usually satisfying, with yoghurt, cheese and ham as well as the standard fare.

Nearby Villa Borghese.

Via Nomentata 28, Rome 00161 (Porta Pia)
Tel (06) 440 3036
Location about one km NE of Via Veneto, with private car parking in garden
Food & drink breakfast
Prices rooms L105,000-L150,000; 30% reduction for children sharing parents' room
Rooms 32 double, one single, 4 family rooms; all with bath or shower; all rooms have colour TV, minibar, air-conditioning, phone
Facilities breakfast room, TV room, bar
Credit cards AE, DC
Children accepted
Disabled no special facilities
Pets not accepted
Closed never
Proprietor Tullio Cappelli

Lazio

Town hotel, Rome

Portoghesi

This is a good example of the kind of sought-after small hotel that may be common in Florence or Venice but is all too rare in Rome: unpretentious, functional but attractively old- fashioned, and fairly priced – at least considering its very central position, which is ideal for the foot-slogging tourist (if not for the motorist). The sights of Rome are distributed all around, with the delightful Piazza Navona and the stunning Pantheon only yards away. Furnishings are simple, service is polite and efficient rather than notably warm. There is a pleasantly sunny breakfast room (with a small terrace), and an overwhelming choice of places for dinner within a short stroll. Recent visitors are enthusiastic, and single out the breakfast for praise.

Nearby Piazza Navona, Pantheon.

Via dei Portoghesi 1, Rome 00186
Tel (05) 6864231
Location just N of Piazza Navona, with roof terrace
Food & drink breakfast
Prices rooms L70,000-L110,000
Rooms 27 rooms, 22 with bath or shower; all rooms have phone, air-conditioning, TV
Facilities breakfast room, sitting-room
Credit cards MC, V
Children accepted
Disabled access possible – large lift/elevator
Pets small ones only accepted
Closed never
Proprietor Mario Trivellone

Town hotel, Rome

Sitea

The Sitea is a well-maintained hotel with only a reception area on the ground floor and its other public areas up on the sixth. Great effort has clearly gone into the elaborate decoration of the bar and sitting-rooms up there, though it is not quite clear which era of Roman history their designers were aiming to evoke. The bedrooms we saw were comfortably furnished in traditional style and generally spacious, with somewhat old-fashioned bathrooms. Many have apparently been renovated.

Nearby Fontana di Trevi, Via Veneto.

Via Vittorio Emanuele Orlando 90, Rome 00185
Tel (06) 475 4696
Location in middle of city, close to Piazza della Repubblica; public garage and car parking nearby
Food & drink breakfast; lunch and dinner available in coffee shop
Prices rooms L145,000-L220,000
Rooms 31 double, 27 with bath, 3 with shower; 6 single, one with bath, 4 with shower; all rooms have central heating, phone, air-conditioning; hairdrier and radio on request
Facilities sitting-room, roof-garden bar
Credit cards AE, DC, MC, V
Children welcome
Disabled no special facilities
Pets accepted by arrangement; not allowed in public rooms
Closed never
Proprietors Giovanni and Giuseppe de Luca

Lazio

Photo: Villa della Rose (facing page)

Town guest-house, Rome

Scalinata di Spagna

The Spanish Steps are a favourite spot for visitors to Rome to sit around soaking up the atmosphere and the afternoon sun, and at the top of them are two hotels – the Hassler (where rooms typically cost L500,000) and, facing it across the piazza, this highly individual little *pensione* (now elevated to 3-star status).

The idiosyncratic character of the place is obvious as soon as you walk in the door, when you come face to face with Cacao, the resident parrot. Beyond the tiny reception area, a corridor dotted with antiques and paintings leads to old-fashioned bedrooms of varying size with bathrooms which by Italian standards are rather plain. For eight months of the year breakfast is served on the roof-top terrace, from which many of the famous sights of Rome can be spotted across the neighbouring roofs, whilst enjoying the early morning sunshine; at other times, a tiny room off reception is brought into play.

Signor Bellia is charming and helpful, and clearly tickled by the wave of publicity his captivating little house has received in recent years, particularly in the United States. His prices are no longer low, yet demand for rooms continues to exceed supply. The rational response is to raise prices further; we hope the temptation can be resisted. Book early.

Nearby Spanish Steps, Villa Borghese, Via Veneto.

Piazza Trinita dei Monti 17, Rome 00187
Tel (06) 679 3006
Location at the top of the Spanish Steps; car parking 50 m away
Food & drink breakfast
Prices rooms L131,500-L191,000
Rooms 10 double, 2 with bath, 8 with shower; 4 single, one with bath, 3 with shower; all rooms have central heating, minibar, radio, phone, air-conditioning
Facilities breakfast room, roof garden
Credit cards MC, V
Children accepted
Disabled no special facilities
Pets not accepted
Closed never
Proprietor Giuseppe Bellia

Lazio

Villa delle Rose

Via Vizenza 5, Rome 00185
Tel (06) 445 1788
Location close to main railway station with small garden; parking for 4 cars, public car park 200 m away
Food & drink breakfast
Prices rooms L91,000-L146,500
Rooms 29 double, 8 single, all with bath or shower; all rooms have central heating, phone, TV
Facilities large sitting-room with bar, breakfast room
Credit cards AE, DC, MC, V
Children very welcome
Disabled access difficult
Pets accepted if well behaved
Closed never
Proprietor Claude Frank

If an economical night or two near Rome's railway station is necessary, this calm old villa certainly takes some beating. The bedrooms are neat, and gradually being improved by the enthusiastic owner Claude Frank (who is Swiss), and there is a grand little bar/sitting-room with marbled pillars and a beautifully frescoed ceiling. Breakfast is served in a cool arched cellar with linen on the tables and bentwood chairs, and there is a shady terrace surrounded by flowers and greenery in the little garden.
Nearby Piazza della Republica, church of Santa Maria Maggiore.

Valadier

The Valadier has almost completely shed its *belle époque* image now; in place of 19thC French is 21stC International – something like a millionaire's yacht. The place has been entirely refitted with marble, mirrors, highly polished wood and electronic gadgetry (you can check your bill on the TV screen in your room). Charming? Well, no, but very impressive and exceptionally comfortable, despite the small size of the rooms. The location, as ever, is one of the best for sightseeing and shopping, and the staff are efficient and friendly.
Nearby Spanish Steps, Villa Borghese.

Via della Fontanella 15, Rome 00187
Tel (06) 361 0559
Location off Via del Corso, close to Piazza del Popolo; garage 100 m away
Food & drink breakfast, lunch, dinner
Prices rooms L230,000-L330,000; suites up to L500,000; meals about L50,000
Rooms 24 double, 12 single, 3 suites, all with bath and shower; all rooms have central heating, phone, minibar, TV, piped music, air-conditioning, electronic safe, hairdrier
Facilities piano/American bar, dining-room, sitting-room, conference rooms; solarium
Credit cards AE, DC, MC
Children welcome
Disabled entrance difficult, but 2 lifts/elevators
Pets small ones only
Closed never
Proprietor Simonetta Battistini

Lazio

Sole al Pantheon

Complete refurbishment in 1988 has at last given the ancient Sole the decor and atmosphere which does justice to its privileged position – to one side of the square in front of the famous Pantheon, one of the few perfectly preserved ancient Roman buildings. It is no exaggeration to say that it has been transformed. The high-ceilinged bedrooms – each named after a famous person who has stayed there – are classically decorated and well equipped, with some lovely antique furniture. The public areas are also elegantly and tastefully furnished, with ornaments and comfortable armchairs set against plain walls and red-tiled floors. Sadly, all this smart renovation has pushed prices to high levels.

Nearby Pantheon, Villa Borghese.

Piazza della Rotonda 63,
Roma 00186 Roma
Tel (06) 678 0447
Location in piazza in front of the Pantheon
Food & drink breakfast
Prices rooms
L200,000-L350,000
Rooms 22 double, 3 single, all with bath; all rooms have

central heating,
air-conditioning, phone, TV,
hairdrier, radio, minibar
Facilities breakfast room, bar
Credit cards AE, DC, MC, V
Children accepted
Disabled lift/elevator
Pets not accepted
Closed never
Proprietor A Giraudini

Castello Miramare

High on the hillside above Formia, with tremendous views of the huge, sweeping bay of Gaeta, stands this modest little folly or 'castle', built in the late 19th century and converted in the 1970s. It is emphatically a restaurant with rooms rather than a hotel – the only sitting area is a claustrophobic hall with a barrel ceiling. The main dining-room runs all along the front of the building, but in summer a glamorous marquee affair is erected on a rear terrace, and there are other little terraces in the gardens for breakfast and drinks.

Nearby Gaeta (8 km); Sperlonga, Terracina, San Felice Circeo all within reach.

Balze di Pagnano, Formia
04023 Latina
Tel (0771) 700138
Location on hill above town, in gardens, with private car parking
Food & drink breakfast, lunch, dinner
Prices rooms L68,000-L112,000; meals from L45,000
Rooms 10 double rooms, one with bath, 9 with shower; all rooms have minibar, colour TV, hairdrier, air-conditioning
Facilities 3 sitting-areas, bar, dining-room; tennis
Credit cards AE, DC, MC, V
Children accepted
Disabled no special facilities
Pets accepted
Closed Nov
Proprietor Carla Celletti

Lazio

Seaside hotel, San Felice Circeo

Punta Rossa

San Felice is an amiable village at the foot of the 550-metre Monte Circeo, which is an isolated lump of rock at the seaward point of a flat area, once marshland but now drained except for zones which have been declared a national park to preserve the flora and fauna. The Punta Rossa lies around the mountain in a secluded setting above an exposed and rocky shore.

The hotel has the form of a miniature village. Reception is in a lodge just inside an arched gateway, and beyond that is a little piazza enclosed by white-walled buildings in rough Mediterranean style. Bedrooms are spread around in low buildings at or near the top of a garden beyond the piazza which descends steeply to the sea. They are pleasant, varying in size, many with colour schemes which look a bit dated; all have balconies with sea views. The main attraction of the suites is their admirable size. The restaurant is part-way down the garden (already bursting with colour when we visited in spring) towards the sea and pool, with views from its terraces.

Nearby Terracina (20 km); Circeo national park.

San Felice Circeo 04017 Latina
Tel (0773) 528085
Location 4 km W of San Felice, isolated on rocky shore; in gardens, with ample car parking
Food & drink breakfast, lunch, dinner
Prices rooms L130,000-L410,000 with breakfast; suites L395,000-L610,000
Rooms 27 double, 6 single, 7 suites; all with bath or shower; all rooms have phone, minibar, colour TV; all double rooms have sea-view balcony or terrace, air-conditioning
Facilities bar, dining-room, terrace, courtyard; outdoor swimming-pool, small beach
Credit cards AE, DC, V
Children welcome
Disabled access difficult
Pets small dogs accepted by arrangement
Closed never
Manager Maria Fiorella Battaglia

Lazio

Internazionale

Despite its central Rome location, the interior of this hotel – in business since 1870 – has something of the feel of a grand British house, with its ornate wooden staircase, chandeliers, plush furnishings and rather muted colour schemes. The styles in the bedrooms tend to be mixed – reproduction antique chairs and tables may clash with a carpet and pictures of rather modern designs. But the Internazionale is comfortable, well-equipped, and, situated only a short walk from the Spanish Steps, could scarcely be better placed for sightseeing.

Nearby Villa Borghese, Piazza di Spagna, Spanish Steps.

Via Sistina 79, Roma 00187 Roma
Tel (06) 679 3047
Location just S of Villa Borghese, E of Piazza di Spagna; with some car parking
Food & drink breakfast
Prices rooms L150,000-L220,000 with breakfast
Rooms 30 double, 21 with bath, 9 with shower; 7 single with shower; 2 suites with bath; all rooms have central heating, air-conditioning, phone, TV, minibar; most rooms have hairdrier
Facilities dining-room, sitting-room
Credit cards AE, MC, V
Children accepted; baby-sitting on request
Disabled no special facilities
Pets not accepted
Closed never
Proprietor Dott. Giuseppe Gnecco

Locarno

This stylish wisteria-covered building is set just off the great oval Piazza del Popolo. The bedrooms are spacious, comfortable and pretty, with good bathrooms. Many have sitting-areas, which is perhaps just as well, since the sitting-room is rather cheerless. In contrast, the walled terrace is light and airy, shaded by pretty white umbrellas and full of greenery – a pleasant place for a quiet drink or just to relax. Only breakfast is available in the hotel, but cafés and restaurants abound in the area.

Nearby Villa Borghese, Pantheon, Castel S. Angelo.

Via della Penna 22, 00186 Roma
Tel (06) 321 6030
Location 100 m from Piazza del Popolo; no private parking but garage service on request
Food & drink breakfast
Prices rooms L129,000-L250,000 with breakfast;
Rooms 23 double, 15 single, all with bath; all rooms have central heating, air-conditioning, phone, TV, hairdrier, minibar
Facilities dining-room, sitting-room, bar; garden
Credit cards AE, V
Children accepted; baby-sitting on request
Disabled lift/elevator
Pets not accepted
Closed never
Proprietor Maria Teresa Celli

Abruzzo

Castello di Balsorano

High on a wooded, rocky hill, the Castello di Balsorano is a
fine-looking 13thC fortress – one of the few to have survived the
Barbarian attacks and earthquakes of the Abruzzo region. Inside,
it still has the atmosphere of a medieval castle, unchanged by the
modern amenities which have been installed. Downstairs there
are grand rooms with coats of armour and shields, swords and
daggers and ancient shotguns. Bedrooms are in similar medieval
style, some with ornately carved baronial beds and silk wall
hangings. In this quite a remote part of Abruzzo it is normally
essential to speak Italian. But the Castello is an exception: Mary
Ricci is English.

Nearby Abruzzo National Park within reach.

Castello di Balsorano,
Balsorano, Sora 67025
L'Aquila
Tel (0863) 95236
Location on rocky hilltop in
village; with private car
parking
Food & drink breakfast,
lunch, dinner
Prices rooms L82,500; suite
L110,000; meals about
L50,000; breakfast L10,000

Rooms 5 double, one suite, all
with bath; all rooms have
central heating
Facilities dining-room, bar
Credit cards not accepted
Children accepted
Disabled access difficult
Pets not accepted in
dining-room
Closed Nov
Proprietors Nino and Mary
Ricci

Mille Pini

Scanno lies surrounded by the 2,000-metre peaks of Abruzzo, the
highest of the Apennine mountains. The Lago di Scanno is the
local beauty spot, and there are hotels beside it; but those with
an eye on the hills should make for this modern hotel (as its
name suggests, surrounded by pines) at the foot of the chair-lift
up to Monte Rotondo. It is simple and neat, in Alpine chalet
style, and quiet at most times of the year. Few foreign visitors
penetrate this far, so don't expect to speak English. A recent
visitor found this 'a very friendly place indeed'.

Nearby Sulmona (31 km).

Via Pescara 2, Scanno 67038
L'Aquila
Tel (0864) 74387
Location slightly out of village,
at foot of chair- lift; in small
garden, with car parking on
quiet road
Food & drink breakfast,
lunch, dinner
Prices rooms L70,000-
L96,000; meals L40,000
Rooms 15 double; 5 single;

one family room; all with
bath; all rooms have central
heating, phone
Facilities dining-room,
sitting-room, games room, TV
room, winter room
Credit cards not accepted
Children accepted
Disabled no special facilities
Pets dogs not accepted
Closed restaurant only, Tue
Proprietor Carmelo Silla

Campania

Hotels in Campania

Campania has three components: the frantic city of Naples (where, somewhat to our surprise, we have succeeded in finding one attractive small hotel – the Miramare, page 185); the extremely popular seaside resorts to the south of Naples on the Sorrento peninsula and the islands of Capri and Ischia (where there is a super-abundance of such hotels); and the coast and countryside away from Naples, where we have drawn almost a complete blank.

Ischia is hard work for the seeker of small hotels. Tourism there was originally and is still closely linked with the island's thermal springs, and large hotels with spa facilities are the norm – accounting partly for the island's domination by German visitors. One of the most popular excursions is to Sant'Angelo on the south coast – a tiny fishing village on a narrow isthmus. Sant'Angelo would be a pleasant place to stay for longer than an hour or two – indeed, it is at its best before the daily coaches arrive or after they depart – and apart from the San Michele (page 177) it has a couple of other hotels which make acceptable bases. The Miramare (Tel (081) 999219) is almost at sea level on the east side of the village, with a big terrace on the waterside which gets the morning sun. Just behind it up the steep hillside, with views over the rooftops from its little terraces, is La Palma (Tel (081) 999215).

On Capri, the Pazziella (Tel (081) 837 0044) is an ex- private villa – small and smart, with flowery terraces and gardens.

Della Baia

This low-lying white building stands well away from the main part of Baia Domizia. Inside, the three Sello sisters have successfully reproduced the peaceful atmosphere of a stylish private villa: spotless white stucco walls, cool quarry-tiled floors and white sofas are offset by bowls of fresh flowers and potted plants, and the antique and modern furnishings blend well together. Bedrooms are no less attractive; all have balconies.
Nearby Gaeta (29 km); Naples within reach.

Via dell'Erica, Baia Domizia
81030 Caserta
Tel (0823) 721344
Location in S part of resort, with gardens leading down to long sandy beach; ample car parking
Food & drink breakfast, lunch, dinner
Prices FB L92,000-L122,000; reductions for children
Rooms 54 double, 18 with bath, 36 with shower; 2 single, one with bath, one with shower; all rooms have central heating, balcony, phone
Facilities 2 sitting- rooms, TV room, bar, terrace, dining-room; tennis, bowls, private beach
Credit cards AE, DC, MC, V
Children welcome
Disabled no special facilities
Pets small, well-behaved ones accepted
Closed Oct to mid-May
Proprietors Elsa, Velia and Imelde Sello

Campania

Converted monastery, Amalfi

Cappuccini Convento

A rickety-seeming elevator from the roadside is your unim-pressive introduction to this extraordinary hotel, perched in an apparently impossible position on the cliff face above Amalfi; not surprisingly, one of its great attractions is the superb views of the rugged Amalfi coast, shared by the flowery, creeper-covered terraces and many of the rooms.

But the other merits of this 12thC monastery soon become clear, too. The public areas are light and airy, with a striking sense of space, many original features retained, and antiques lining the wide hallways. The salon/bar has Oriental rugs on tiled floors, with comfortable pink-covered armchairs and sofas, a newly built brick fireplace and a piano adding to the clubby atmosphere. The large dining-room is a delight, with superb vaulting and columns, crisp white tablecloths and bentwood and cane chairs on a tiled floor. The bedrooms are mostly large and charmingly furnished with antiques; most have tiled floors with rugs, and quite a few have both a sea view and a balcony.

The recently restored cloisters are the cool, dignified venue for occasional piano and other recitals.

Nearby Grotta dello Smeraldo (4 km); Ravello (7 km); Sorrento (33 km).

Amalfi 84011 Salerno
Tel (089) 871877
Location 300 m from middle of Amalfi, high up on cliffs, reached by lift/elevator up from main road; garden and private car parking at road level
Food & drink breakfast, lunch, dinner
Prices rooms L70,000-L150,000

Rooms 46 double, 7 single, all with bath or shower; all rooms have phone
Facilities dining-room, sitting-rooms, bar, solarium, conference facilities; beach
Credit cards AE, DC, V
Children accepted
Disabled no special facilities
Pets accepted
Closed never
Proprietor Alfredo Aielli

Campania

Converted monastery, Amalfi

Luna

The middle of Amalfi is crowded and bustling, and the most desirable hotels lie just outside it or well above it up on the rockface. The Luna Convento is one of the former – about five minutes' walk uphill from the cathedral. It occupies two separate buildings, separated by the winding coast road – one of them an old Saracen tower perched right on the sea.

The hotel opened in 1825 (it is one of the oldest in Amalfi), and has been in the same family for five generations. But you only have to step inside to see that the building's history goes back much further than the 19th century. The unique feature is the Byzantine cloister enclosing a garden and ancient well. The arcade serves as a quiet and civilized sitting area and breakfasts are served within the actual cloister – a delightful spot to start the day. You have the choice of modern or traditional bedrooms, and for a premium you can have your own private sitting-room. Lunch and dinner (specialities are cannelloni, *crêpes* and fish risotto) are taken either in the vaulted restaurant in the main building, where large arched windows give beautiful views of the bay, or better still across the road where the terrace and parasols of the tower restaurant extend to the water's edge. The swimming-pool forms part of the same complex – as does the somewhat incongruous disco.

Nearby cathedral of Sant'Andrea and cloisters of Paradise (in Amalfi); Valle dei Mulini (1 hr walk); Ravello (6 km).

Via P Comite 19, Amalfi 84011 Salerno
Tel (089) 871002
Location short walk from middle of resort, overlooking sea, with private garage
Food & drink breakfast, lunch, dinner
Prices rooms L80,000-L160,000; FB L130,000-L150,000; 20% reduction for children under 6, sharing parents' room

Rooms 45 double, 5 single, 5 family rooms; all with bath; all rooms have minibar, phone
Facilities 2 dining-rooms, 2 bars, Byzantine cloister; swimming-pool, disco
Credit cards AE, DC, MC, V
Children welcome
Disabled 2 lifts/elevators
Pets accepted, but not in restaurant or by pool
Closed never
Manager A Milone

Campania

Seaside hotel, Capri

Flora

On the edge of the fashionable little town of Capri, the Flora looks out to the sea and the ancient cliff-top Certosa di San Giacomo. It is a modest but well cared-for little hotel (recently refurbished to gain an extra star), immersed in greenery and flowers, with calm and spacious bedrooms (many with balconies sharing the view) and an attractive sun-terrace. Breakfasts are excellent, and the lack of a dining-room is no problem – there is a wide choice of restaurants within easy strolling distance.

Nearby Carthusian monastery of San Giacomo, Augustus gardens, beach at Marina Piccola.

Via Federico Serena 26, Capri 80073 Napoli
Tel (081) 837 0211
Location about 200 m from middle of Capri town; with flowery terrace and fine sea views; no private car parking
Food & drink breakfast
Prices rooms L240,000
Rooms 16 double, one single, 7 family rooms, all with bath; all rooms have

air-conditioning, TV, minibar; most rooms with terrace, phone
Facilities breakfast room, sitting-room, bar, terrace
Credit cards AE, DC, MC, V
Children accepted
Disabled access difficult
Pets accepted
Closed Nov to Feb
Proprietor Virginia Vuotto

Seaside hotel, Capri

Luna

In comparison with some of the ritzy alternatives on Capri, the Luna strikes you as somewhat old-fashioned – in the nicest sense. A delightful path shaded by vines forms the entrance to the hotel; inside, public rooms are spacious, quiet and civilized, with beautiful views of the sea from the dining-room terrace, and bedrooms have the sort of space and comfort you expect from a top-class hotel. The setting is one of the most desirable on the island – perched on cliffs plunging down to the dark blue water and facing the strange islets of the Faraglioni.

Nearby old town of Capri; Certosa di San Giacomo.

Viale Matteotti 3, Capri 80073 Napoli
Tel (081) 837 0433
Location about 250 m from middle of Capri town, on cliffs; in large garden
Food & drink breakfast, lunch, dinner
Prices rooms L145,000-L320,000 with breakfast; meals L50,000
Rooms 46 double, 2 single, all with bath; all rooms have

air-conditioning, phone, minibar
Facilities dining-room, 4 sitting-rooms, TV room, bar, terrace, conference facilities; swimming-pool
Credit cards AE, DC, V
Children accepted
Disabled no special facilities
Pets accepted, but not allowed in dining-room
Closed Nov to Mar
Proprietor Luisa Vuotto

Campania

La Pineta

Despite its increase in size (and gloss) over the years, the Pineta retains what was always its greatest asset – the location. 'Pineta' means pine-wood and the modern, low-lying buildings lie right among the trees, on a hillside overlooking the sea and the rocky south coast of the island. Flowery terraces shaded by pines and the spacious balconies of the apartments focus on this spectacular panorama. Breakfasts are buffet-style, and the pool-side restaurant caters for the latest of risers, serving tempting meals from noon to 5pm.

Nearby town of Capri (3 minutes' walk); Marina Piccola (2 km).

Via Tragara 6, Capri 80073, Napoli
Tel (081) 837 0644
Location among pines close to the middle of town; no private car parking
Food & drink breakfast, lunch; dinner at Ristorante Campanile in Capri town
Prices rooms L85,000-L250,000; lunch about L40,000; special weekly rates
Rooms 40 double, 8 single, 6 family rooms, all with bath; all rooms have central heating, air-conditioning, TV, phone, minibar
Facilities breakfast room, bar, piano bar, 3 terraces; gym, sauna, heated outdoor swimming-pool
Credit cards AE, DC, MC, V
Children accepted if well-behaved
Disabled no special facilities
Pets small ones accepted
Closed never
Proprietor Costanzo Vuotto

Villa Sarah

A steep walk up from the middle of Capri will bring you to the Villa Sarah – a whitewashed building among the vines, well away from the bustle of the town. (Carry on along the path and you come to the remains of the Villa Iovis, one of 12 palaces on the island belonging to Tiberius – local guides will tell you he kept a different mistress in each one of them.) Originally the Villa Sarah was built by an English aristocrat and though much modernized, it still has the friendly air of a private home. Rooms are cool, whitewashed and simple, and the only public area is the breakfast room – though most guests prefer to take breakfast on the terrace, soaking up the morning sun.

Nearby Capri town (500 m); Villa Iovis (30 minutes' walk).

Via Tibero 3/a, Capri 80073 Napoli
Tel (081) 837 7817
Location on road leading from middle of Capri town to Villa Iovis; with shady garden
Food & drink breakfast
Prices rooms L80,000-L160,000
Rooms 12 double, 8 single, all with bath or shower; all rooms have phone
Facilities breakfast room, terrace
Credit cards AE
Children accepted
Disabled no special facilities
Pets dogs not accepted
Closed Nov to Mar
Proprietor Sga C Vuotto

Campania

Seaside hotel, Capri

Scalinatella

No expense has been spared in the creation of this small, exclusive hotel. A spotless white building with a profusion of arches and oriental ornamentation, it feels distinctly Moorish. Inside a world of cool luxury awaits you. Every corner is air-conditioned and the rooms have all the trimmings that you might expect for the very high price you will be paying – telephones in the bathroom, private terraces and beds that disappear into alcoves, converting your rooms into a sitting-room by day. Furnishings vary from the simple and refined to the extravagant and perhaps over-rich. But there are few other flaws in this luxury hotel. Its location, with beautiful views to the Carthusian monastery of San Giacomo, leaves little to be desired; the garden and pool (where buffet lunches are served) are immaculate. The hotel was refurbished in 1989.

Nearby Monastery of San Giacomo (overlooked by hotel); Capri town (about five minutes' walk).

Via Tragara 10, Capri 80073 Napoli
Tel (081) 837 0633
Location on Punta Tragara road; with garden and ample car parking
Food & drink breakfast, buffet lunch by pool
Prices rooms L150,000-L420,000 with breakfast
Rooms 30 double, all with bath and jacuzzi; all rooms have air-conditioning, phone, TV, minibar
Facilities sitting-rooms, breakfast room, bar; swimming-pool, tennis
Credit cards not accepted
Disabled no special facilities
Pets accepted
Closed Nov to mid-Mar
Proprietors Morgana family

Campania

Seaside villa, Capri

Villa Krupp

After the bustle of Capri town, the Augustus gardens are a welcome retreat, terraced on a gentle hillside above the sheer cliffs and little beaches of Marina Piccola. Quite high up is the Villa Krupp, a serene white villa whose main claim to fame is that both Lenin and Gorky lived here for a while – you can still see the desk where they wrote. There are no public rooms, but bedrooms are bright, clean and mainly spacious, with floral tiled floors and the occasional rug. Walls are whitewashed and there are some pretty antique pieces and wicker chairs with cushions. Each of the rooms has a balcony, and breakfasts are taken on a terrace overlooking the gardens and the sea.

Nearby middle of Capri a few minutes' walk; Marina Piccola.

Via Matteotti 12, Capri 80073 Napoli
Tel (081) 837 0362
Location in the Augustus gardens, up from the middle of Capri town
Food & drink breakfast
Prices rooms L58,000-L116,000
Rooms 12 rooms, all with bath or shower; all rooms have balcony
Facilities small terrace
Credit cards V
Children accepted
Disabled not suitable
Pets not accepted
Closed never
Proprietor Sga Settanni

Seaside hotel, Capri

Villa Brunella

The Brunella was built in 1970 and its modern façade has no great distinction. What really makes the place is its setting, perched on terraced slopes in the south-east of the island, with superb views of rugged cliffs and azure waters. You can admire the views from the balcony of your room, from the terrace where a buffet lunch is served, or from the pool which lies below the hotel. The atmosphere is relaxed and the bedrooms are spacious, light and modern. Sadly, for most travellers these attractions count for little, because Sg. Ruggiero apparently has no hesitation in dishonouring reservations when it suits him.

Nearby beach of Faraglioni, Carthusian monastery of San Giacomo, Capri town.

Via Tragara 24, Capri 80073
Tel (081) 837 0122
Location on terraced slopes, overlooking sea and cliffs, a few minutes' walk from Capri town; no proper road or car parking
Food & drink breakfast, lunch, dinner
Prices rooms L100,000-L120,000; meals about L35,000
Rooms 18 double, all with bath; all rooms have central heating, air-conditioning, phone; 5 rooms have sitting-area
Facilities 2 sitting-rooms, 2 bars, swimming-pool, panoramic terrace
Credit cards AE, V
Children accepted
Disabled no special facilities
Pets not accepted
Closed Nov to mid-Mar
Proprietor Vincenzo and Brunella Ruggiero

Campania

Converted monastery, Ischia

Il Monastero

Ischia Ponte gets its name from the low bridge giving access from the 'mainland' of Ischia to the precipitous islet on top of which stands the original settlement of Ischia, known collectively as the Castello although it consists of several buildings. One of these is an old monastery which is now run as a simple but entirely captivating *pensione*.

A lift reached by a tunnel into the rock of the island takes you up to the Castello (though there are steps as an alternative). Discreet signs bring you to the locked door of the *pensione*, and a ring on the bell summons the amiable *padrone*. Up a final flight of stairs and at last you are there. Many paintings hang on the plain walls of the hallway and the neat little sitting-room. The dining-room has satisfyingly solid wooden furniture. Bedrooms are monastically simple; some are reached from inside, some from the outside terrace, which gives a breathtaking view of the town and island of Ischia.

We have no first-hand experience of the food, and half-board is inescapable; but we know that the cooking is good enough to keep the Monastero full in spring and autumn when other hotels are half-empty.

Nearby Castello d'Ischia.

Castello Aragonese 3, Ischia Ponte 80070 Napoli
Tel (081) 992435
Location on island E of Ischia town, linked by causeway
Food & drink breakfast, dinner
Prices DB&B L43,000-L58,000
Rooms 15 double, 1 single, 13 with bath or shower
Facilities dining-room, TV room, large terrace
Credit cards not accepted
Children accepted
Disabled not suitable
Pets not accepted
Closed mid-Oct to mid-Mar
Proprietor Ciro Eletto

Campania

La Villarosa

This is a sharp contrast to the Monastero in every way: it is immersed in a jungle of a garden right in the heart of the little town of Ischia, and its great attraction (apart from the garden and pleasant little pool) is its series of delectable sitting-rooms, beautifully furnished with comfortable armchairs and ornate antiques. The bedrooms are, by comparison, rather plainly furnished, but perfectly acceptable.

The light, welcoming restaurant upstairs leads out on to a terrace overlooking the garden and the roof-tops of Ischia, and meals are served there in summer. Only full board terms are offered, and regrettably we have no evidence about the standard of cooking – so anyone who books in for more than a night or two is clearly taking a risk.

Like many hotels on the island, the Villarosa offers thermal treatments of various sorts – though the atmosphere is far removed from that of the traditional spa hotel. (The 'Scottish shower' mentioned in the brochure is presumably a localized drizzle.)

Nearby port of Ischia (500 m); Castello d'Ischia (2 km).

Via Giacinto Gigante 5, Porto d'Ischia 80077 Napoli
Tel (081) 991316
Location 200 m from lido; with limited car parking
Food & drink breakfast, lunch, dinner
Prices FB L95,000- L115,000
Rooms 34 double, 20 with bath, 14 with shower; 6 single, all with shower; all rooms have central heating

Facilities sitting-room, bar, dining-room, TV room, terrace; thermal outdoor swimming-pool, sauna
Credit cards MC, V
Children not suitable
Disabled access possible – lift/elevator to bedrooms
Pets not accepted in public rooms or dining-room
Closed Nov to Mar
Proprietor Paolo Amalfitano

Campania

Belvedere

You could not hope for a more perfect position for a hotel; perched on the edge of a cliff with magnificent views of the Amalfi coast. It is possible to argue that there is more to the Belvedere than the belvedere; it has just a bit of style (glazed verandas dripping with vines and geraniums, sitting-rooms with velvet chairs on oriental rugs) and a friendly atmosphere (created by a small and attentive staff). But in the end the setting is the thing. Bedrooms are nothing more than adequate; but apparently all have balconies. A path leads down through a rocky terraced garden to a fair-sized swimming-pool.

Nearby Amalfi; Ravello (13 km); Positano (14 km).

Strada Statale 163, 84010 Conca dei Marini
Tel (089) 831282
Location on cliff edge, 6 km W of Amalfi on coast road; with garden and car parking
Food & drink breakfast, lunch, dinner
Prices rooms L100,000-L125,000; meals L45,000
Rooms 35 double, all with bath; one single with bath; all have central heating, phone
Facilities 2 dining-rooms, sitting-room; swimming-pool
Credit cards AE, MC, V
Children accepted
Disabled no special facilities
Pets not accepted
Closed Oct to Apr
Proprietor Angelo Lucibello

San Michele

This villa-style building is not a remarkable hotel in itself. The bar/sitting-room has a tile floor and a dark, comfortable atmosphere, with deep modern armchairs; the dining-room is more traditional, with a terrazzo floor, raffia-seated chairs and a shady terrace; bedrooms too have tiled floors, small rugs and modern (though not ugly) furniture – and each has a small balcony. The real attraction is the exceptionally peaceful location and lush gardens; there are thermal facilities neatly tucked away, lovely terraces with plenty of tables and chairs and a delightful swimming-pool set among pine trees.

Nearby boats to Ischia town.

Sant'Angelo, Isola d'Ischia 80070 Napoli
Tel (081) 999276
Location on rocky headland with garden; access by foot only: public car parks (one paying, once free) 5 minutes' walk away
Food & drink breakfast; lunch and dinner in season
Prices rooms L100,000-L180,000
Rooms 39 double, 5 single, all with bath or shower; all rooms have phone
Facilities hall, bar, conference facilities, 2 terraces; sea-water pool
Credit cards not accepted
Children accepted
Disabled not suitable
Pets accepted
Closed Nov to Mar
Proprietor Claudio Iacono

Campania

L'Ancora

This modern and unpretentious hotel shares the views of the famous and over-priced Syrenuse, next door – and its close proximity to the heart of the resort. The public areas are large, light and simply furnished, with rather loud tiled floors. The spacious dining-room opens out on to the terrace, which overlooks the sea and gets the sun for most of the day; it is partly shaded by a creeper-covered awning. The bedrooms, most of which have balconies overlooking the sea, are traditionally decorated. They are sparsely furnished and seem quite large, but what furniture they have is well chosen and there are rugs on the tiled floors. Bathrooms are clean, tiled and in good order. A pool is apparently planned; heaven knows where they'll put it.

Nearby Amalfi (17 km); Sorrento (17 km); Ravello (23 km).

Via C Colombo 36, Positano 84017 Salerno
Tel (089) 875318
Location a short walk from middle of resort, with private car parking
Food & drink breakfast, dinner
Prices DB&B L90,000-L110,000
Rooms 18 double, all with bath; all have phone, minibar, TV, some air-conditioning
Facilities sitting-room, dining-room, terrace
Credit cards AE, DC, MC, V
Children accepted
Disabled no special facilities
Pets accepted, but not in dining-room
Closed mid-Oct to Mar
Proprietors Savino brothers

Marincanto

Like most hotels in Positano, the Marincanto is no bargain. But for a hotel of its category, the rooms in the main building are surprisingly spacious and well furnished (those in the annexe are less impressive). The views from the flowery terraces of dazzling blue seas and the colourful houses of Positano jostling on the hillside are hard to forget. There is no restaurant, which is probably an advantage in a resort where half-board terms may be a rip-off and good food is abundant. The public rooms are confined to an open-plan reception and sitting area – breakfast is taken on a pretty sea-view terrace. Several flights of steps lead down to a pebble beach. In a resort where parking is a problem, the hotel car park is a bonus – but watch the charges.

Nearby Amalfi (17 km); Ravello 23 km); Sorrento (17 km).

Positano 84017 Salerno
Tel (089) 875130
Location built into hillside directly above sea and beach; with terrace and private (paying) car park
Food & drink breakfast
Prices rooms L90,000-L110,000
Rooms 25 double, all with bath or shower; all rooms have phone, minibar
Facilities sitting-room, bar
Credit cards AE, DC, MC, V
Children accepted
Disabled no special facilities
Pets dogs not accepted
Closed mid-Oct to week before Easter
Proprietor Sga Celesti Manna

Campania

Miramare

On the steep hill to the west of the beach and the fishing boats, the Miramare is a series of old fishermen's houses joined to make a charming and thoroughly comfortable hotel. The sitting-room has a vaulted ceiling, Oriental rugs, antique furniture and lots of plants and flowers. The dining-room is a delight – a glassed-in terrace with bougainvillaea hanging from the ceiling trellis, smart modern chairs and a memorable view shared by all tables. Each bedroom has a balcony overlooking the sea – and in some cases even the bath gives a view

Nearby Amalfi (17 km); Ravello (23 km).

Via Trara Genoino 25-27, Positano 84017 Salerno
Tel (089) 875002
Location 3 minutes W of main beach; with private parking for 10 cars
Food & drink breakfast, lunch, dinner
Prices rooms L70,000-L260,000 with breakfast; dinner L50,000
Rooms 10 double, 3 single, 5 suites; all with bath and shower, central heating
Facilities dining-room, bar, 3 sitting-rooms
Credit cards AE, MC, V
Children not encouraged
Disabled not suitable
Pets not allowed in dining-room
Closed never; restaurant Nov to mid-Mar
Proprietor Sg. Attanasio

La Tonnarella

Perched high on cliffs at the western extremity of Sorrento's sweeping bay, La Tonnarella enjoys superb sea views from its restaurant and flowery terraces. (It is apparently named after a lookout tower from which fishermen could spot approaching shoals of tuna fish). The restaurant is at the heart of the operation, and the sitting-room, although charmingly furnished with antiques, is on the small side; but the bedrooms are more numerous and more attractive than is usual in most Italian restaurants-with-rooms. A lift takes you down the cliffs to a small private beach, far below. Signor Gargiulo is unfailingly courteous.

Nearby Naples, Vesuvius, Pompeii, Capri and Ischia all within reach.

Via Capo 31, Sorrento 80067 Napoli
Tel (081) 878 1153
Location about 1 km from middle of resort, on cliffs overlooking the sea, with lift/elevator to beach; private car parking
Food & drink breakfast, lunch, dinner
Prices rooms L60,000-L70,000; DB&B L50,000-L60,000; FB L60,000- L70,000; meals L25,000
Rooms 16 double, 2 family rooms, all with bath; all rooms have central heating
Facilities dining-room, bar, TV room
Credit cards AE, DC, MC, V
Children welcome
Disabled no facilities
Pets small ones accepted in bedrooms and in dining-room
Closed Dec to 10 Mar
Proprietor Carlo Gargiulo

Campania

Seaside hotel, Positano

Palazzo Murat

Most hotels in this picturesque and fashionable little resort are ranged up the steep hills either side of the ravine leading down to the sea. Such positions are fine for views, but imply strenuous climbs back from the beach or the middle of the resort. The Palazzo Murat is by no means viewless, but it is much more in the heart of things – just inland of the *duomo*, and reached by one of the pedestrian alleys lined with trendy boutiques.

The main building is a grand L-shaped 18thC *palazzo*, easily identified from most parts of the resort by its pitched, tiled roof. Within the L is a charming courtyard – a well in the middle, bougainvillea trained up the surrounding walls, palms and other exotic vegetation dotted around – where you can take breakfast (though in spring early risers will find it sunless). Along one side of this courtyard run the interconnecting sitting-rooms, which are beautifully furnished with antiques.

Bedrooms in the *palazzo* itself are attractively traditional in style – some painted furniture, some polished hardwood – and have doors opening on to token balconies (standing room only). We have not seen rooms in the more modern extension on the seaward side of the main building, but most of them do have the attraction of bigger balconies.

A breakfast-only hotel could scarcely be better placed: Positano's many restaurants are mainly congregated behind the beach, a short stroll away.

Nearby tour of Amalfi coast and Sorrento peninsula.

Via dei Mulini 23, Positano 84017 Salerno
Tel (089) 875177
Location in heart of resort; paying car park nearby
Food & drink breakfast
Prices rooms L160,000-L180,000
Rooms 28 double, all with bath and shower, phone,

balcony, radio, minibar
Facilities sitting-room, TV room, terrace, bar
Credit cards AE, DC, MC, V
Children accepted
Disabled access difficult
Pets small ones only accepted
Closed Nov to Easter week, but open for Christmas week
Proprietor Carmela Cinque

Campania

Villa Franca

Provided you are not worried by heights, or by remoteness from the centre of things, this smartly traditional hotel – all arches, white walls and tiled floors – has much to commend it. The position, high on the western side of the Positano ravine, gives an excellent view of the resort and the coast beyond from the windows and terraces; the bedrooms and public rooms are spacious and comfortable. A reporter found the proprietors and staff welcoming, and the food satisfying and freshly prepared. There is a private bus to and from the beach at certain times.
Nearby Amalfi (17 km); Sorrento (17 km); Ravello (23 km); boat trips to Capri.

Via Pasitea 318, Positano
84017 Salerno
Tel (089) 875735
Location on main road above middle of Positano, with fine sea views
Food & drink breakfast, dinner
Prices rooms L90,000-L190,000 with breakfast; meals L50,000-L60,000
Rooms 28 double, 1 single, all with bath or shower; all rooms have central heating, radio, satellite TV, phone, air-conditioning
Facilities dining-room, bar terrace; swimming-pool
Credit cards AE, MC, V
Children welcome
Disabled not suitable
Pets accepted, but not allowed in dining-room **Closed** never
Proprietor Mario Russo

Giordano Villa Maria

With its views down to the sea, the shady garden restaurant of this charming old villa is not surprisingly popular for lunch and dinner, and there is a traditionally furnished dining-room for cooler days; bedrooms are simple but comfortable. Guests have the use of a large modern pool at the nearby Hotel Giordano, which is under the same ownership. Carla Palumbo will patiently talk you through the menu in excellent English.
Nearby Amalfi (6 km); sights of Vesuvius, Pompeii, Sorrento within reach.

Via Santa Chiara 2, Ravello
84010 Salerno
Tel (089) 857170/255
Location on path to Villa Cimbrone, in garden; private car parking available
Food & drink breakfast, lunch, dinner
Prices rooms L66,000-L132,000 with breakfast; suites L165,000- L198,000; DB&B L88,000- L99,000 (min 3 days)
Rooms 10 double, 5 with bath, 5 with shower; 2 single, with shower; 2 family rooms, both with bath; all rooms have central heating, phone; TV and minibar on request
Facilities dining-room, TV room, lounge bar, sitting-room, heated swimming-pool, hydromassage
Credit cards AE, MC, V
Children accepted at proprietor's discretion
Disabled no special facilities
Pets not accepted
Closed never
Proprietor Vincenzo Palumbo

Campania

Marmorata

Despite the address, the Marmorata is not up in the hill-top town of Ravello, but set on the rugged shoreline. Originally a paper mill, the building has been smartly converted into a four-star hotel with a nautical design theme. It is stylishly modern, cool and comfortable. Large windows make the most of the sea views, and the main terrace is perched directly above the water.

Nearby Ravello (6 km); Positano, Sorrento within reach.

Strada Statale 163, Localita Marmorata, Ravello 84010 Salerno
Tel (089) 877777
Location 3 km E of Amalfi; on hillside below coast road, with private car parking
Food & drink breakfast, lunch, dinner
Prices rooms L90,000-L280,000 with breakfast
Rooms 38 double, 2 with bath, 36 with shower; 3 single, 2 with bath, one with shower; all rooms have central heating, colour and satellite TV, radio, minibar, air-conditioning, phone
Facilities hall, dining- room, bar, conference room; terraces, solarium, sea- water pool
Credit cards AE, DC, MC, V
Children accepted
Disabled access difficult
Pets accepted if well behaved
Closed never
Proprietors Camera d'Afflitto family

Parsifal

Wagner was one of the many illustrious visitors who stayed at Ravello's Villa Rufolo, and the gardens there are said to have been the inspiration for the second act of the opera from which this little hotel takes its name. No doubt Wagner would have been equally inspired by the stunning sea-views from this simple but charming little hotel. It was converted from a monastery, and part of the cloister, along with Corinthian columns and vaulted ceilings, have been preserved. Home-made pastas, cannelloni and *crêpes* are the specialities of the house, and you can enjoy them on a creeper-clad terrace.

Nearby Villa Rufolo and Villa Cimbrone at Ravello; Amalfi (7 km); Positano (18 km); Pompeii within reach.

Via G d'Anna 5, Ravello 84010 Salerno
Tel (089) 857144
Location in quiet street on fringe of town; car parking on street
Food & drink breakfast, lunch, dinner
Prices rooms L70,000-L95,000; meals L28,000
Rooms 15 double, 8 with bath, 4 with shower; 2 single, one with shower; 2 family rooms with bath; all rooms have central heating
Facilities sitting-room, dining-room, terraces, cloister
Credit cards AE, DC, MC, V
Children accepted
Disabled no special facilities
Pets accepted, but not in dining-room
Closed 7 Oct to end Mar
Proprietor Nicola Camera

Campania

Caruso Belvedere

The Caruso Belvedere is one of several hotels in this justly popular beauty spot which have been converted from old *palazzi*. Ever since it opened in 1903 it has been in the capable hands of the Caruso family. The grandeur may have faded somewhat and the rooms cannot be called luxurious, but unaffected, informal charm is the key to its success.

Many of the original features, such as the Corinthian columns and marble pillars, still survive; the antiques, faded sofas and open fireplaces are entirely in keeping with the setting. When we last visited, bedrooms were perhaps simpler than you might expect, but most of them have been refurnished in the last couple of years. The restaurant is simple, light and spacious, but its best feature is the summer terrace commending sensational views of the rugged coast and the Gulf of Salerno. We lack recent reports about the food, though most people seem to enjoy the wines that come from the Caruso's own vineyards.

Perhaps the most romantic feature of all is the terraced garden, with its timeless views of the sea far below.

Nearby Villa Rufolo, Villa Cimbrone; Amalfi (7 km).

Via San Giovanni del Toro 52, Ravello 84010 Salerno
Tel (089) 857111
Location 500 m from the main piazza, with garden; public car parking in front of hotel
Food & drink breakfast, lunch, dinner
Prices rooms L112,000-L153,000 with breakfast; DB&B L105,000- L129,000
Rooms 22 double, 2 single, all with shower; 2 family rooms, both with bath; all rooms have central heating, phone
Facilities dining-room, bar, TV room, solarium
Credit cards AE, DC, MC, V
Children welcome
Disabled no special facilities
Pets small ones only accepted, and not in public areas
Closed never
Proprietor Paolo Caruso

Campania

Palumbo

A Moorish-inspired *palazzo*, built for a nobleman in the 12th century, the Palumbo was bought by a Swiss hotelier in the mid-19th century and is still run by his family. No expense has been spared in its conversion to a five-star hotel, but what distinguishes it from most other hotels of its category is its understated luxury and elegance.

Public rooms focus on a 13thC inner courtyard where Corinthian-topped columns, oriental arches and a profusion of flowing plants provide a cool, civilized sitting-area. The restaurant is equally elegant, though more French than Moorish, with its peach tablecloths, gilt mirrors, mouldings and bentwood chairs. But on fine days the choice location for breakfast, lunch or candlelit dinners is the restaurant balcony, where you look down over terraced vineyards to dazzling blue seas below. Various other balconies and terraces (hung with vines and roses) share this same stunning panorama. Throughout the hotel there are beautiful antiques and paintings – including what is purported to be a Caravaggio. Bedrooms are light and airy and tastefully furnished with antiques, tiled floors and rugs. Those in the annexe are more modern in style, but, for anyone on a tighter budget, are much cheaper.

Nearby Villa Cimbrone, Villa Rufolo; Amalfi (7 km).

Via San Giovanni del Toro 28, Ravello 84010 Salerno
Tel (089) 857244
Location perched on cliffs; with garden, sun terrace and private car parking
Food & drink breakfast, lunch, dinner
Prices rooms L215,000-L360,000; DB&B L184,000-L257,000
Rooms 21 double, 3 suites; all with bath; 7 rooms are in annexe close to main building; all rooms have phone, TV, minibar
Facilities sitting-rooms, bar, dining-room
Credit cards AE, DC, MC, V
Children accepted
Disabled not suitable
Pets dogs not allowed in dining-room
Closed never
Proprietors Vuilleumier family

Campania

Miramare

This waterfront hotel, a couple of blocks from the very grand Excelsior in Santa Lucia (as in the song) is handy for ferries to the islands, and for several of the major sights. Rooms are cleverly designed to make the most of their compact dimensions, and are reached by the most elegant, creaky old lift we have encountered. Good breakfasts are served in the smart, light penthouse dining-room with views of the famous bay, surrounded by a roof terrace. Staff are friendly and helpful. Prices cannot be called low, but are reasonable by local standards.

Nearby Palazzo Reale and Castel dell'Ovo.

Via Nazario Sauro 24, Naples 80132
Tel (081) 427388
Location in Santa Lucia
Food & drink breakfast, dinner
Prices rooms L180,000-L220,000 with breakfast
Rooms 27 double, 4 single; all with bath or shower; all rooms have air- conditioning, phone, TV, minibar, trouser- press
Facilities sitting-rooms, bar, dining-room, TV room
Credit cards AE, DC, MC, V
Children welcome if well behaved
Disabled ground-floor bedrooms
Pets welcome if well behaved
Closed never **Proprietors** Enzo and Bibi Rosolino

Capo la Gala

The Sorrento coast road is squeezed between mountain and sea, but space has been found on the steep hillside below to create this neat modern hotel, arranged in a series of terraces. On the first level down from the shady car park and reception are double-bedded rooms, reached from an interior corridor; below that are twin-bedded rooms reached via an outdoor terrace; all are uniformly done out with tiled floors, plain walls and pretty cane furniture. Just above sea level are the fair-sized pool and restaurant – a pleasant spot for serious sunbathing.

Nearby Pompeii (10 km); Sorrento (10 km); Naples (34 km); Capri (30 min by boat); Ischia (one hr by boat).

Via Luigi Serio 7, Capo la Gala, Vico Equense 80069, Naples
Tel (081) 879 8278
Location 3 km N of Vico Equense, below coast road, in steep gardens with undercover car parking
Food & drink breakfast, lunch, dinner
Prices rooms L135,000-L180,000; DB&B L145,000-L190,000
Rooms 18 double, all with bath and shower; all rooms have phone, minibar, balcony with sea-view
Facilities 3 bars, dining- room, TV and video room, games room; swimming-pool (thermal sulphur spring fed), sauna, solarium, private beach
Credit cards AE, V
Children flexible attitude
Disabled lift/elevator available
Pets at proprietors' discretion
Closed Nov to Mar
Proprietors Antonio and Maria Savarese

The 'heel' of Italy

Hotels in the heel

To say that good small hotels in the heel of Italy are difficult to find is a wild understatement. It would be nearer the truth to say that they don't exist. The half-dozen hotels which have full entries in the following pages are the best you will find, but none of them is particularly captivating. Some alternative recommendations may be helpful.

Lecce is a city of Baroque architecture which is well worth exploring; the Risorgimento (Tel (0832) 42125) is in a splendid central building, but way overdue for refurbishment. Otranto has a brand new hotel – the Albania (Tel (0836) 811830) – fairly traditional from the outside but positively clinical within. If your ambition is to make it right to the southern tip of the heel, you could aim for L'Approdo (Tel (0833) 753016), a well-run seaside holiday hotel at Marina di Léuca.

None of the major cities of the area is particularly alluring; each has a handful of routine big hotels. But if circumstances dictate a night in Foggia the place to head for is the Cicolella (Tel (0881) 3890), which has an attractive restaurant, star-rated by Michelin. To the north at Peschici, on the other side of the Gargano peninsula from our Mattinata recommendation, is the Gusmay (Tel (0884) 94032), a civilized and peaceful beach hotel surrounded by pines.

Alba del Gargano

Mattinata is a lively little resort a short bus-ride from the beach; both the town and this part of the coast have escaped major development. The hotel itself is low-rise and unobtrusive; inside it is simply, but not starkly, decorated and furnished. The high-points of a stay here are al fresco dining in the courtyard (the emphasis is on fresh fish) and going out in one of the sons' motorboats for a tour of the spectacular coast.

Nearby spectacular coast of Gargano peninsula; Monte Sant'Angelo (19 km).

Corso Matino 102, Mattinata 71030 Foggia
Tel (0884) 4771
Location at end of main street; garage and car parking in courtyard
Food & drink breakfast, lunch, dinner
Prices rooms L38,400-L120,000 with breakfast; air-conditioning L15,000; reductions for children under 6
Rooms 20 double, all with shower; 3 single, all with shower; 16 family rooms; all rooms have phone; 9 rooms have air-conditioning
Facilities dining-room, outdoor dining area, TV room, games room, bar
Credit cards V
Children welcome
Disabled some bedrooms on ground floor
Pets small ones accepted, but not in certain rooms
Closed restaurant only, Nov to 1 Apr
Proprietor Francesco Piemontese

The 'heel' of Italy

Trulli **hotel, Alberobello**

Dei Trulli

The 'heel' of Italy has only one major tourist attraction: *trulli* – tiny stone buildings with conical, pointed roofs, usually joined in jolly little groups to make up multi-roomed houses. In Alberobello, a whole sector of the town consists of *trulli*, making it the natural goal of most visitors to the heel – though there are plenty of *trulli* dotted around the countryside, too.

The Dei Trulli offers *trulli* enthusiasts the irresistible opportunity to go the whole hog – not just to peer at these quaint dwellings but actually to stay in one. The hotel is a sort of refined holiday camp – it consists of little bungalows, each partly contained in a *trullo*, set among pines and neat flower beds. You get a small living-room as well as a spacious bedroom and compact bathroom, plus seats outside your front door.

There is a rather plain restaurant staffed by waiters whose charming demeanour quickly evaporates when problems arise. The cooking is competent, but the price for half-board is unreasonably high; the hotel does not publicize a bed-and-breakfast rate, but will quote one on request – and there are restaurants in the town (within walking distance, through Alberobello's main *trulli* zone).

Nearby coast (15-20 minutes by car).

Via Cadore 28, Alberobello 70011 Bari
Tel (080) 721130
Location 5 minutes' walk from middle of Alberobello; with private car parking
Food & drink breakfast, lunch, dinner
Prices rooms L77,000-L170,000; DB&B L120,000-L135,000
Rooms 28 double apartments, 11 with bath, 17 with shower; 11 family apartments all with bath and shower; all have TV, phone, sitting-room, minibar
Facilities dining-room, bar; swimming-pool, playground
Credit cards AE, V
Children welcome
Disabled no special facilities
Pets small ones only accepted
Closed never
Manager Luigi Farace

The 'heel' of Italy

Country hotel, Fasano

La Silvana

This friendly, family-run hotel (not to be confused with the much larger Sierra Silvana, in the same hill-top resort community) makes a useful and economical base from which to explore the *trulli* district – Alberobello, where you will see the best examples of these distinctive buildings, is only a short drive away. It is a modern though not brand-new place, with clean, spacious but plainly furnished rooms – some with large balconies and attractive views. The big restaurant attracts many non-residents, and there is a wide tiled terrace with sun-shades. Most important of all, the proprietors are welcoming and helpful.

Nearby Alberobello (15 km).

Viale dei Pini 87, Selva di Fasano, Fasano 72010 Brindisi
Tel (080) 933 1161
Location 2 km W of Fasano, in wooded residential area; with ample car parking and garage
Food & drink breakfast, lunch, dinner
Prices rooms L68,000-L70,000; DB&B L65,000-L70,000 (minimum stay 3 days)
Rooms 13 double, most with bath or shower; 2 singles; 3 suites with bath; all rooms have central heating
Facilities dining-room, TV room, terrace
Credit cards V
Children welcome
Disabled not suitable
Pets accepted, but not allowed in dining-room
Closed restaurant only, Fri in winter
Proprietor Anna Palmisano

Seaside hotel, Castro Marina

Orsa Maggiore

Castro Marina is a small resort and fishing port midway along the dramatic and beautiful rocky strip of coast which forms the bottom of Italy's heel. The Orsa Maggiore is situated a little way out along the coast road heading north: a modern building high above the sea, its modest grounds dotted with many olive trees. The hotel is run amiably and competently by five brothers, who inherited it from their mother. It is a straightforward place – well kept, with the occasional antique alongside the everyday furniture – with a high reputation locally for its food (wedding feasts are a regular weekend hazard).

Nearby Lecce (48 km); fine drives along coast to N and S.

Litoranea per Santa Cesarea 303, Castro Marina 73030 Lecce
Tel (0836) 97029
Location 500 m N of Castro Marina, with ample private car parking
Food & drink breakfast, lunch, dinner
Prices rooms L55,000-L750,00; FB L35,000- L96,500
Rooms 30 double, 28 with bath, 2 with shower; all rooms have central heating, phone, small terrace
Facilities dining-room, hall, bar, 2 sitting-rooms, veranda
Credit cards AE, DC, MC, V
Children accepted if well behaved
Disabled no special facilities
Pets well behaved ones accepted **Closed** never
Proprietors Ciccarese family

The 'heel' of Italy

Covo dei Saraceni

This is a modern hotel close to the heart of the attractive little resort of Polignano, but on a secluded promontory. It overlooks a rugged little cove where once, presumably, the Saracens invaded Apulia; now it is a popular shingly sand beach. The building, on several split levels, copies the traditional flat-roofed style of these parts and is painted white; inside it has a nautical atmosphere owing to a predominance of blue and white. Bedrooms are bright and modern, some with terraces. A competitively priced alternative to the Grotta Palazzese, although of limited appeal for the longer stay.

Nearby Alberobello (30 km).

Via Conversano 1, Polignano a Mare 70044 Bari
Tel (080) 740696
Location on cliffs, close to middle of town; with large car park
Food & drink breakfast, lunch, dinner
Prices rooms L34,000-L84,000; DB&B L55,000-L67,000
Rooms 25 double, 1 single, all with shower; all rooms have air-conditioning, phone, TV, minibar, radio, sea view
Facilities dining-room, bar, sitting-room, TV room, terrace; solarium
Credit cards AE, DC, MC, V
Children accepted
Disabled no special facilities
Pets accepted
Closed never
Manager Vito Consoli

Il Melograno

'The Pomegranate' was, until quite recently, a working farm. Olives, pomegranates and mulberries now find their way to the hotel kitchens, along with other local produce, to be transformed into sumptuous dishes for which Il Melograno is justly famous. The hotel has more doubled in size since it opened in the mid-1980s, and the emphasis is now on conferences rather than holidaymakers. But this detracts little from the charm of the place, secluded behind white walls, dotted with quiet courtyards and tree-lined paths, its rooms beautifully decorated and graced with splendid antiques (owner Camillo Guerra is an ex-antique-dealer). And in this part of Italy such stylish hotels are a rarity.

Nearby Monópoli; Bari (55 km); Bríndisi (60 km).

Contrada Torricella, 70043 Monópoli
Tel (080) 808656
Location in quiet setting, 2 km SW of Monópoli, just W of SS16; with gardens and car parking
Food & drink breakfast, lunch, dinner
Prices rooms L240,000-L320,000 with breakfast; lunch/dinner L50,000
Rooms 33 double, all with bath; 4 family rooms, all with bath; all have central heating, air-conditioning, phone, TV, hairdrier, radio, minibar
Facilities dining-room, sitting-room; tennis, swimming-pool
Credit cards AE, DC, V
Children accepted
Disabled no special facilities
Pets accepted **Closed** Nov
Proprietor Camillo Guerra

SOUTHERN ITALY

The 'toe' of Italy

Area introduction

Hotels in the 'toe'

For travellers heading south with time to spare, the SS18 makes a slow-paced alternative to the A3 motorway, sticking to the eastern coast south of Lagonegro where the motorway takes a long detour inland. Two of our three recommended hotels are at the northern end of this stretch of coast, and there are a few places further south that are worth bearing in mind. At Diamante is the Mediterranean-style Ferretti (Tel (0985) 81428), with terraces overlooking the sea and a highly reputed restaurant. The 65-room Grand Hotel San Michele (Tel (0982) 91012) at Cetraro is rather more swish – a well-restored old house in an attractive informal garden on cliffs above the beach. 90 km inland is the Barbieri (Tel (0981) 948072), worth a stop for excellent Calabrian fare and views of the medieval village of Altomonté.

The main tourist attraction of the toe, however, is on the other side of the A3 – the magnificently wild landscape of the Sila mountains east of Cosenza and north of Catanzaro. Each of these towns has a handful of acceptable hotels. In the mountains south of Catanzaro is the delightfully pretty village of Stilo. At its heart is the San Giorgio (Tel (0964) 775047), a 17thC palace, high on our agenda for inspection. The owner, Francesco Caperi, is the director of a theatre company; his English-speaking wife and other members of the company 'help run and animate' this attractive 14-room hotel.

Seaside hotel, Maratea

Villa Cheta Elite

This gracious art nouveau building stands out from the modern blocks that characterize so much of the Italian coastline. It would merit attention even in the most competitive region; in the south, it is a veritable oasis. The villa lies among flowery terraces, enjoying beautiful views of the precipitous wooded west coast of Basilicata. Inside, lace table-cloths, chintz sofas and carefully chosen period pieces create the air of a private home. The Aquadros are relaxed and charming hosts.

Nearby Maratea (8 km); spectacular corniche road.

Via Nazionale, Acquafredda di Maratea 85041 Potenza
Tel (0973) 878134
Location 1.5 km S of Acquafredda, in gardens overlooking sea; private car parking
Food & drink breakfast, lunch, dinner
Prices rooms L65,000-L120,000; DB&B L80,000-L120,000
Rooms 16 double, one with bath, 15 with shower; 2 family rooms, both with shower; all rooms have central heating, phone
Facilities dining-room with sea-view terrace, TV and reading-room, bar
Credit cards AE, DC, MC, V
Children welcome if well behaved
Disabled access difficult
Pets small ones only accepted; allowed in dining-room in low season only
Closed mid-Oct to Mar
Proprietors Marisa and Lamberto Aquadro

The 'toe' of Italy

Santavenere

The Santavenere lies just outside the charming old town of Maratea, close to the sea, and is undoubtedly one of the most refined hotels of the deep south, furnished throughout in impeccable taste. The building is low-lying and arcaded, set on a promontory with lawns stretching to cliffs which plunge down sheer to the sea. The beach is not far away, but it is pebbly and the hotel's garden, pool and terrace are all so inviting there is not much temptation to stray far. Inside, the public rooms boast a fine collection of antiques, and prettily upholstered sofas – the sort you might find in an elegant country home. Bedrooms are equally inviting, with many of them enjoying sea views from a terrace or balcony.

Nearby old town; dramatic coastal scenery.

Fiumicello di Santa Venere, Maratea 85040 Potenza
Tel (0973) 876910
Location close to beach in Maratea; with garden and private car parking
Food & drink breakfast, lunch, dinner
Prices DB&B L190,000-L250,000
Rooms 40 double, 13 single, all with bath; all rooms have phone, TV, minibar; half the rooms have terrace or balcony
Facilities sitting-rooms, dining-room, bar, terrace; swimming-pool, tennis, beach
Credit cards AE, DC, MC, V
Children accepted
Disabled no special facilities
Pets not accepted
Closed Oct to Apr
Manager Davide Maestripieri

Baia Paraelios

Few hotels in the deep south of Italy can boast a setting as fine as that of the Baia Parelios, on a promontory overlooking a bay of fabulous white sands washed by crystal-clear waters. It consists of bungalows, staggered on the hillside above the bay, each one with a terrace and sitting-room. The communal areas are the prettily furnished reception area at the top of the hill, an inviting pool and open-air bar in the middle of the complex, and a dining-room and sitting-room down by the beach.

Nearby fishing port of Tropea.

Parghelia, Tropea 88035 Catanzaro
Tel (0963) 600004
Location W of Parghelia; in gardens; private car parking
Food & drink breakfast, lunch, dinner
Prices FB L190,000-L275,000; reductions for children
Rooms 72 bungalows, all with bathroom; all rooms have sitting-room, terrace, phone, ceiling fan
Facilities dining-room, sitting-room, open-air bar; swimming-pool, tennis, boutique, massage room, chapel
Credit cards AE, DC, V
Children welcome
Disabled no special facilities
Pets accepted if well behaved
Closed 4th week Sep to 4th week May
Proprietor Adolfo Salabe

West Coast

Town hotel, Erice

Elimo

Traditional and modern, local and oriental – you will find all these styles (and more) in this smart and highly unusual little hotel. The Tilotta family refurbished the old stone building and opened it as a hotel in 1987. Each of the 21 bedrooms has been given an individual character, followed through to the last detail, and public areas have also been meticulously refurbished. The restaurant, with snazzy black chairs against a tiled floor and white walls, offers good-value food, especially in local fish dishes.
Nearby Trapani (14 km), with daily car ferry service and hydrofoil to the Egadi islands; Segesta temple.

Via Vittorio Emanuele 75, Erice 91016 Erice
Tel (0923) 869377
Location in middle of town; with roof garden, and car parking 150 m away
Food & drink breakfast, lunch, dinner
Prices rooms L94,600-L100,000; lunch/ dinner L40,000-L45,000
Rooms 17 double, 16 with bath, one with shower; 2 single with shower; 2 family rooms with shower; all have central heating, phone, TV, minibar
Facilities dining-room, sitting-room, bar, terrace
Credit cards AE, DC, V
Children accepted if well-behaved
Disabled no special facilities
Pets not accepted
Closed never
Proprietor Mario Tilotta

Town hotel, Erice

Moderno

Erice is in every sense remote from the tourist haunts of eastern Sicily – a medieval town with paved streets perched on a rocky outcrop at the north-western extremity of the island. The place to stay is the Moderno – in the heart of the town, and run with flair and warmth by the Catalano family. Some parts of the hotel are, as its name suggests, smartly modern – notably the split-level sitting-room – but some bedrooms are elegantly traditional, and there are pictures, ornaments and plants everywhere. The sunny terrace gives fine views.
Nearby Trapani (14 km) (with daily car ferry service and hydrofoil to the Egadi islands); Segesta temple (35 km).

Via Vittorio Emanuele 63, Erice 91016 Trapani
Tel (0923) 869300
Location in middle of town
Food & drink breakfast, lunch, dinner
Prices rooms L55,000-L100,000; DB&B L80,000-L90,000
Rooms 33 double, 10 with bath, 23 with shower; 7 single, all with shower; all rooms have central heating, phone
Facilities dining-room, sitting-room, bar, terrace
Credit cards AE, DC, V
Children accepted
Disabled lift/elevator
Pets small ones only accepted, but not in public areas
Closed never
Proprietor Giuseppe Catalano

East coast

Villa Paradiso

Next to the public gardens and close to the heart of historic Taormina, the Villa Paradiso also has the advantage of a glorious panorama along the coast and across to the hazy cone of Etna. The only drawback to the location is that it is on a main road, which means some noise for back rooms and major problems with parking in high season. The hotel is a well-maintained white building, and the public rooms have all the style and atmosphere of a private villa: white arches, patterned carpets on tiled floors, stylish sofas and an imaginative collection of prints, paintings and watercolours. The restaurant on the fourth floor makes the most of the views, and the food is distinctly above average. Every bedroom has a balcony, and inevitably the most sought-after are those at the front with sea views. The majority are larger than you would expect from a *pension*; some have attractive painted furniture. You can reach the beaches by cable-car or – more conveniently – the hotel minibus, which takes you to the Villa Paradiso Lido (free facilities for guests).

Nearby Greek theatre, Corso Umberto and public gardens; excursions to Etna.

Via Roma 2, Taormina 98039 Messina
Tel (0942) 23922
Location on SE edge of town; small public car park next door, paying garage nearby
Food & drink breakfast, lunch, dinner
Prices DB&B L90,000-L152,000
Rooms 33 double, 19 with bath, 2 with shower; 3 single, all with shower; 9 suites, all with bath; all rooms have central heating, air-conditioning, phone, radio
Facilities 2 sitting-rooms, bar, dining-room, terrace
Credit cards AE, DC, MC, V
Children welcome; special meals and baby-sitting on request
Disabled access possible – some ground- floor rooms
Pets small cats and dogs only accepted
Closed early Nov to mid-Dec
Proprietor Salvatore Martorana

East coast

Arathena Rocks

For peace-lovers the gardens and pool of the Arathena Rocks provide an attractive alternative to the busy sands of Giardini-Naxos; and there is swimming in the sea from the rugged black lava rocks or a man-made private beach. Rooms throughout the hotel are light and cheerful, with whitewashed walls and painted furniture. The dining-room overlooks the garden and sea, as do some bedrooms. The friendly Arcidiacono family speak English, and will do their best to make sure that your stay here is an enjoyable one.

Nearby Taormina; excusions to Etna.

Via Calcide Eubea 55, Giardini-Naxos 98035 Messina
Tel (0942) 51349
Location 5 km SW of Taormina on private road, overlooking own gardens and sea; with private car parking
Food & drink breakfast, lunch, dinner
Prices DB&B L80,000- L88,000
Rooms 42 double, 10 single, all with bath or shower; all rooms have phone

Facilities 2 sitting-rooms, dining-room, bar, snack-bar by pool; sea-water swimming-pool, tennis
Credit cards MC, V
Children welcome; special meals on request
Disabled no special facilities
Pets dogs not accepted in dining-room
Closed Nov to Mar
Proprietors Arcidiacono family

Villa Fiorita

Built into the rock high on a mountain terrace, the Fiorita is a small hotel with a grand panorama of the bay below Taormina. Bedrooms are spotlessly clean and surprisingly well equipped for a hotel of its category. Downstairs there are various sitting-rooms, though the main attractions in summer are the outdoor terraces, garden and pool. And for those who prefer the beach the funicular down to sea-level is only a couple of minutes' walk away. The Fiorita is principally a bed-and-breakfast place, but evening snacks are served on request.

Nearby Greek theatre, beach (via funicular).

Via L Pirandello 39, Taormina 98039 Messina

Tel (0942) 24122
Location about 5 minutes from middle of resort, on NE side; with garden and (paying) garage
Food & drink breakfast
Prices rooms L90,000
Rooms 24 double, 23 with bath, one with shower; all rooms have air- conditioning, phone, colour TV, radio,

minibar
Facilities sitting-room, breakfast room, games room, sauna, heated swimming-pool
Credit cards AE, MC, V
Children not encouraged
Disabled no special facilities
Pets not accepted
Closed never
Proprietor Antonietta Colombo Papa

East coast

Seaside villa, Taormina

Villa Belvedere

The Belvedere is a simple but stylish hotel which has been in the same family since 1902, with each generation making its changes without altering the inherent charm of the place. Currently in charge is Frenchman Claude Pécaut and his Italian wife, both of them friendly and helpful.

One of the villa's great assets is its location. It is close to the middle of Taormina, commanding a spectacular panorama of the bay and the slopes of Etna to the south. Ask for a room at the front, and preferably one with a terrace. Not only do the few rooms at the back of the hotel lack these superb views – they are also noisy and gloomy by comparison.

Flowery gardens lead down to a small pool where the setting and poolside bar (snacks and light lunches) tempt guests to linger all day and postpone the more serious business of sight-seeing. There is no proper restaurant, but this can scarcely be considered a drawback given the choice down the road in central Taormina. And the hotel does have two prettily furnished draw-ing-rooms, an indoor bar and a spacious breakfast room. All in all, a sound choice for a reasonably priced family hotel when you don't want to be tied down by meals.

Nearby Greek theatre, Corso Umberto, public gardens; excursions to Etna, half or whole day.

Via Bagnoli Croce 79,
Taormina 98039 Messina
Tel (0942) 23791
Location close to public gardens and old town, with garden and parking space for 15 cars
Food & drink breakfast
Prices rooms L55,000-L146,000 with breakfast
Rooms 39 double, 3 single, all with bath or shower; all rooms have central heating
Facilities 2 sitting-areas, 2 bars, breakfast room; swimming-pool
Credit cards MC, V
Children accepted if well behaved
Disabled no special facilities
Pets welcome
Closed Nov to Feb
Proprietor Claude Pécaut

East coast

Seaside villa, Taormina

Villa Sant'Andrea

The Villa Sant'Andrea was originally built and furnished by an aristocratic English family. It was converted to a hotel in 1950, but even after modernization it still has the stamp of a rather elegant turn-of-the-century English home. Flowery fabrics (largely Sanderson), cool colours and a few carefully chosen antiques combine to create a light and inviting interior – helped by the big windows that overlook the bay. Some of the guest rooms are a little old-fashioned in comparison with the rest of the hotel, but the front rooms with terraces are hard to beat for views. The bars and dining-rooms, in contrast, are crisply Continental.

The hotel stands among luxuriant sub-tropical terraces just above the pebbly beach of the bay of Mazzaro (deck-chairs and parasols are provided for guests). One of the restaurants is right on the beach, and you can lunch or dine here in the shade of palm trees overlooking the bay – an inviting spot both by day and night, when you can watch the fishing boats glide silently out to sea. The main restaurant is kept fresh by sea breezes wafting through the white arches which frame the bay.

Nearby Greek theatre, Corso Umberto and public gardens of Taormina, all reached by cable car; excursions to Etna.

Via Nazionale 137, Mazzaro, Taormina-mare 98030 Messina
Tel (0942) 23125
Location on NE side of town, in gardens overlooking private beach; parking for 30 cars
Food & drink breakfast, lunch, dinner
Prices rooms L110,000-L256,000 with breakfast; DB&B L159,500- L192,500; reductions for children under 12
Rooms 56 double, 44 with bath, 12 with shower; 3 single, one with bath, 2 with shower; all rooms have central heating, air-conditioning, phone
Facilities 2 dining-rooms, 2 bars, sitting-room; windsurfing, rowing-boats
Credit cards AE, DC, MC, V
Children accepted
Disabled no special facilities
Pets not accepted
Closed Nov to late Mar
Manager Francesco Moschella

South coast / Aeolian islands

Villa Athena

Agrigento was one of the richest cities of the ancient world, and the unique feature of the Villa Athena is its amazing setting – right in the Valley of Temples, where the ruins rise in isolated splendour (the Temple of Concord is directly in view).

From an 18thC villa it has been converted into a smart four-star hotel. The façade is classical and handsome. Sadly, the interior is somehow much more modern than you might expect and the atmosphere does tend towards the impersonal. But this is well outweighed by the beauty of the site – the grounds, the pool, the palms and the terraces where you can eat looking across to the timeless temples.

Nearby Valley of Temples.

Via dei Templi 33, Agrigento 92100
Tel (0922) 23833
Location 3 km south of Agrigento, in the Valley of the Temples with own garden and ample car parking (supervised)
Food & drink breakfast, lunch, dinner
Prices rooms L98,000-L140,000
Rooms 35 double, 6 single; all with shower; all have central heating, air-conditioning, radio, TV, phone
Facilities dining-room, bars, terrace, swimming-pool
Credit cards AE, MC, V
Children accepted; baby-sitting available
Disabled no special facilities
Pets accepted
Closed never
Proprietor Francesco d'Alessandro

Villa Diana

Lipari is the largest of the volcanic Aeolian islands, and among its attractions are picturesque fishing villages, deep clear blue seas and the charming town of Lipari. The Pensione Diana is a skilfully restored villa whose ample terraces and quiet gardens overlook Lipari and the bays that frame it. It is a family home, furnished and looked after with care; there are antiques, paintings and ceramics in the dining-room, and some of the bedrooms have antiques too. Dinners include a variety of local dishes, served with wines made on the island.

Nearby Norman cathedral, Bishop's Palace (Eolian Archaelogical Museum), and other old buildings of Lipari.

Via Tufo, Lipari, Isole Eolie 98055 Messina
Tel (090) 981 1403
Location about 15 minutes from middle of Lipari; in garden, with private parking
Food & drink breakfast, dinner
Prices rooms L35,000-L65,000; meals L30,000
Rooms 11 double, 8 with bath, 3 with shower; 2 single, both with shower
Facilities dining-room, terraces, bowls
Credit cards V
Children welcome
Disabled no special facilities
Pets welcome
Closed Nov to Mar
Proprietor Anna Calabrese Hunziker

Inland Sardinia

Country hotel, Oliena

Su Gologone

The Barbagia, in the heart of mountainous Sardinia, is a region which the locals say has never been tamed. The landscape is wild, the villages remote and bandits still thrive – though tourists are unlikely to encounter them.

The hotel is a low-lying white villa, covered in creepers, surrounded by flowing shrubs and set in a landscape of rural splendour: wooded ravines, fields of olives, pinewoods and the craggy peaks of the Supramonte mountains. It feels isolated, and it is; but the Su Gologone is far from undiscovered. Once, only a few adventurous foreign travellers found their way here; now, they come for the peace, or indeed for the food alone, which is typically Sard: cuts of local meats, roast lamb and the speciality of roast suckling pig – you can watch it being cooked on a spit in front of a huge fireplace. The wines are produced in the local vineyards. The dining-room spreads in all directions – into the vine-clad courtyard, the terrace and other rooms, all in suitably rustic style. The bedrooms are light and simple, again in rustic style, in keeping with the surroundings. Walls are whitewashed, floors are tiled and there are lovely views.

Despite its size and range of facilities, the Su Gologone still feels small and friendly, and in most respects still typically Sard. **Nearby** Gennargentu mountain range; Monte Ortobene – a 21-km drive.

Oliena 08025 Nuoro
Tel (0784) 287512
Location 8 km NE of Oliena, in remote mountain setting with private parking
Food & drink breakfast, lunch, dinner
Prices rooms L54,000-L68,000 DB&B L68,000-L88,000; FB L82,000- L102,000
Rooms 61 double, 4 family rooms, all with bath; all have central heating, phone, air-conditioning, colour TV; 15 rooms have minibar
Facilities 5 dining-rooms, 2 bars, conference room; disco, swimming-pool, tennis, bowls, riding, mini golf
Credit cards AE, MC, V
Children accepted
Disabled no special facilities
Pets accepted
Closed Nov to Feb
Proprietor Giuseppe Palimodde

Photo: Sporting (facing page)

Costa Smeralda

Cappricioli

The Capriccioli is a small, simple, family-run hotel, and its modest prices are a fraction of what you pay at the five-star luxury places on the Costa Smeralda. The Azara family have been here for a quarter of a century, starting with just a restaurant. The rustic villa-style building lies among the windswept *macchia*, close to a pretty beach of white sands. The style is predominantly rustic, but in the restaurant, nets, boats and anchors provide the setting for *Risotto Pirata* and other local dishes. The key attraction is the restaurant terrace, with beautiful views of the coast.

Nearby sandy beaches of the Costa Smeralda.

Cappricioli, Porto Cervo
07020 Sassari
Tel (0789) 96004
Location in Cala di Volpe area, overlooking beach; with ample car parking
Food & drink breakfast, lunch, dinner
Prices DB&B L96,000-L167,000
Rooms 24 double, 3 with bath, 21 with shower; 4 single, all with shower; all rooms have central heating
Facilities dining-room with terrace, 2 bars, 2 TV rooms; tennis, beach with windsurfing
Credit cards AE, MC, V
Children welcome
Disabled no special facilities
Pets not accepted
Closed Oct to Apr
Proprietor Martino Azara

Sporting

The Sporting is another little Costa Smeralda oasis of luxury. Its series of neo-rustic houses lie on a peninsula, with sea views all around. The style is one of simple elegance, with beams, tiled floors and white stucco walls providing the setting for spotless white sofas and benches scattered with cushions. The atmosphere is quite clubby – it is popular with the wealthy yachting fraternity who moor their boats in the marina next door. Bedrooms with white walls and cushioned wicker seats are cool and restrained, and all have a terrace overlooking the sea.

Nearby beaches of Costa Smeralda.

07026 Porto Rotondo, Olbia
Sassari
Tel (0789) 34005
Location 15.5 km N of Olbia on a peninsula between sea and marina; with garden and ample car parking
Food & drink breakfast, lunch, dinner
Prices DB&B L220,000-L345,000
Rooms 27 double, all with bath; all rooms have minibar, phone, balcony
Facilities dining-room, barbecue, piano bar; sea-water swimming-pool, beach, boat hire, water-skiing, windsurfing, tennis
Credit cards AE, DC, MC, V
Children accepted
Disabled no special facilities
Pets not accepted
Closed end Sep to mid-Apr
Manager Hans Steurer

Costa Smeralda

Resort village, Porto Cervo

Pitrizza

The smart playground of the Costa Smeralda is liberally endowed with luxury hotels, but there is one that stands out from the rest: the Pitrizza. What distinguishes it (apart from its small size) is its exclusive, intimate, club-like atmosphere. No shops, disco or ritzy touches here. Small private villas are scattered discreetly among the rocks and flowering gardens, overlooking a private beach. Rooms are furnished throughout with immaculate taste, some of them amazingly simple. The style is predominantly rustic, with white stucco walls, beams and locally crafted furniture and fabrics. Each villa has four to six rooms, and most have a private terrace, garden or patio. The core of the hotel is the club-house, with a small sitting-room, bar, restaurant and spacious terrace where you can sit, enjoying the company of other guests or simply watching the sunset. A path leads down to the golden sands of a small beach and a private jetty where you can moor your yacht. Equally desirable is the sea-water pool, which has been carved out of the rocky shoreline.

There is of course a hitch to the Pitrizza. The rooms here are among the most expensive on the entire Italian coastline.

Nearby beaches of the Costa Smeralda; Maddalena archipelago.

Porto Cervo 07020 Sassari
Tel (0789) 91500
Location 4 km from Porto Cervo, at Liscia di Vacca; ample car parking
Food & drink breakfast, lunch, dinner
Prices DB&B L303,000-L438,000; reductions for children sharing parents' room
Rooms 21 double, 6 single, one suite; all with bath; all rooms have air-conditioning, minibar, phone, TV, radio; most rooms have terrace or patio
Facilities bar, dining-room, terrace; sea-water swimming-pool; beach, water skiing, boat hire, windsurfing, private mooring
Credit cards AE, DC, MC, V
Children accepted
Disabled no special facilities
Pets not accepted
Closed Oct to mid-May
Manager Sg. P Tondina

Costa Smeralda / East coast

Balocco

For those who cannot afford the five-star luxury that typifies the Costa Smeralda, the Balocco is a more than satisfactory four-star substitute. It is a small, well-equipped hotel and, unlike most along this stretch of coastline, it is conveniently situated only a short walk from the shops and chic harbour of Porto Cervo. Sub-tropical gardens lead down to the swimming-pool, and from the bedrooms and terraces there are fine views of the sea and the yachts which frequent the port. The building is typically Mediterranean – white, tiled and built on various levels. Walls are whitewashed, and furnishings are a mix of modern and rustic. Every room has a terrace or balcony.

Nearby Porto Cervo; Maddalena archipelago.

Via Liscia di Vacca, Porto Cervo 07020 Sassari
Tel (0789) 91555
Location overlooking sea and port of Porto Cervo, in gardens with ample car parking
Food & drink breakfast
Prices rooms L110,000-L240,000 with breakfast
Rooms 34 double, 12 with bath, 22 with shower; all rooms have phone, TV, air-conditioning, balcony or terrace
Facilities hall, TV room, bar; swimming-pool, terrace, solarium
Credit cards AE, DC, MC, V
Children welcome
Disabled access difficult
Pets not accepted
Closed mid-Oct to Apr
Proprietor Antonio Verona

Don Diego

On an unspoilt stretch of coastline, the Don Diego faces the islands of Tavolara and Molara, with a well-equipped beach and jetty on the shore below. The hotel consists of individual Mediterranean-style cottages scattered amongst the *macchia* and flowering gardens, each with its own terrace; the rooms are comfortably furnished and blissfully quiet. The main building houses the public rooms, attractively furnished in rustic style, including a restaurant where fish is the main speciality.

Nearby Olbia (15 km); Costa Smeralda.

Località Costa Dorata, Porto San Paolo, Vaccileddi 07020 Sassari
Tel (0789) 40007/006
Location 1.5 km SE of Porto San Paolo on the coast; in gardens, with private car parking
Food & drink breakfast, lunch, dinner
Prices DB&B L130,000-L150,000
Rooms 49 rooms, all in independent villas, all with bath or shower; all rooms have phone
Facilities dining-room, sitting-room; swimming-pool, tennis, beach
Credit cards not accepted
Children accepted
Disabled no special facilities
Pets dogs accepted, but not allowed in dining-room
Closed never
Manager Sg. di Geronimo

West coast / North coast

Villa las Tronas

Lying on its own little rocky peninsula, the Villa las Tronas looks more like a castle than a hotel – which is not so surprising when you discover its background. Not so long ago it was a holiday home of the former royal family of Italy. Inside, as one might expect, the furnishings are suitably palatial. Ornate chandeliers, moulded ceilings, gilt mirrors create a grand, rather formal setting, and bedrooms are soberly elegant. Gardens surround the hotel and you can swim off the rocks below. But the main beach of Alghero lies well to the north.

Nearby Porte Conte and Neptune's Grotto (24 km).

Via Lungomare Valencia 1, Alghero 07041 Sassari
Tel (0789) 975390
Location standing in gardens on rocky coastline close to old town, with private car park
Food & drink breakfast, lunch, dinner
Prices DB&B L120,000-L160,000; FB L135,000-L190,000; 20% reduction for children under 7 sharing parents' room
Rooms 25 double, 12 with bath, 13 with shower; 5 single, 3 with bath, 2 with shower; all rooms have central heating, minibar, colour TV, phone
Facilities 2 sitting-rooms, dining-room, bar, writing-room; bowls
Credit cards AE, DC, MC, V
Children accepted
Disabled access difficult
Pets not accepted
Closed restaurant only, winter
Proprietors Masia brothers

Shardana

Santa Teresa di Gallura is a small, busy town on the rugged northern tip of Sardinia, looking across to the cliffs of Corsica. The stylish Shardana lies well out of town, on a quiet hillside close to a sandy beach. Accommodation is mainly in separate bungalows, laid out among the myrtle and juniper, with rooms furnished in an attractive rustic style. A restaurant specializing in fresh fish, a piano bar and a comfortable sitting-area are located in the central clubhouse, along with a handful of bedrooms. The pool is small but prettily set on the sea side of the hotel, and there are water sports on the beach.

Nearby Maddalena archipelago.

Capo Testa, Santa Teresa Gallura 07028 Sassari
Tel (0789) 754031
Location 2.5 km from Santa Teresa Gallura
Food & drink breakfast, lunch, dinner
Prices rooms L80,000-L180,000
Rooms 51 rooms (45 in bungalows), all with bath or shower, phone, minibar
Facilities dining-room, bar (piano bar in Jul and Aug); swimming-pool
Credit cards not accepted
Children accepted
Disabled not suitable
Pets small ones accepted in bedrooms
Closed Oct to May
Manager Nicola Lupo

Reporting to the guides

Please write and tell us about your experiences of small hotels, guest-houses and inns, whether good or bad, whether listed in this edition or not. As well as hotels in Italy, we are interested in hotels in Britain and Ireland, France, Spain, Portugal, Austria, Switzerland, Germany and other European countries, and those in the eastern and western United States.

The address to write to is:

> Chris Gill,
> Editor,
> *Charming Small Hotel Guides,*
> The Old Forge,
> Norton St Philip,
> Bath, BA3 6LW,
> England.

Checklist

Please use a separate sheet of paper for each report; include your name, address and telephone number on each report.

Your reports will be received with particular pleasure if they are typed, and if they are organized under the following headings:

> Name of establishment
> Town or village it is in, or nearest
> Full address, including post code
> Telephone number
> Time and duration of visit
> The building and setting
> The public rooms
> The bedrooms and bathrooms
> Physical comfort (chairs, beds, heat, light, hot water)
> Standards of maintenance and housekeeping
> Atmosphere, welcome and service
> Food
> Value for money

We assume that in writing you have no objections to your views being published unpaid, either verbatim or in an edited version. Names of major outside contributors may be acknowledged in the guide.

If you would be interested in looking at hotels on a professional basis on behalf of the guides, please include on a separate sheet a short CV and a summary of your travel and hotel-going experience.

Index of hotels

Index of hotel names

In this index, hotels are arranged in order of the first distinctive part of their name; very common prefixes such as 'hotel', 'albergo', 'il', 'la', 'dei', 'delle' and 'du' are omitted. Less common prefixes, and words such as 'Casa', 'Castello' and 'Villa' are not.

Index of hotels

Index of hotels

Index of hotel locations

In this index, hotels are arranged by the name of the city, town or village they are in or near. Hotels located in a very small place may be indexed under a larger place nearby.

Index of hotel locations

Index of hotel locations